MANAGING
CLIENT/SERVER

DOLF ZANTINGE
PIETER ADRIAANS

 syllogic

▲▼ Addison-Wesley

Harlow, England • Reading, Massachusetts • Menlo Park, California
New York • Don Mills, Ontario • Amsterdam • Bonn • Sydney • Singapore
Tokyo • Madrid • San Juan • Milan • Mexico City • Seoul • Taipei

© Addison Wesley Longman 1996

Addison Wesley Longman Limited
Edinburgh Gate
Harlow
Essex
CM20 2JE
England

and Associated Companies throughout the world.

Cover designed by Op den Brouw, Design & Illustration, Reading
and printed by Oxted Press Ltd, Oxted, Surrey
Typeset by Meridian Colour Repro Limited, Pangbourne
Printed and bound by Biddles Limited, Guildford and King's Lynn

First printed 1996
Reprinted 1997

ISBN 0-201-87749 X

British Library Cataloguing-in-Publication Data
A catalogue record for this book is available from the British Library

Library of Congress Cataloging-in-Publication Data is available

Managing Client/server

FOREWORD

Dolf Zantinge has a broad experience of setting up large client/server projects. At present, he is a director at Syllogic, an organization which has built up several years of experience in the preparation and implementation of large scale datawarehouses, based on client/server applications in internationally operating organizations.

Pieter Adriaans studied philosophy and mathematics in Leiden. He has been active in the research of artificial intelligence and relational database systems since 1984. In 1992, he received a PhD in computer science. At present, he is a director at Syllogic, where he is responsible for the development of tools for the management of client/server systems and databases. The basis for Syllogic's activities in this area is the integration of datawarehousing with intelligent database and systems managment tools.

PREFACE

Client/server technology is currently receiving an enormous amount of attention. Syllogic has built up a broad basis of experience in the implementation of client/server systems over the last few years. We regularly receive requests from clients to record our knowledge systematically on paper. This book is meant, in part, to satisfy those clients' needs.

Client/server is a method by which information system programs and data are divided between a client computer and a server computer. In the client/server concept, data is stored on a central system in a network. This system is the server. Multiple clients make use of this server to request, store and change data. However, the entire application manifests itself to the user, as a single program. In a traditional environment, the entire application runs on a single system. This system is burdened with tasks that are important only to the local user: for example, screen operations, error messages, and input consistency checks. In a client/server environment this sort of task is carried out by a local system. This means not only that the individual user receives better service, but that there is less load on the server, which is entrusted only with those tasks for which it is optimally suitable. As the application is divided over various types of system, a flexible environment is created, which allows each system its own specific contribution.

The client/server concept is now becoming important for many organizations as a result of the emergence of PCs, computer networks and relational databases. There is, however, a lot of confusion about client/server capabilities and the problems accompanying implementation of such a concept in an organization. The wrong image of client/server often exists: client/server implementation is, for example, primarily defended as a cost-cutting operation. At the same time, much has been written about client/server, but few organizations have as yet had actual experience with it. The existing literature about client/server focuses, mainly on the technical aspects of client/server implementation: How are things done?

Which protocols and scripts must be used? This kind of approach is, of course, necessary and useful, but more strategic information on this development is also necessary. In this book, we explain client/server environments primarily from a management perspective: Where does attention need to be focused during client/server implementation? What are the limiting conditions? Which techniques are used?

We have consciously avoided an overly in-depth discussion of technical aspects: not only because this sort of information changes so rapidly, but also because a bird's eye view is more useful from a management perspective. The organization and, in particular the individual employee, must be the center of client/server implementation.

It is important to recognize that diverse forms of client/server exist. A database application is usually built up out of three layers: data, processes and user interface. Client/server systems can be distinguished based on the way in which these three layers are divided over the various systems. In this book, a number of different client/server strategies will be discussed. Each form has its own approach. In the simplest client/server form, only the user interface on the client is handled. The most advanced form works with distributed databases. This form of client/server architecture distributes, in addition to the user interfaces and the processes, the data over various systems. Ensuring data integrity in such an environment requires close attention, both during design and implementation, and during the actual use and management of the system.

The ability to identify the various forms of client/server is essential to the introduction of client/server architecture. Each form has different technical requirements. Implementation of client/server technology will, in most cases, exert considerable influence on the structure of the organization. Management of systems can be decentralized; divisions can bear responsibility for their own application developments within the organization; new communication possibilities arise between the various levels of the organization. This leads to more complex management problems in the areas of security, version management, and backup strategies. A new generation of products will be introduced to solve these issues.

In order to optimally implement client/server technology, in-depth knowledge of hardware and software requirements, networks, database technology, management tools and various communication protocols, as well as possible combinations of the above (interoperability), is absolutely essential. The use of fourth generation programming languages within the client/server concept is also linked to specific conditions.

These and many other questions related to client/server implementation within an organization are handled in this book. The book is meant for DP managers, students, consultants and professionals who want to orient themselves to the world of client/server technology. It offers a typology of client/server architectures and provides an overview, for each type of architecture, of the various benefits and difficulties of client/server.

FOREWORD ix

Many people and organizations have helped this book to come into being. We should like to thank each and every one of them. We are especially grateful to Oracle, CA Ingres, Sybase, IBM, Sun, Compuware, Cabletron, as well as to the large number of companies we were able to assist in implementation of client/server environments: KLM and its information managers deserve special mention here.

In addition, several people deserve special mention: Frans Bolk and Thea van Breenen for producing the figures and for editing the text; Lisa Birthistle for her corrections and suggestions for textual improvements, Larry England for his comments on the book, Kay Madnani, Fiona Gleeson and their team for their support on the documentation concerning data warehousing, Roel Fiolet, Fred Bohlander, Timor Slamet and Frank de Bruijn for many fruitful and interesting discussions about the client/server concept. Lastly, we would like to thank Marion Bruijns and Rini Adriaans, without whom this book would not have been possible.

Houten, May 1996
Dolf Zantinge, Pieter Adriaans

Trademark notice

Apple® and Macintosh® are registered trademarks of Apple Computers Incorporated.

Burroughs™ is a trademark of Unisys Corporation.

CORBA™ is a trademark of Object Management Group.

DB/2™, IBM™, IBM PC™, OS/2™, Presentation Manager™ and Visual Age™ are all trademarks of International Business Machines Corporation.

DEC™ is a trademark of Digital Equipment Corporation.

INGRES™ is a trademark of Ingres Corporation.

Intel™ is a trademark of Intel Corporation.

LAN Manager™, Microsoft™, MS Windows™, SQL/Server™, and Windows NT™ are all trademarks of Microsoft Corporation.

Lotus Notes™ is a trademark of Lotus Development Corporation.

Motif™ is a trademark of Open Software Foundation.

Motorola™ is a trademark of Motorola Corporation.

NetWare™ and UNIX™ are trademarks of Novell Inc.

Oracle™ is a trademark of Oracle Corporation UK Limited.

Sun™ is a trademark of Sun Microsystems Inc.

Sybase™ is a trademark of Sybase Incorporated.

X/OPEN™ is a trademark of X/OPEN Group of Companies.

Xwindows™ is a trademark of MIT.

CONTENTS

Chapter 1

The rise of client/server

Introduction

Client/server is not only a technology but, more importantly, a way of thinking about distributed information handling in your organization.

The role of the end user is changing and becoming more important. He will become more independent from the central information technology (IT) department; he will need to access all kinds of information; and he will want to manipulate this information locally. This must be done by hardware and software products that can work together, and this can only be created by client/server technology.

Client/server technology is a concept in which computers, linked by a network, work together. One computer, the server, can carry out a given task at the request of another computer, the client, while both computers retain their independence. This allows tasks to be distributed over several systems, each of which can then carry out those tasks which most closely correspond to its speciality. From the user's perspective, this system appears to be a single system. Actually, in principle, client/server is nothing more than a division of labor applied to computers.

The benefits of a division of labor are self-apparent. People can carry out a wide variety of different tasks. In prehistoric times, everyone built his own hut, hunted his own prey and repaired his own bearskin. This organization of work did not have a positive effect on the quality of life. We have our own complex society and its comparative luxury and safety could only be developed based on the

1

distribution of tasks to the people with the most suitable education and qualifications to carry out those tasks. In this way, everyone carries out the tasks best suited to them, and a society with distributed functions and optimal cooperation can exist.

From isolated system to optimal cooperation

Computers are multipurpose. Calculation, databases, word processing, data communication and multimedia can all run on the same system. Most organizations use them for word processing on the personal computer with the database sited on the mainframe. We could say that we are now in the prehistoric period of the computer age. The existence of this situation is not really surprising. Until just a short time ago, each computer was doomed to an isolated, lonely existence, because the network technology and software necessary for communication with other computers did not exist. Some of that technology and software does now exist, but it is apparent that the most important developments are still to come. The future will see the realization of worldwide networks and data highways, developments which will significantly affect the way in which we use computers and the way we organize our labor, as well as having a significant effect on our culture in its entirety. Systems will no longer be isolated, but will be able to communicate with each other. Wherever people can be found, optimal communication will shortly be possible and carrying out tasks will become a more worldwide activity – the birth of the 'Global Village' concept. The idea behind the global village is that modern communication media will allow people to maintain social contacts similar to those in a village, but on a worldwide scale: for example, a daily conversation with an acquaintance in the USA, an exchange of recipes with a friend in Japan and maintenance of close contacts with a circle of friends that is geographically spread around the world. This will all be possible, while at the same time we may hardly know our own geographically local neighbors.

To take advantage of these developments, organizations will have to change their information systems. Companies that do not create a flexible environment which can grow along with requirements related to system communication and integration will in future encounter problems. The client/server concept makes such a flexible environment possible.

These are developments which transcend the interests of individual companies and even individual countries. Many automation department managers are asking themselves whether they should switch over to client/server applications. The question is actually not whether that should be done, but when and how. The necessity of switching over to a client/server information facility arises not only from pressure within the organization, but more importantly, due to pressures from society itself, a society which, with regard to its citizens' mobility, has reached its boundaries and which will therefore become increasingly dependent on a division of labor facilitated by data communications. Organizations which remain rooted in the prehistoric period of the computer age, organizations which do not realize an infrastructure that can take advantage of these developments, will remain dependent on information systems which do not contribute to the support of the organization, irrevocably leading to the loss of these organizations' right to exist. The role of the end user is changing: with a computer system at the office or at home, a user can be connected with all kind of servers and work in any place. He must be able to connect his local system to the network, and must have access to the information he needs. He will be connected to his bank, which could be thousands of miles away in any country, and in a second he will be able to place an order in the computer system of some kind of organization elsewhere in the world. Organizations who don't make this type of connection possible will lose market share, because communication in the future will be done by networks supported by client/server technology.

The influence of new products

Our image of what the future will bring is always made by extrapolating on existing trends. What strikes one most in such extrapolations is that it is extremely difficult to determine which trends are more or less permanent and which trends will change. Noticing a trend is one thing – evaluation of the value of that trend within the context within which it occurs is quite another. If people 150 years ago could have imagined the huge cities we now live in, they would probably also have foreseen an immense manure problem because of the increase in the number of horse-drawn vehicles. The trend in this example is the increasing intensity of transportation. The context within which the trend occurs, however, is dramatically different. We have switched over from the use of draft animals to motorized transport. The arrival of the car was inconceivable at that time. People 150 years ago would find it impossible to imagine the impact the car would have on our culture, varying from the growth of the tourist industry to the establishment of commuter cities. This demonstrates how difficult it is to evaluate the true worth of technological developments. Attempts to estimate the value of technological developments are, however, always useful. As our image of the future becomes sharper, we can better manage our actions. This is valid not only for individuals but, even more importantly, for organizations. A strategic image of the future is immensely important in making the right decisions in a world which is changing ever more rapidly.

It is a good idea to bear this sort of thing in mind as we think about the importance of the client/server phenomenon. We are entirely convinced that, now the computer has existed for some 40 years, we stand on the brink of a new automation gulf which will have a much deeper influence on our society than everything which has preceded it. That a trend is easy to identify and that the context and the actual value of that trend are less easily quantified is also valid here. We can easily identify the trends: more computers, the ability to perform more complex calculations, more powerful networks and more information. But the dimension behind these trends is much more drastic. Until now, automation has not really changed the way in which people organize their work. The large infrastructural information systems in most organizations are largely simulations of manual administration systems based on formulas. The PC has invaded the workplace and the work of the individual employee has changed somewhat. He types his own letters, maintains his own diary and carries out calculations more quickly, but his desk remains in the same building as 30 years ago. The typing pool has disappeared and the archive has been modernized, but the structure of the organization has not changed fundamentally. The power structure, the geographic spread of companies, ideas about the division of labor, employee career paths and company culture are essentially more than 100 years old. The pressures of ongoing intensification of economic traffic and information technology developments will facilitate changes in the actual organization. At present, the contours of developments which will considerably change our society in the coming decades are becoming clear. Overly detailed prophecies of what the future will bring remain risky, but we cannot afford to ignore the future. The degree of penetration of automation linked to technical developments in the area of networks has reached saturation point, leading to a slow change in the function of the computer. It is changing from an information storage and manipulation medium to a communication medium, and a medium with an increasingly direct influence over an organization's production resources.

History has taught us that technological developments in the area of communication media have the greatest and most unexpected effect on culture. Think of the invention of paper, the printing press, the telephone, radio and television. Now there is a new worldwide development: client/server and distributed processing.

When Edison drew up a list of the application possibilities for his newest invention, the gramophone, he placed recording music in fifth place. The great inventor was far more interested in recording speeches made by statesmen and in sending oral letters. Since that time, a whole new industry has arisen around the distribution of music, and without doubt the invention of the gramophone played an essential role in the development of this new industry. Why is it so difficult to predict the impact of a new technology on our society? Predictions are extrapolations from existing trends. One of the reasons seems to be that it is almost impossible to understand the changed context of many trends. Why did Edison not think that the distribution of music would become the most important function of the gramophone? Simply because at the time the music industry did not exist in the form in which we now know it. Music was first and foremost 'live music'. You went out in the evening especially for music. Music in the workplace was unthinkable at that time. We must try to avoid that pitfall in our evaluation of client/server applications and data communication. On the other hand, the first contours of the possibilities and consequences for organizations which have introduced the concept are now visible, considerably facilitating our predictions.

Closer analysis of the influence of the telephone, television, the automobile and other developments in our society makes it clear that the simple fact that something is technically possible is of less importance to our prediction of its influence and the secondary effects of such developments than the broad social acceptance of such developments. In the time when just 1000 US citizens had a television, the medium was of merely marginal importance, despite the cleverness of the technology itself. Only when every household was equipped with a television did the impact of the new medium become clear. It turned out to influence political processes, education and culture. Completely new industries come into existence around such a medium. In this way, even new power structures can come into being, structures which control the new medium, control public opinion and thereby wield considerable political power. At the same time, we see that such a medium can exert this kind of social effect only if its introduction is facilitated by other, catalytic developments. For example, the pervasive influence of television on our society cannot be explained by the technology alone. The rapid development of electronics, the emancipation of large groups of the population, and the development of the mass culture and financial structures also played an important role in supporting the introduction of the new technology. The introduction of a new technology is accompanied by a broad basis of dependent services and products which exert a positive influence on each other and speed up the acceptance of this technology.

New communication resources

Changes in the area of communication and information recording have turned out to have an enormous impact on our culture. Society exists by the grace of organized communication processes. In ancient Greece and Rome, urban complexes became possible only once the invention of paper had enabled the maintenance of complex administrative systems. A new technology can spread only if a given infrastructure exists to allow that spread. The infrastructure for computers is not yet at its optimum. Only when computers are linked to each other via powerful networks, which enable the inexpensive transmission of images, sound and data, will the social impact of informatics be felt completely. At present, a variety of infrastructure realization initiatives are already in full swing. Examples are the data highway plans of Al Gore in the USA and initiatives by Microsoft boss Bill Gates for a worldwide satellite network for wideband data communication.

The market

Every organization is dependent on a market, the environment within which the organization must manage to survive. Each market has its own internal dynamics: some hardly change, while others change rapidly. The organization that can take the quickest advantage of market needs is the organization most likely to survive. The structure of an organization is attuned to the market. If the market changes, the organization will have to adjust its own structure. Good information facilities are important for both internal adjustment to market changes, and for communication with the market. What is good information? Information quality is determined by three factors:

- *Integrity:* it must be correct.

- *Topicality:* it must be recent.

- *Completeness:* it must contain all relevant aspects.

Every organization is dependent on an information system for the processing of information. An information system is a system which ensures that all levels of the organization consistently receive good-quality information. An information system is the totality of equipment, programs, people, procedures and databases which the organization needs to carry out its tasks. An information system must meet the following requirements to ensure information quality:

- *Maintainable:* the market forces organizations to change. Maintenance of the information system must not hinder organizational change.

- *Scalable:* the system must be able to grow along with the organization, allowing investments to be spread over time.

- *Integrable:* seamless integration of new technological developments in the existing architecture must be possible.

- *Manageable:* simple and efficient management of the system must be possible.

One can see already from the requirements mentioned above that an information system is vitally important to an organization. Until just a short while ago, an information system was seen as a cost post which did not contribute to production, a view which is now undergoing a fundamental change. Information is increasingly seen as a product in itself. In addition, information can directly influence other product factors, such as labor, capital and machines. The business cycle can be shortened by a good information system. Machines can be controlled directly by the information system. Market developments force companies to change their organizational structure, and these developments will be increasingly initiated by information technologies. For this reason, an information system is not only important for the internal control of an organization, but also for maintaining contact with the market. This means that organizations without adequate information systems will lose contact with the market and will cease to exist.

Take, for example, the advertisements and product information which many companies now distribute via mailings and folders. In future that will happen largely via electronic media, and that has a number of consequences. Not only will companies be forced to participate in this sort of development, because they will otherwise be unable to get their information to the consumer, but the consumer will be able to compare the goods supplied via electronic media, enabling him to consistently purchase at the lowest price possible. Intensified communication possibilities will result in tougher competition.

Information cycle

Until now, the information systems of large organizations were largely mirror images of manual, form-based administrations. The organizational form which accompanies these methods of administration is hierarchical. In hierarchical organizations, large groups of people carry out complex tasks. Characteristic of such organizations is that decision making authority rests at the top of the organization. To make the right decisions, the top of the hierarchy must have access to the right information. This information is assembled at the bottom of the organization, and travels a long road before reaching the right people in the organization. Decisions also travel a long road before reaching the people who must actually carry out operational implementation of the decisions. One could speak of an information cycle (Figure 1.1): the information turnover time within an organization; the time between the moment at which the need for information arises and the moment at which the information becomes available and decisions based on the information are implemented. As more intermediate layers develop, the information time cycle gets longer and the quality of the information decreases.

The more layers an organization possesses, the longer the information cycle will be. Since topicality is an important information quality factor, this means that information quality decreases in organizations with more layers. The information system becomes a cumbersome and expensive mechanism, leading to a decrease in the organization's capacity to react to new market developments. To combat this effect, many companies split themselves into smaller, relatively independent business units, resulting in a shorter information time cycle. Such an operation can succeed only if the information systems are also modified. The hierarchical structure of an organization is often mirrored in the information system. We can think, in these terms, of article codes, standard reports, fixed accounting rules, unique identification numbers, and so on. Independent business units must have their own autonomous information systems, however, which can adjust

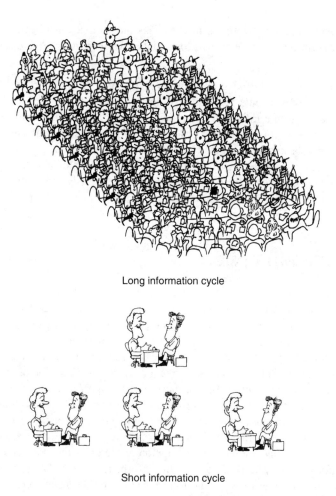

Long information cycle

Short information cycle

Figure 1.1 Long and short information cycle.

themselves to changing market conditions. At the same time, the parent company needs to regularly receive standard reports. The underlying systems must, therefore, be linked, without negatively affecting information quality. The information system must allow lightning quick changes to the individual business unit's information to allow for changes in the market, without disturbing communication between the units. The old mainframe and minicomputer technology is entirely inappropriate for this, as it would lead to extremely high maintenance costs and long maintenance cycles. At present, the maintenance cycles of a great number of companies are too long, hindering any reactions to market developments. During a bank merger a short time ago, the programming time necessary to combine the two banks' information systems was estimated at 3600 man years. An average mainframe from the 1970s represents an investment in software development of approximately $200 million. Many of these systems are so complex that they have become almost impossible to maintain. Modification of quite elementary aspects of a bank application or an airline reservation system (for example, an increase from two to three positions in a date field) can quickly cost millions of dollars, and is sometimes not viable at all. Many mainframe applications must be replaced before the year 2000 simply because they cannot handle the date rollover.

Organizations exist in a continually changing environment: the viability of an organization in the long run is closely linked to the organization's ability to change to meet the needs of the outside world. The information system of an organization is a mirror image of the organization's internal structure, a structure that is largely defined by its interaction with its environment. Until a short while ago, many organizations were able to exist under the fictional supposition that an information system is a static entity. Under this supposition, maintenance of the information system was a necessary evil, and the life-expectancy of the information system was limited. This was mirrored in the structure of the programs, which were linked as closely as possible to each other, leading to a hopelessly tangled and, in time, unmanageable jumble of sources. In the 1990s, however, social developments happen so quickly that few organizations can still permit themselves such a view of information systems.

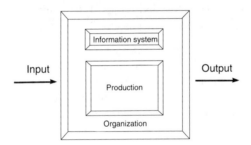

Figure 1.2 Information system as an organization model.

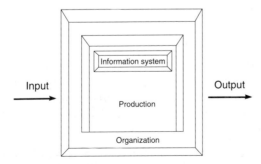

Figure 1.3 Information system as part of production.

Most information systems are not flexible, while the relationship between the information system and the organization is becoming increasingly important. Organizations will have to communicate and cooperate far more intensely with each other via their information systems, which, in turn, will cause these systems to change.

The future

Can we say anything worthwhile about future developments? In general, the consequences of new technology can be placed in the following categories:

- *First-order effect: replacement.*
  Traditional technologies are replaced by new technologies.

- *Second-order effect: intensification.*
  Introduction of inexpensive, efficient, high quality technologies leads to increased use.

- *Third-order effect: dependence.*
  Intensification leads to the existence of new social and organizational structures which exist solely by grace of the use of technology.

The introduction of motorized transport is a good example: a first-order effect was the replacement of traditional transportation methods such as the horse and buggy by more efficient methods: train and automobile. A second-order effect was an increased use of the new transportation methods. Travel became more popular, purchase of foreign products became easier, and so on. A third-order effect was the creation of social structures dependent on the existence of an infrastructure for intensive transport: commuter cities, shopping centers, vacation resorts, office parks, and so on.

These effects can also be discerned in the use of information technology. Malone and Rockart (1991) see a more efficient coordination of activities as the most important aspect of information technology. In the light of this view, we can distinguish three effects of the use of computer technology:

- A first-order effect is the reduction of coordination costs through the replacement of old technologies. In the past, organizations were dependent on large groups of clerks, bookkeepers and typists to coordinate their tasks. These coordination tasks are now largely carried out with fewer people with the help of the computer.

- A second-order effect is the intensification of coordination processes within the organization as a result of the availability of IT. Due to the introduction of computers, reports, balance sheets and memos can be drawn up and distributed more quickly than in the past. Balance sheets are now more frequently requested and communication is carried out more intensively.

• A third-order effect is the change to organizational structures which are dependent on more intensive coordination.

At present, larger organizations are already unable to function without information technology. An airline company's dependence on its reservation system is so great that a system failure lasting just a few hours could lead to bankruptcy. This dependence can only increase in the future and spread to all levels of society.

The work of a doctor, for example, will also change. The doctor of the future will have his own information system which not only contains all of his patient data, but which he also uses to communicate with hospitals, research centers, health insurance companies and colleagues. X-rays appear directly from the laboratory on screen. Blood test results are immediately evaluated by an on-line tissue analysis system. If the doctor is unsure of something, he can consult colleagues on-line. Many consultations will occur via data communications. In Japan, a toilet has already been introduced that can analyze human waste and which is directly linked to the family doctor. The doctor of the future will have to invest in these types of techniques if he wants to continue to function, not just to avoid personal expense, but simply because society will demand this of him. Health insurance companies, banks and laboratories will accept, and send, their information only via data communications.

We can find other examples in the area of education, where the computer will also create a new dependency. Students will communicate at home, via the computer, with various educational institutions. Traditional school books will largely cease to exist in their present form, replaced by multimedia applications or by books which can be modified ad hoc according to the requirements of specific students. This will lead to individualization of education. The student of the future will be able to determine his own course of study. The school as a physical building will disappear, replaced by education centers geographically spread over wide distances.

Many industries will have to modify their functions or disappear. The videotheque in its present form is doomed to extinction. In the future, every family will be able to call up a variety of services via interactive television, including a selection of interactive films. Food and clothing will also be ordered interactively via the television, and orders will be checked automatically against credit levels.

This illustrates the social pressure exerted upon organizations to modify their information systems. Information managers will have to take this sort of development into account. If the information manager does not create a flexible infrastructure that is able to profit from these developments, the chances are that the organization will exclude itself from further market participation.

There is no doubt that the intensification of coordination in our society can have great advantages: more information will be available, allowing better education; information will be distributed more quickly; companies will be able to easily make use of new technologies; international cooperation and operations will be easier; services will be more easily geographically spread; working at home will become easier, decreasing the need for transport; and so on.

It is also clear, however, that these new technologies are accompanied by pitfalls. To participate in society people will need access to the technology. The enormous increase in the amount of information available is accompanied by the very real danger of a correlated decrease in the quality of that information. Increasing amounts of personal information will be accessible by the general public. In the future, organizations will be able to automatically request information on what people eat and read, which films people see, what they buy and with whom they communicate.

GOLDEN RULES

- New information systems will become a part of the production environment in an organization.

- Integration of software products is a requirement for organizations.

- End users will become more involved in integrating the software, and will become more independent of the local datacenter.

- Large organizations will become more dependent on the information structure in their organization.

- Only organizations that are able to integrate their software at end user level are able to respond to the market (an infrastructure based on client/server technology is able to support this).

- Organizations can only respond quickly if they work with open systems and with new technologies.

Chapter 2

The advance of client/server

Introduction

Before looking at the technical and organizational details of client/server technology, it may be helpful to sketch the last 30 years' developments in the automation field. This overview of developments allows us to more easily place the client/server concept, especially if we have some insight into the influence of various hardware and software products on each other. Market demand has speeded developments and, at the same time, ensured increasingly that international agreements came into being to regulate the standards necessary for the development of client/server.

From assembler to object oriented

Machine code was used to program the first software. Those machine code programs were written in what are now called the first generation programming languages. Programs written in such languages are almost completely unreadable without the help of machines, and a great deal of specialized knowledge was necessary to write programs. A more readable format was quickly found: assembler. In assembler, the second generation programming languages, the machine instructions are programmed in a readable format and later translated into machine code: so-called assembly. The advantages are readily apparent, but there were also great disadvantages. Since assembler was still based on specific machine instructions, a separate assembler dialect had to be learned for each type of computer. In addition, assembler was mainly focused on what a machine could do and not on what the programmer wanted. If a programmer wanted the machine to carry out a given process 10 times, he had to write a program which established a counter in the memory, instructed the counter to increase each time, and wrote the new quantity to the memory. That is naturally rather roundabout, which is why languages were designed that were independent of individual computer platforms. In these so-called third generation languages, the programmer has a number of abstract constructions, such as counting loops and if-then statements, at his disposal. He can focus entirely on the core of the program without worrying about the details of the machine on which the program will be run. Once the program is finished it is compiled, which means translated into a specific machine-readable code. Any COBOL program, for example, can be run on any given computer if a good compiler is available.

Third generation languages are multipurpose. They can be used to write anything, varying from a complex optimization algorithm to a financial administration system. If, however, we use great amounts of changeable data, we notice that it is inefficient to store this data in the program itself. To efficiently manipulate large databases, separate programs were designed: database management systems (DBMSs). The introduction of databases allowed the standardization of a great deal of the programming work. Anyone who has ever written an administrative application in a third generation programming language knows that such an application entails writing a large number of fairly repetitive routines: programs which gather information from disks, or write information to disks, or to the screen, programs which print out lists and check user input. The need for more powerful commands to directly manipulate data and screens and to define lists quickly arose. The use of database systems led, in time, to a new abstract layer above the third generation languages: fourth generation programming languages. Applications can quickly be built with the help of these new languages. In many cases, definition of a simple data model is enough to create an elementary administrative system. Of course, once one knows what files make up a system and how those files are related to one another, one can automatically generate the file structure, the input screens and the print routines.

The fourth generation languages are not the final stage in the development. They flow, almost without a gap, over into a new concept: object-oriented programming. Fourth generation languages are also still based on the traditional distinction between programs and data. The data is passively stored in a database and lies in wait to be processed by the active procedural part of the application, the program. The problem with this traditional view is that maintenance of programs is very difficult. In an environment with a frequently changing structure, not only do data definitions often need modification, but the programs which process the data need frequent maintenance. Object-oriented programming tries to offer a solution to this dilemma by eliminating the age-old distinction between data and program. Programs are divided into so-called objects, which are partial applications containing both data and programs. Objects communicate with each other by sending messages. The main idea is that objects are relatively independent. New programs are developed by creating new objects. Objects can easily be exchanged between programs. An object in a program is easily exchanged for another object which can process the same messages. Software becomes much more robust and software maintenance becomes simpler using this approach. Object-oriented programming is an approach which can easily be linked to client/server technology, and which strengthens the client/server concept. After all, client/server does not possess a hierarchical structure, but a combination of separate programs.

Mainframe

Within automation, the mainframe is well known as a computer that is used for the management of large database files, and which enables the execution of thousands of transactions at the same time. We thus find the mainframe in environments where hundreds of thousands of users need to continually access database files. Mainframes are especially important in the financial, insurance and government worlds, and in the transport and chemical industries. In part due to the mainframe, thousands of transactions per day can be processed by banks. Salaries have not been paid in cash at most organizations for years, but are paid using automatic credit bookings processed by computer. The financial world would never have been able to grow at such a spectacular rate without the help of mainframes. Mainframes are mainly found in organizations which possess large databases. Since most mainframes came from IBM, a reasonable level of database and programming language standardization exists in the mainframe world. Many products were delivered by a single hardware manufacturer, leading almost as a matter of course to some degree of standardization.

The mainframe is able to support thousands of users at any given moment due to its special operating system. This operating system must be able to optimally control the central processor, to establish thousands of terminal links, to manage thousands of printers and to facilitate communication with other computers. This is all centrally handled by a single computer. The tasks are usually quite comprehensive, and skilled personnel are required to coordinate the various activities with one another, and to manage the entire process. Without specialized system management software, it is almost impossible to keep a mainframe running.

Although the mainframe offers enormous centralized power, users need local service, service other than that for which the mainframe is meant and for which it is suitable.

Mainframe maintenance

The mainframe turned out to be too expensive for certain processes and not flexible enough. Maintenance of mainframe applications also continues to be an enormous cost post. The hierarchical database is especially complex and expensive to maintain. Third generation languages are not flexible enough according to modern-day standards to link new applications to existing applications and databases. Maintenance is an extra bottleneck, especially when applications must be converted or ported to other computers or program languages. Publication of new releases often means modification of existing applications, with considerable consequences for the stability of these applications. At present, the maintenance of existing applications at some large organizations accounts for 60% of the system-related time expenditure. This is occurring at a time when there is a great need for the automation of business processes. The mainframe is continually being fitted with new possibilities, and is certainly not standing still in its evolution. The 1980s, for example, saw new insights into the arrangement of databases. The relational database, a concept already developed at the beginning of the 1970s by Codd and Date, began to be used. Relational database technology is based on mathematical insights from set theory and relational algebra.

IBM introduced the relational database DB/2 as an answer to the hierarchical database. Other suppliers also began to make use of the relational database principle. Oracle was one of the first in the market to commercially introduce a relational database, and it was quickly followed by Ingres and Sybase. This development was also made possible by programming language evolution. The programming language C, for example, became popular at the beginning of the 1980s and offered developers new possibilities. Since modifications in the mainframe can have enormous consequences for existing applications, mainframe departments are unable to respond quickly to new developments. Upwards compatibility is a condition for many clients' new computer purchases, as very few organizations can afford to quickly write off this kind of investment. It remains, however, extremely difficult to introduce new developments into a mainframe environment, since in many cases, software written in the 1960s and 1970s must be retained.

Many mainframe sites are wrestling with problems rooted in the past. It is often difficult to adequately maintain existing programs; the original source codes are no longer available and the programmers have changed function or job. This leads to particularly great difficulties, as in the 1990s a number of fundamental technological innovations become generally accepted. Users want graphics possibilities in, for example, word processing and spreadsheets, and the demand for database applications continues to grow. The mainframe's operating system is unsuitable for many of these functions.

This has all led to a demand for new multifunctional operating systems. The mainframe possesses a very heavy-duty operating system which is suitable for supporting a great number of users. It is, however, not open, and it is suitable only for the supplier's specific hardware line. The desire to transfer applications to other platforms has lead to a new generation of operating system.

Minicomputer

The minicomputer was the 1970s' answer to the demand in the market for computer power for special applications at the department level, or for small and medium sized business. The administrative departments of many organizations had an urgent need for inexpensive computers for process automation. Other forms of database-oriented application were also in demand. Minicomputers which supported technical research work were also introduced in the market. The programming language Fortran was especially popular in research circles. These machines, however, were also very limited in functionality.

Although the mainframe market was controlled chiefly by IBM, the mid-range market consisted of a variety of competitors: DEC, Honeywell, Bull, Burroughs, and so on. One of the more striking phenomena in the mid-range market was the fact that each supplier again had its own operating system, which was closed to the competitors' products and usually to other types of computers from the same supplier. These proprietary systems made it difficult for many organizations to expand without substantial conversion costs.

Personal computer

The beginning of the 1970s saw the introduction into the market of the first micro-chips which could serve as the computer's central processing unit by companies such as Motorola and Intel. This made it relatively easy, with a bit of knowledge and a soldering kit, to build a simple computer. The personal computer (PC) was born.

Apple was the first large PC manufacturer. The first PCs were not equipped with a hard disk, with all programs read into the memory and run via a floppy disk drive. IBM quickly introduced its own variant of the PC: the IBM PC, and later the IBM XT. The arrival of word processors and new programs such as spreadsheets spurred the demand for more powerful PCs.

Compilers for programming languages such as C were developed. The personal computer was fitted with special cards which allowed the user to run simple graphics applications. The demand for local applications was so great that a large market came into existence for a variety of standard software, software which strained the PC's capacity to its very limits.

In the mid-1980s IBM introduced its new operating system, OS/2, the first real multitasking operating system for PCs. Users were now able to carry out several tasks at the same time, for example printing, calculations and data communications.

Many minisystem suppliers felt directly threatened by this development, one of the reasons that minisystem suppliers embraced the UNIX standard at the end of the 1980s. Independent investments in new operating systems had become unjustifiably large. UNIX supported networks, graphical interfaces and databases, and seemed to be an ideal system to switch over to, for a variety of reasons. The success of a number of market newcomers also began to play a role. A whole new segment came into existence: workstations. These machines, which fell between the PC and the minisystem, were originally used primarily for research applications, but gradually penetrated the business market segment. Sun is one of the most important players in this market, and has stimulated the acceptance of UNIX systems in the business world enormously.

PC operating systems

Desktop operating systems

There are currently millions of personal computers in use throughout the world. The popularity and power of the PC changed the IT world enormously. The real role for the end user began with the advent of the PC. This popularity was partly dependent on the user-friendliness of this computer. One of the first companies who started to sell a very user-friendly user interface was Apple, and its user interface remains one of the best in the world. It started to work with windows and objects at a very early stage. One of the problems with this software was that it was very dependent on the hardware platform. With PCs using the first Intel processors we saw DOS emerge as the dominant player in the area of desktop operating systems. DOS did not support any multitasking, nor did it have any windows capabilities. At the end of the 1980s, though, there was an increasing demand for window-oriented software for Intel platforms, and this gap in the market was filled by Microsoft Windows.

Windows

Microsoft started to ship its first Windows software in the mid-1980s, but it took some time before the end user could work really effectively with this product. The reason was that the world was waiting for the Intel 386 processor to give the processing power needed, and for cheaper memory prices. The real success of Windows started at the beginning of 1990. Five years later, most of the PC software in the world is working with Windows.

The demand for more computer power at the desktop was limited to memory and the 16-bit operating system. Windows 3.1 is still a 16-bit programming interface, but its successor, Windows 95, is a 32-bit multitasking operating system. Windows 95 really means the end of the DOS world.

With a window interface the end user can be much more flexible, and productivity is increased. The world of client/server with multimedia, graphical interfaces, advanced graphical interfaces and working with modular software are all made possible using this interface.

One of Microsoft's strongest selling points is that it can build a lot of very good and user-friendly software for its Windows interface. With sophisticated spreadsheets, word processors and office products, Microsoft has pushed the market into using its Windows product. The products are well integrated and well accepted in the marketplace.

The more powerful the personal computer becomes, the more powerful the desktop operating systems will be. At this stage we can already see that desktop operating systems can be connected to all kinds of other computer systems, that they can be used as file servers or as operating systems on large computers. The role of the small office computer has been taken over by the current personal computer, and the operating system to support this is now sometimes based on these desktop operating systems.

Windows NT

Microsoft introduced Windows NT in 1993. Market analysts expected this product to take over the Novell and UNIX server tasks, and at present there is a growing market share for NT, but it is not as big as many had predicted. Windows NT is a 32-bit operating system, and is on the market as Windows NT Workstation and Windows NT Server. Windows NT is a good operating system for personal computer servers in local area networks (LAN). A major aspect of the NT world is that it works not only on Intel processors, but also on RISC processors and on DEC Alpha systems. Another key element of NT is that all other Microsoft products, such as word processors and other office products, can be worked with. Again, it is well integrated, which means that in small office environments Windows NT is particularly successful. Both Novel and Microsoft will play an important role in this world. Microsoft is offering its SQL/Server as its relational database in local area networks, a database which is based on the Sybase database engine. The next generation of LAN servers from Microsoft is known as Cairo, and will support object orientation.

OS/2

When we talk about an existing user-friendly 32-bit desktop operating system, we can look at the current versions of OS/2 from IBM. With the first release of OS/2 in 1988 we could see the new world of user interfaces on Intel processors. This product is a single-user, multitasking operating system, capable of running on several applications simultaneously. IBM is now selling several versions of OS/2, like OS/2 Warp, OS/2 LAN Server for managing a server, and the Communication Manager for connections to hosts.

The problem with OS/2 has been the limited number of applications, like word processors, spreadsheets and standard applications, that run on it. This is now changing, and we can see many more applications running on OS/2 than in the past. Like Microsoft, it can work with its own relational databases.

IBM supports the DB/2 database on OS/2 with OS2/2. This database is a part of the DB/2 family, and is a complete relational database. Like Microsoft with Windows 95 and Windows NT, we can see today that IBM offers a complete set of products like multimedia, CICS, databases and word processors, and in its latest version OS/2 supports multiple processor techniques. Groupware like Lotus Notes or other products can all run on OS/2. The problem with OS/2 is that Microsoft offers a complete set of advanced software products from spreadsheet and word processors to complete office tools in its product line, while IBM offers only a limited number of tools. This means there are far fewer standard applications that run on OS/2 than are available in the Microsoft world. The market has traditionally preferred the Microsoft Windows world to that of OS/2. This may change with products like OS/2 Warp and Lotus Notes.

Groupware products

A new generation of software products will become very important for the end user: that is, the world of groupware products like Lotus Notes. Groupware offers users the flexibility to work with and integrate products like mail, databases, agenda, spreadsheets, applications and connectivity to other systems in their organization.

The world of groupware products is a world of graphical user interfaces where you can develop your own applications with simple macros. The groupware products allow you to share all the information in your organization with other end users. Messages are sent to and from employees and connected in different applications. Groupware products operate using client/server technology, and make it possible to connect your desktop world to other applications within an organization.

Groupware products are typically end user products with great possibilities. End users can work at home or in the field, connect themselves to the server and find the information they need, and send back their own information, which can in turn be used by other end users connected to the groupware products. The programs are flexible and easy to manipulate, and integration of the information in these programs is very easy.

PC networks

The PC has become extremely popular, due partially to enormous price decreases and the great number of standard software packages currently available. The PC possessed enough power and flexibility to make many investments in mini systems superfluous. The enormous increase in the number of PCs resulted in a rapid proliferation of local applications, printers, modems and standard software without the capacity to exchange data easily. This situation threatened to develop into unacceptable islands of automation, resulting in high costs along with a lack of manageability. Each PC needed its own printer and standard software, which meant substantially increasing PC usage costs.

A solution for this issue was the creation of networks. A PC network can be used in a variety of ways, some of which – listed in order of their degree of technological advancement – follow:

- *Printer sharing:* several PCs use a single printer which is controlled via the network.

- *File sharing:* files resident on one PC can be accessed by another. Useful for word processing environments.

- *Program sharing:* PCs can run programs, including executables, which are resident on other PCs.

- *Multi-user database:* the system includes a central server with a database that can be accessed by several PCs.

At first it was quite unclear which network products would play an important role. In the space of just a few years, however, the market leaders became apparent: LAN Manager from Banyan and NetWare from Novell in particular played an important role in ensuring user-friendly operation of the most common database, word processing and spreadsheet software on the PC within a PC network. This LAN software is acceptable in smaller but not in larger environments.

Network software based on existing PC architectures, however, inherits all of the greatest disadvantages of the limited underlying PC architecture: inadequate multi-user facilities, a limited degree of multitasking, inadequate security and poor backup and recovery facilities. These are all aspects which were reasonably well arranged in UNIX. UNIX is a multifunctional operating system, and it quickly became obvious that it had great potential for use at both workstations and on networks. This led to a broad acceptance of UNIX outside of the research market. UNIX was the first open operating system capable of meeting many of the requirements of network organizations.

Sun was especially good at exploiting the power of UNIX. Sun introduced its own hardware line, which was well suited for graphics applications and could also be used as a central network server. Universities and research centers worldwide were able to make excellent use of the Sun workstations. All of the activities which could be carried out on a PC could also be carried out on these work-stations, but the possibilities far exceeded those of the PC.

LAN servers and client/server

Client/server and LAN operating systems like Novell, LAN Server from OS/2, Windows NT and UNIX are compatible in many cases, but there are also some very important differences. Novell, LAN Server and Windows NT offer good capabilities in small departments. In the field of large client/server systems, with hundreds or thousands of users, we can see that only UNIX supports the high level connections needed for the server's tasks. New operating systems built to support personal computers in LANs could also support all kinds of server tasks like data-base, security, communication and authorization, on-line transaction processing (OLTP), distributed computing environment (DCE), multiprocessing techniques, distributed computing, advanced graphical user interfaces, clustering and heavy networking jobs, but not always as well as UNIX. In this world of heavy server tasks, the UNIX world is still developing and continues to dominate the market. UNIX will be used to build large client/server sites for many years to come because of the need for very powerful operating systems and highly skilled people who are able to connect all these servers. The UNIX world will take over many tasks from the mainframe world because it is capable of supporting mainframe tasks on the server. In particular, in a large client/server environment it is very important that servers are entirely controlled by the network and system manage-ment products.

UNIX

The UNIX operating system was written in 1969 at AT&T Bell Laboratories to simplify the work of AT&T's researchers. It is written in the C programming language, which, with its simple basic structure, is relatively easy to implement on a new computer. In this way, an open operating system was developed which could easily be transferred over to other platforms. The purchase price of the operating system was fairly low, one of the reasons for its great popularity with many universities. Universities often created their own versions of UNIX by adding their own code. The University of Berkeley deserves special mention in this connection. UNIX was, until a short while ago, a registered AT&T trademark. For this reason, many suppliers use other names for UNIX: DEC, for example, calls it ULTRIX, and IBM's version is called AIX. The many different names have led to some confusion in the market, but the belief that various packages exist is a misunderstanding: the various versions actually differ very little from each other.

UNIX has achieved revolutionary growth in the past few years. This is partly due to its extraordinary performance on the new generation of RISC processors. Some of the advantages of UNIX are:

- UNIX systems are open to various hardware platforms.

- It is not processor dependent.

- It offers outstanding graphics performance.

- It offers good processing performance.

- It offers good network facilities and can communicate with many other computers.

- It runs on both large and small computers.

At the end of the 1980s, the splintered character of the UNIX market and the many versions of the operating system began to hinder further acceptance of uniform standards. The market clearly needed further standardization. The interests of the various suppliers turned out to be irreconcilable, and two camps came into being: UNIX International and the Open Software Foundation (OSF). The differences in the viewpoints of the two organizations seemed minimal to outsiders, but for a long time a merger remained impossible for commercial reasons. Almost all of the larger software suppliers joined forces with OSF. Sun, however, with several other suppliers, including AT&T, joined forces with UNIX International.

This all changed in 1993. First, the network supplier Novell took over the AT&T UNIX System Laboratory, giving Novell all rights to AT&T UNIX. Novell used this takeover to attempt to penetrate the larger network environment market, a strategically important market for the company. Ultimately, UNIX International and OSF united forces in Unified UNIX. The partners offered their source code to the X/Open group, which certifies suppliers if they meet agreed upon standards. This cooperation was partially motivated by the threat embodied by Microsoft in its Window NT. An international UNIX standard finally came into being, so it is now possible to run the same UNIX on various hardware platforms, and the portability of UNIX software is ensured.

Databases

A database is a collection of data stored according to a preset structure. A database does not always have to be stored in the computer: a simple index card system is also a database, as is a large collection of data stored in a computer which enables thousands of users to carry out search operations simultaneously. A good computer database allows changes to be made to data without endangering data integrity. Any kind of information important to the organization can be stored in a database.

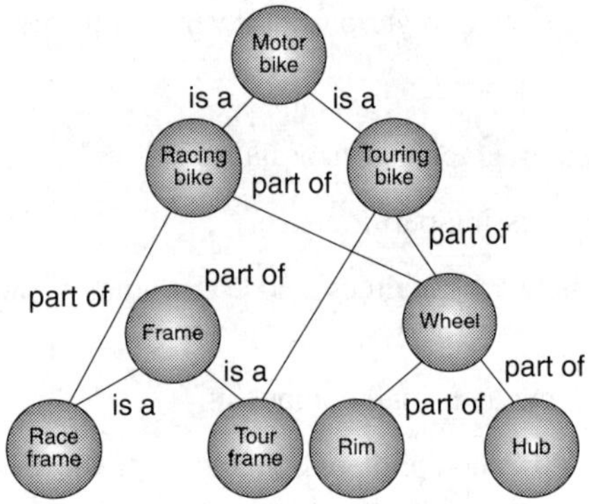

Figure 2.1 Structure of a motorbike world.

There are various types of database:

- file management system
- hierarchical database
- network database
- relational database
- object-oriented database.

File management

To explain the relationships between these databases we will give a simple example. The motorbike world displays a structural description of a bike database (Figure 2.1). There are two types of bike. The relationships between the two types are shown with an 'is-a' relationship. Bikes are made up of various components. The component relationship is called a 'part-of' relationship. Each type of database stores this information differently. The oldest and simplest form is the file management system, where each field is sequentially stored in a large file on a disk, known as a flat file (Figure 2.2).

```
........bike 1/wheel 1/rim 1/hub 1/wheel 2/rim 2/
hub 2/frame 1/union/bike 2/wheel 3/rim 3/hub 3/
wheel 4/rim 4/hub 4/frame 2/union............
```

Figure 2.2 File management system.

If information is needed, the information search operation begins, similar to a word processing file, at the very beginning of the file and continues sequentially until the information is found. It is obvious that this method cannot work quickly. If relationships between data must be defined and more than one system must work with the data at the same time, data manipulation occurs very slowly. The risk of damage to data integrity is also high. Of course, indexes can be created, allowing faster work, but these require considerable maintenance.

Hierarchical database

Larger databases are also often inefficient because many pieces of data have to be stored more than once. Take a database with company contact persons: of course, we want to store each contact person's address. Certain companies may, however, have more than one contact person. If we store all of our data in a single file, that file will contain the same address several times. That is very inconvenient if one of the companies moves because we will have to input the new address in several places in the file. This is called a one-to-many relationship. A single company has many contact persons, so these one-to-many relationships occur quite frequently. In addition, it is extremely important to recognize these relationships in connection with the consistency of the under-lying database. The file management system did not meet requirements on a number of points.

The first answer to this problem was the hierarchical database. In a hierarchical database, such as IMS, data is ordered according to a tree structure. It is obvious that relationships are easier to manage in this way. Each record can have a number of 'children,' the children can also have children, and so on (Figure 2.3).

Children inherit all their parents' dependencies. By allowing the logical organi-zation of the data to correspond to the physical location on the disk, a hierarchi-cal database can be searched extremely quickly. The design of hierarchical databases is also based on the need for speedy data search operations. All infor-mation is divided into classes which demonstrate a one-to-many relationship. This is then also the problem with these databases. If the structure is changed, a great part of the data also changes, leading to very time-consuming, expensive maintenance.

Network database

The tree structure is an excellent format for the storage of one-to-many relation-ships, but the world does not consist solely of this kind of relationship. More complex forms also exist: for example, the relationship between products and their suppliers. A product has several suppliers, and each supplier delivers several

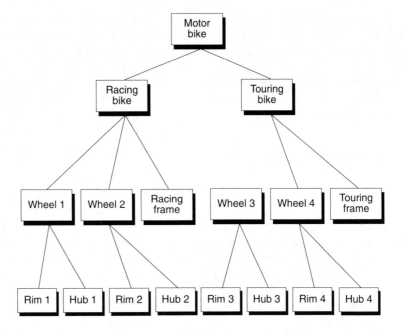

Figure 2.3 Hierarchical database.

products. Such relationships are called many-to-many. To efficiently model this kind of relationship, the network database (Figure 2.4) was developed, for example IDMS. Network databases also have their disadvantages, however.

Relational database

There was a need for a database model capable of physically storing data independent of its logical structure. The answer was the relational database (Figure 2.5). This database was developed in the early 1970s by E. F. Codd, and has been continually improved since that time. The relational model is based on insights into set theory and algebra. Data is organized in tables, which consist of columns and rows (records). With the aid of relational algebra, new tables can be defined based on existing tables. Data in tables is uniquely identified using keys, allowing easy definition of one-to-many and many-to-many relationships. We examine this phenomenon more in depth in the chapter on relational databases. The arrival of the relational database was ushered in by a new, fairly user-friendly programming language, Structured Query Language (SQL), which is based on relational algebra. This language can be used to define databases (via the data definition language, DDL), to manipulate data (via the data manipulation language, DML). The clear, structured form of the relational database has also influenced database design techniques.

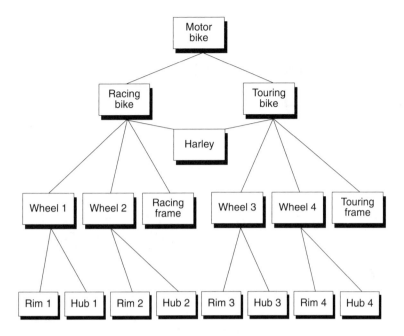

Figure 2.4 Network database.

At first, the relational database was not as quick as hierarchical databases, but various optimization techniques have made the relational database exceptionally fast. The relational database can execute transactions very quickly for a large number of users simultaneously. In some cases, the relational database is actually faster than the hierarchical database. The great advantages of relational databases are the ease of maintenance and the user-friendly manipulation via SQL. In addition, one-to-many and many-to-many relationships are easily defined in relational databases. Table structure modification can often be carried out after the fact, with minimal effort.

Object-oriented database

The introduction of relational databases, in turn, lead to some unexpected consequences. The relational database was brought onto the market by independent software suppliers who had a great interest in ensuring that their databases were able to run on the largest possible number of platforms. The separation of the database manager from the operating system was further carried out, resulting in a more portable database, and allowing the database to grow from the PC to the mainframe. In fact, these developments made the choice of the correct database for the client more important than the choice of the right database for the operating system or computer.

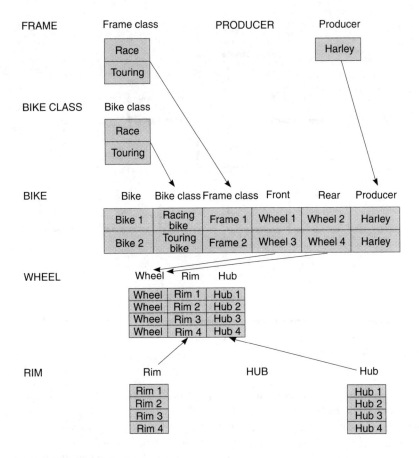

Figure 2.5 Relational database.

In addition to the relational database, we can see another development, the object-oriented database (Figure 2.6). The characteristics of such databases are:

- *Storage of information in objects*: objects can be much more complex than traditional databases. They contain not only information, but also knowledge about how to process that information.

- *Message passing:* objects communicate with each other by sending messages.

- *Encapsulation:* objects are autonomous. Objects have no access to each other's internal structure, except by sending messages.

- *Inheritance:* objects are included in a hierarchy of classes which inherit characteristics from each other.

There are few object-oriented databases used for infrastructural information systems. They are often used, however, in specialized systems such as databases under Case tools and information systems. Suppliers of relational systems will add object-oriented facilities to their products in the coming years. The object-

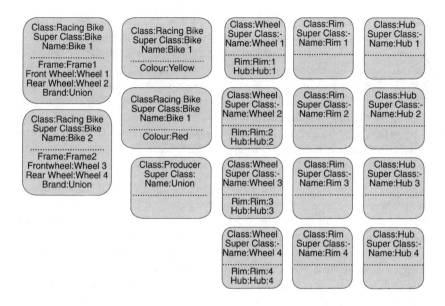

Figure 2.6 Object-oriented database.

oriented database's future as an independent application is questionable. That does not change the fact that the object-oriented philosophy displays many similarities to client/server ideas. The relationship between client and server systems is also based on message passing, during which the underlying systems retain a relatively high degree of autonomy. Many client/server applications are also object-oriented.

Fourth generation languages and databases

The popularity of relational databases also had another side-effect. Once a standard method had been found to store and search for data, methods become available to standardize other parts of programs. Elementary input screens and printouts, for example, can be directly based on the underlying data tables. Many of the tests and checks necessary to monitor database consistency can be defined in SQL. The arrival of the relational database led to the development and introduction of a new generation of programming languages. These fourth generation languages were different from their predecessors, which had no multipurpose environments. Fourth generation languages are specifically focused on building complete applications based on standard models. Various operations which were easily written in third generation languages, such as sorting algorithms, are almost impossible in fourth generation languages, but screen definitions and list specifications are quite easily programmed. The difference in programming style between the third and fourth generation languages is that in third generation languages all procedure components had to be written line by line. An application consists of a set of procedures which are linked by, for example, a user interface within which various applications can be controlled via a menu. Via an application programming interface (API), for example, access to a database or library can be gained. Many fourth generation languages do not use this type of procedure. Code is not usually written line by line. Standard statements are often contained in the standard software in the form of triggers, procedures or macros. In addition, a mere request for certain information is usually sufficient to get that information: the computer itself decides where and how to gather the information.

Almost all suppliers of fourth generation languages work with SQL as the programming language for an underlying relational database. This is partly because SQL has become an international standard. Working with a fourth generation language has therefore become very attractive. A database can easily be modified and transferred to other hardware platforms. Fourth generation languages (4GL) have turned out to be an ideal answer to the third generation languages such as COBOL and PL/1. The ease with which standard applications can be programmed in fourth generation languages saves considerable time. Most fourth generation languages can be used on several relational databases, and also run on various hardware platforms. This results in applications which are less dependent on the hardware and software on which they are used. The ideal of portable software came yet another step closer.

Usually, 4GL products are accompanied by an excellent screen painter which automatically builds the screens without necessitating user programming. These screens can be easily modified to meet new specifications, are often portable, and can be used on the different terminals of the various suppliers. Most fourth generation languages are based on the three-schema architecture, which is the first international step towards standards in software building. This architecture consists of three levels: screens or graphical user interfaces; the processes or procedures which are built with the help of triggers, macros or SQL statements; and the link with a relational database. The basis of this architecture is detailed in an International Standards Organization (ISO) report written in the 1980s. Three-schema architecture consists of:

- *External scheme*
  An external scheme determines how the system manifests itself to the user: for example, screens and reports. The external scheme enables the user to communicate with the system.

- *Conceptual scheme*
  The conceptual scheme details the relationship with the structure of the underlying database. This scheme also contains the constraints to which the database must conform. These are expressed in triggers and macros.

- *Internal scheme*
  This is the structure of the database. It determines how the data is physically stored.

As a result of this structure, the separation of database, procedures, user interface and operating system is becoming more and more common. No longer is everything hard coded and linked by a tangled jumble of program code. Applications are built in modules which communicate with each other. This development has made it possible to divide applications into loose components. In principle, a user interface may also be cut loose from the rest of the program, as long as communication exists between the user interfaces and the rest of the program. This means that an application's user interface can be resident on another computer, under the condition that adequate communication remains possible. Suddenly, because of the arrival of relational databases and fourth generation languages, the client/server concept became relevant. Of course, splitting programs into modules did not originate with the use of the fourth generation languages, but these languages have certainly exerted an important influence on the process. The greater portability of applications written in fourth generation languages is quite important in this regard.

Growth toward client/server

A historic overview of a number of important trends in the computer market reveals that a number of market developments point toward client/server computing, developments which are interdependent. The attention currently enjoyed by the client/server concept is entirely natural when seen in this light.

The arrival of the PC made the creation of an intelligent workstation possible. Whereas, in the past, certain tasks could only be carried out using a central processor, today tasks can be divided between a central and a distributed processor. Finally, intelligent work, such as working with a graphical interface, can be carried out at the local workstation. This new functionality does, however, place new demands on the hardware. Special computers are now being developed which are suitable for special tasks: for example, graphics computers which control various complex graphics programs, but also control communication servers and printer servers that can process great quantities of data. The rapid proliferation of operating systems and processors in our example makes efficient system management very difficult for many organizations, so the expenses related to training and application conversions are rocketing.

The demand for standardization is increasing, and a number of suppliers are taking the lead, working together in the areas of operating systems and exchanging applications. Due to the pressure on the market, quick reactions are vital. Many organizations can no longer finance these changes without making use of internationally accepted standards. The computer industry has seen unbelievable capacity growth, and prices remain under pressure. Hardware suppliers increasingly purchase their processors centrally from a few large suppliers, and very few manufacturers still produce their own processors. Just a few organizations, such as Intel, Motorola, Sun, HP and IBM, can still finance this. The market for memory chips is becoming increasingly centralized, with just a handful of organizations, including IBM, able to actually produce memory themselves.

Operating system standardization brings a number of parties in the market closer together. Hardware and software from various manufacturers can be exchanged without problems, and thus the concept of interoperability is born. Due to the introduction of networks, process execution can be optimally distributed over the organization, which in turn leads to a greater demand for specialized processors.

The final development in this chain is the introduction of the relational database. SQL facilitates application portability. Applications can be split into the user interface, processes and database. Networks which allow PC applications to communicate with database servers come into existence. The only thing missing to ensure a good provision of information service in such an environment is a good concept to link everything together and to make the total package manageable. Filling this gap is the mission of client/server and distributed technologies.

GOLDEN RULES

- Mainframes can become a part of a client/server architecture; they will be used as a database server and an on-line transaction processing system.

- The world of proprietary systems will come to an end; there is space left for them only if they are able to work in an open environment.

- The personal computer will take over many tasks in an organization, and the influence of the personal computer will increase; for that reason, it needs a multitasking operating system.

- Groupware products will become very strategic, as they are able to collect a lot of information in the organization at the end user's desk. Groupware products, multitasking operating systems using graphical user interfaces, allow it to connect all the information systems within the organization.

- Relational databases and object-oriented databases will play a strategic role in the client/server environment.

- Client/server is the concept that links all the information systems together, and they are set up in such a way that they can communicate with each other.

Chapter 3
Cost justification

Return on investment

Before every new investment, the return on investment must be carefully examined. Usually, the first implementation of the client/server concept will involve the purchase of various new hardware, software and network products: management tools, fourth generation programming languages and relational databases, gateways, training, and the re-engineering or reconstruction of applications. This can demand investments which quickly exceed current IT budgets. A healthy return on investment must, of course, balance out these new investments. If one looks only at the difference in depreciation expense between the new and the existing environment, one gets a distorted idea of the actual costs. In many cases, the traditional and new environments will need to run in parallel for a certain amount of time. The costs will then definitely rise during the inception phase. Setting up a good infrastructure for client/server can be taken care of most effectively by a software integrator specialized in client/server implementation. If process organization does not go well during the inception phase, the chance is high that costs will be unnecessarily high, and that recouping the investment will take much longer than necessary. Each investment must be placed in the framework of the organization's present and future needs (Figure 3.1).

Everyone knows that the investment in a typewriter is much lower than the investment in a PC, laser printer, word processor and the training necessary to effectively use this kind of equipment. The efficiency advantages of the latter investments, however, are so great that the return on investment in a PC is many

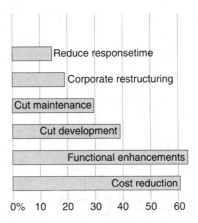

Figure 3.1 Motivation to switch to a client/server environment.

Cost reduction and functional enhancements are the main motivations driving mainframe replacement by client/server configurations. (Customer response OTR market analysis 1995.)

times larger than the return on investment in a typewriter. The capabilities of the PC and word processor are so much broader than those of a typewriter that comparison is simply impossible. The user of a PC can carry out far more tasks than the user of a typewriter, and the ability to call up an existing file and modify it to fit current needs implies enormous increases in efficiency.

The same is true of a well implemented client/server environment. Organizations which are considering client/server implementation are wise to first devise a good plan for the infrastructure. This serves as a growth path which can later be adjusted to account for changes in the user demands or the environment. Reviewing only short-term investments, and ignoring long-term investments, can lead to dramatic developments in the future. Since few companies have switched over to a complete client/server environment, most organizations look only at the short-term cost increases. Organizations which have taken the step into a total client/server environment now see their costs quickly decreasing, after the initial period of educational construction and adjustment. Their applications are built more quickly, and the organizations can react more quickly to the wishes of their users. The old systems can slowly but surely be retired. Improvements on the workfloor will lead to considerable cost savings.

Special aspects of client/server implementation

Implementation of the client/server concept involves a number of particular aspects which must be considered when making a price comparison. We will briefly discuss these aspects.

Maintenance and conversions

Maintenance is an important aspect of the cost evaluation of a client/server environment. The maintenance of traditional systems is a cost post that is reaching unacceptable proportions in many organizations. In the past few years, the cost of maintaining mainframe environments has risen rapidly. Many organizations currently spend 60% of their system-related time in performing maintenance. Many applications built in the 1960s and 1970s are now hopelessly out of date. These applications are usually built in assembler, PL/1 or COBOL, and the source code is difficult to maintain because they were written using old-fashioned development techniques. The developers of these applications are usually no longer present in the organization, or have received other job functions. The system documentation is often out of date, or has actually disappeared completely. In many cases, costs will increase even more if the organization is forced to change in response to quicker changes in the market than in the past. Much software contains hardware-dependent code; screen and printer control, security and other components are programmed with hard code. In such an environment, existing applications slow down the organization's progress. Maintenance is postponed, and in the long run the information system changes from a business support to a millstone around the organization's neck.

The greatest difference between the traditional and client/server environments is that the software is usually split up into fixed components, making future maintenance simpler. In a well set up client/server environment, the developers take future maintenance into consideration. The programs are split into loose modules, and typical client/server techniques are used. Interaction between software modules occurs via client requests and server responses. Adherence to the principle of modular construction prevents hard coding of printers, security and authorizations. Calling up business rules, changing terminals, user interfaces and many other components must be set up to enable easy modification to the system, for example with the use of remote procedure calls (RPC) or by using reusable object technology.

Hard coding of program dependencies, the forceful coupling of these with each other, as we usually see in the traditional environment, impairs flexibility so seriously that the software will have to be drastically modified in the long term. This is also one of the dangers of re-engineering to a client/server environment. It may be true that hardware prices necessitate this step, but the organization must first carefully consider the role of existing programs if a client/server environment is to be implemented at a later stage in business operations.

Maintenance with 4GL

The rise of fourth generation languages will lead to an extensive repositioning in the setup of information systems. These languages are especially suitable for building standard applications, and guarantee a high degree of portability and openness. They can be especially valuable, as they can drastically decrease the enormous costs associated with conversions to other platforms.

A number of 4GL suppliers, including Oracle, Informix, Sybase, Ingres, Powerbuilder, Gupta and many others, have begun to tune their development environments to meet the requirements of client/server environments. Separate servers are being developed for the execution of most functions. Separate servers execute tasks for business rules, applications, printers, multimedia, gateways, replicators and databases. Maintenance of these software products opens a completely new dimension. Maintenance costs can usually be decreased to half of the costs involved in maintaining the old, traditional environment. Changes in operating systems or user interfaces have already been taken care of by these suppliers, which leads to a decrease in maintenance costs.

Conversions

The conversion of traditional environments to a new computer or to a new operating system is a topic in itself. The costs involved in conversions can be incredibly high, as conversions usually involve considerable investments in addition to normal maintenance. The issue is even more complex in situations in which the information systems of various organizations must be combined to form a single system: for example, in cooperation efforts between two companies. There are a number of conversion programs on the market which can translate program code to other programming environments. Many third generation programs are now being converted to fourth generation programs, but this creates situations which do not always lead to the desired results. Third generation languages are procedurally constructed, and the printer and terminal control must be separately programmed. Fourth generation languages usually use standard routines to carry out these tasks. In addition, 4GLs are usually able to work with SQL and triggers, but these are not recognized in 3GLs. Often, the conversion of simple programs is possible, or the underlying database can be converted, but conversion of a hierarchical database can lead to great problems. The fact that a program has been re-engineered does not mean that the program is optimally tuned to a client/server environment, or that the program has been improved. Re-engineering is often merely a cosmetic change; the old structure of the program remains unchanged. A menu-controlled program, for example, can be equipped with a graphical interface, but without fundamental changes to the underlying dialog, that remains a rather useless exercise. A COBOL application with a hierarchical database can be adapted to a relational system, but the old database navigation structure remains in the program, with all the inherent consequences for maintenance. In many cases, completely rewriting such a program can be cheaper in the long run.

In the present stage of automation, analysis and design of systems should actually already take future maintenance and modifications to the organization into account. The information systems of the future must be dynamically constructed based on client/server techniques so that modifications can be implemented more quickly and costs can be kept under control. The costs of future conversions must be more closely considered when examining investments in automation; they must certainly be included in any comparison of traditional environments and client/server. This comparison has already been made by many organizations, and has positively influenced them to switch over to open environments.

Business cycle

The business cycle concept is used to determine the amount of time it takes an organization to produce and sell products: the quicker this sort of business process can be carried out, the more cost effective the organization. The business process includes all kinds of phases. The implementation of the client/server concept can have a positive effect on the business cycle. We will examine this in more depth in an example.

An organization has built up an inventory using its own financial resources. This inventory on-hand must be sold as quickly as possible at a profit. Several variables can affect this process, including the following:

- Inventory on hand must quickly be replenished in case of shortages.

- Inventory levels must not be too high, as this has a negative effect on liquidity.

- Orders must be filled on time.

- Invoicing must occur on time.

- Accounts receivable must be carefully monitored so that payments are received on time.

All the components in the entire process must be well connected. There are various interactions between these processes. The consequences of mistakes are often quite considerable, and these consequences can in turn lead to new problems. Various procedures for returning received goods, for example, or making modifications to the invoices for those goods, can impose enormous pressure on the organization, and can have enormous consequences for the financial results of the organization. To be able to direct this process, it is important that business processes are adequately mapped out. In most traditional environments, an inventory system functions along with an invoicing system. Many transactions are also processed by hand: updating inventory receipts, placing orders, invoicing based on sales receipts, and so on.

This can be set up differently in a client/server environment. All data is stored in a relational database. The system knows the average length of time a particular product is on hand in inventory, allowing orders to be generated automatically and sent via data communication to the supplier. Each workstation is equipped with a terminal, and manual input is practically eliminated. Catalogues can be automatically put together and sent electronically to a prospective client, who can request, with the help of multimedia, both visual and audio information on the products. Management possesses decision support systems which allow it to request timely information on the organization at the highest, most abstract levels. Modular construction of such an environment allows modifications to be carried out locally. Data can be easily requested by word processing and spreadsheet programs.

Of course, this is all possible on a mainframe as well, but on a mainframe programs are usually hard coded and not modular. The user is more dependent on existing input and output stations, and is limited in his use of various modern techniques. The local workstation interface with the mainframe is usually simple with high overhead costs.

The implementation of the client/server concept can have a positive influence on the business cycle and on the quality of workstation support.

Software limitations

Software has undergone an enormous development over the last few years, and the market offers a wealth of trustworthy, powerful standard products. A selection of the software products presently in use includes:

- graphical applications supported by Windows
- data warehouses and decision support
- case tools
- object oriented
- multimedia
- query tools
- office tools
- relational databases
- animations
- groupware products.

The choice and combination of these products is an important aspect of the construction of a client/server environment. Each software product must be flexibly integrated in the organization, and organizations are beginning to look more closely at the way in which the various products are integrated with each other. Computer-aided design/computer-aided manufacturing (CAD/CAM) applications, for example, must integrate with relational databases. Office tools work with electronic mail and fax machines, and query tools work with word processors and spreadsheets. The combination of this software is of vital importance, and partially determines the flexibility, cost of maintenance and level of productivity achieved. If software is necessary to support business processes, the organization must carefully consider that software's contribution to future productivity. Software which may limit future processes, or make these processes unnecessarily complex, should not be implemented. Each investment made must be weighed and balanced against present and future requirements. An open environment with client/server will provide the best guarantee for software capacity and future growth and the flexibility of the organization.

Management tools

The costs of management of a client/server environment should not be under-estimated. According to many critics, the management of client/server environments is far more expensive than the management of traditional environments. If version management and software distribution functions are also carried out on PCs and local workstations, the costs can be much higher than in a traditional environment. In the past, all functions, including security, authorization, software and version management, could be centrally regulated. The fact that software must be purchased for each local system also results in considerable expense. Many advice bureaus also maintain that the cost of maintaining a workstation used by a large number of users is more expensive in the long run with the client/server concept than with a simple single terminal connection (Figure 3.2).

In the past, the organization was able to manage the entire environment from a single location. At present, however, hundreds or even thousands of different systems must be controlled from various locations. To make this kind of installation manageable, a whole new generation of software products is being developed. Network management, system management and database management tools are especially helpful in carrying out client/server management tasks. Comparative studies of client/server and traditional environments have demonstrated that investment in the client/server concept is returned completely within one or two years, and that the costs of management thereafter hardly rise at all, even if the size of the client/server environment increases considerably. In general, we have

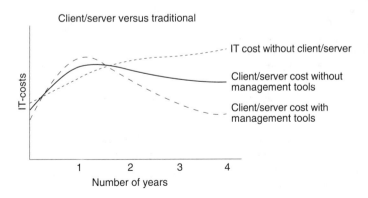

Figure 3.2 Cost justification.

noticed a dramatic decrease in management costs in well supported environments, just one or two years after implementation of client/server. Some of this cost decrease can be ascribed to the dismantling of the original traditional environment and completion of the switch-over to client/server.

Management tools work well only if you have set up a good architecture and standards; only this combination offers you a good management environment.

Workstation automation

One aspect of the client/server concept which usually receives inadequate attention, but which is of great importance in the implementation of the concept, is the role of the user. The role of the user can also provide extra impetus for the implementation of the client/server environment.

In organizations in which the user has no influence on processes, demotivation often occurs. The idea that the working conditions of the individual employee can be drastically changed without him having the slightest influence on such changes also plays an important role in employee demotivation. The user is of great importance for the acceptance of the system and evaluates the user friendliness of the graphical user interface, the integration with office and query tools, word processors, spreadsheets and other products. The most important gain from client/server implementation usually lies in the increase of productivity at the workstation. This means that the individual user is an important link in the success of client/server projects. Favorable implementation of the client/server concept leads to an enormous increase in productivity at the workstations in many organizations. This productivity increase allows the investment in local workstations to be quickly recouped. In some cases, organizations have seen an increase of 50% in productivity. If the user sees that he can exert a positive influence over the entire implementation of client/server, acceptance will be higher and the introduction stage can be considerably shortened.

GOLDEN RULES

- Traditional information systems are unable to cover the current requirements of a modern organization.

- The current maintenance cost of traditional systems will turn to 60–80% if they want to support the new demands within an organization. Only modern techniques based on client/server techniques are able to support this.

- Conversions of traditional computer systems are extremely expensive, and give hardly any technical benefit.

- Modern computer architectures can support a short business cycle.

- The cost of a client/server environment will give you an extra investment at the beginning.

- Client/server will increase your maintenance costs due to the large number of hardware and software systems dependencies.

- Maintenance costs of client/server can be controlled only if you are using a good architecture, standards and management tools.

- Network and system management tools are a must in a client/server environment.

- The return on investment on a client/server system will start within one to two years; the cost reduction will be considerable after this period.

- A good client/server environment can improve your business cycle time.

Chapter 4

Client/server concepts

Definitions

The client/server concept remains in constant fluctuation. We have devised the following definitions (Figure 4.1):

- Client/server is a distributed software architecture within which systems are divided into autonomous processes, allowing clients to request functions which are then carried out by the server. In such an environment, the end users are more flexible and they can manipulate the data they need on a local system.

- Client/server is a concept in which tasks are distributed over clients and servers, allowing tasks to be carried out by those machines which are most suitable for task execution.

Each organization will have its own individual interpretation of a client/server environment. This is because the client/server architecture is dictated by the structure of the organization, which in turn is formed by the market within which it operates. Due to the concept's openness, there are countless software products – each with its own possibilities and limitations – on the market for each client/server architecture. Each organization will have to draw up its own management policies to successfully introduce a client/server architecture. First and foremost, client/server involves software. As the size of the organization increases, the complexity of management issues increases correspondingly. The

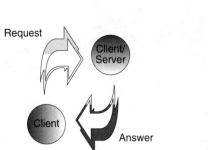
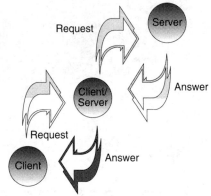

Figure 4.1 Different functions of clients and servers.

organization must implement clear and flexible policies to enable permanent, controlled growth. The organization must also be set up in such a way that adherence to the policy is unavoidable.

The client/server concept is based on a dialog between the client and server. A client passes a given request on to the server and the server executes a task. Each task is processed on a client or server is executed by a software module. The software modules in a client/server concept are able to work together. The server takes action only after having received a software request from the client. There are many different types of software modules that can run on a server. The server tasks do not in fact necessarily have to run on different machines. A short overview follows:

- *Printer server* is used for printing documents.

- *File server* is used to store files accessed by many users: for example, word processing files.

- *Database server* uses a database for data storage and processing.

- *Application server* is used to store an organization's applications, which are distributed to various clients. An application server can also be used to run specific applications.

- *Communication server* processes communication between various networks, protocols and computers. This server can also be used to manage networks.

- *Transaction processing server* executes line transactions. This server is mainly used to carry out speedy bulk transactions, and often supports a great numbers of users.

- *Multimedia server* is used to run specific multimedia applications. This server is used to store drawings, photos, film, audio, and so on.

- *Batch server* executes special batch assignments.

More than one server can carry out the same task within an organization. For example, each department may have a printer server and several database servers. In principle, a single machine is sufficient to carry out multiple server tasks. A single server can be used for database, batch and printer activities.

The basic principle of client/server is that the client is a computer which requests action of one or more servers. Servers are, in turn, able to activate other servers, given the fact that servers can send requests to other servers. In this way, servers suddenly become clients. A database server, for example, can send a request to a printer server to print a document. This results in a distributed method, often called distributed computing.

The client/server concept will eventually result in a form of enterprise computing whereby all the hardware and software systems can work together and the information is available at the place where the end user needs it.

Software distribution

To allow software to run on a client and a server, but still be organized as a single application, the application must be split up into the appropriate components. This demands special attention from the software developer. Most 3GL applications are not very modular in structure: screen structure, disk and printer control, communication ports and terminal links are all encoded in the application, and are closely linked to each other. Libraries are often used, which contain the code for a number of standard functions. An application written in a third generation language consists largely of a great number of files which must all be present on the same machine in order to work properly. Specific interaction with the operating system, for example for print and screen function support, is often programmed. The link between the operating system and the links between the various files prevent the use of such applications within a client/server environment. A client/server application must always have a modular construction, as modularity allows the various parts of the application to be distributed over several systems.

Client/server versus the mini and mainframe

One of the advantages of the client/server concept is that it can be implemented in stages. Most organizations already possess enough PCs and a network with which the PCs can be linked. During the first implementation stage, many tasks can be carried out on a single server. As the organization grows, another computer can be placed next to the first server to take over some of its tasks. This differs, for example, from a mainframe, where investments are often made in capacity expected for the coming years, which means that any future infrastructure is often financed at the very inception of the system.

Another advantage of the client/server concept is that it allows application-focused thinking. If a specific computer is necessary to carry out graphics functions, it can be included in the client/server architecture without any problem. Large central systems often do not allow the addition of such functions without fundamental changes being made to the system architecture.

The client/server concept allows step-by-step investments to be made only as they are needed. In addition, avenues are opened to local execution of specific tasks, without these tasks affecting the rest of the organization. A department in an organization, for example, may need a graphics application with a database that communicates with the central database. Graphics workstations, which are optimally suited to the tasks required of them in this department, can be purchased and installed in this department while the database communicates with the organization's central database. This eliminates the need for a large central system on which all of the applications run. Cooperation is created, but without a hierarchy. Departments can remain autonomous, but intercommunication is optimal.

All of this illustrates the possibilities of the client/server concept: intercommunication, autonomy and optimal data availability. The concept grows along with the organization's needs, and investments are thus matched to the organization's needs. The payback period for hardware and software is shorter. Applications which have already been purchased can usually remain in use, and these applications, in turn, can communicate with other applications. This results in an environment which can generate the following benefits, if appropriately set up:

- decentralized computing;

- use of computers for tasks for which they are optimally suited;

- gradual growth, no oversizing;

- optimal support for departments/units;

- existing equipment can remain in use;

- cost savings;

- software investments better guaranteed;

- user possibilities increased;

- investments in powerful minis and mainframes not always necessary;

- heterogeneous hardware and software platforms can communicate with each other;

- greater availability;

- fewer performance problems;

- greater technical possibilities, including graphics.

These advantages, however, are available only to companies that create a good infrastructure. All parts of the system must be well tuned to work optimally together. The client/server architecture is often seen as the answer to the mainframe, but this is not always true, and it is greatly dependent on the organization. A large bank would not be too quick to modify its mainframe and completely implement the client/server concept. Client/server can certainly lead to a change in the tasks of the mainframe, but it is independent of two concepts with which it is sometimes confused:

- down-sizing, and

- right-sizing.

Down-sizing is a process in which migration from a larger mainframe system to one or more smaller systems occurs. These are usually more powerful UNIX-oriented systems, which are able to take over a part or all of the mainframe's functions.

Right-sizing is a process in which the most suitable computer is used to perform a specific task. The strongest points of a special computer are taken into account when choosing the special tasks which that computer will be used to carry out.

Both down-sizing and right-sizing can be achieved using the client/server concept. This is, however, not absolutely necessary. Down-sizing a mainframe, for example, does not necessarily mean that the client/server concept is being implemented. In such a case, all application processes can continue to be carried out on a UNIX server, while no use is actually made of clients as we know them in the client/server concept.

Hopefully, the client/server concept has been explained clearly, so the chapter continues with a more in-depth explanation of the conditions which must be met for successful implementation of the client/server concept.

Conditions for implementation

As previously mentioned, client/server policies must be drawn up before the actual implementation of a client/server architecture. These policies are dependent on a variety of variables, including the organization, the hardware and software choices made, and, of course, the relationships with the existing infrastructure.

Experience in the implementation of client/server technology within larger organizations reveals that the importance of an overall policy is often underestimated. Companies with a number of PCs in a LAN do not necessarily think of important management tasks such as security, performance, tuning, software distribution, version management and other system tasks. The logic of these tasks is more obvious to companies with mainframes. These tasks are usually relatively well organized in the mainframe environment. Mainframe personnel, however, are plunged into an open world with all kinds of new possibilities, such as graphical user interfaces, PCs and all kinds of 4GL products and Case tools. The two extremes need to grow toward each other in the client/server environment. It is true that the LAN manager in a Novell network carries out some of these functions, but environments with a large number of PCs, minis and mainframes have correspondingly complex demands. The security and quality of the environment require far more attention. Client/server technology encompasses not only a technical side, but also an organizational side: it cannot be implemented without a struggle – organizations must grow into the concept.

A number of variables which are very important during client/server implementation are discussed below:

- networks
- relational databases
- fourth generation languages
- object-oriented technology
- network and system management
- client/server concepts
- analysis and programming within client/server
- links with mainframes and minis
- international standards
- the organization.

These subjects are discussed here briefly, and in more depth in later chapters.

Networks

Client/server communication occurs over networks. The clients and servers must find each other, and they must speak and understand the same language. The number of communication possibilities is quite broad, and is dependent on many factors, including network infrastructure, network protocols and operating systems.

Databases

One of the most common forms of client/server uses relational databases. This concept encompasses many possibilities, but ANSI/SQL, two phase commit, distributed databases and stored procedures demand special attention. Models of business processes can be stored in the database, and these models must be borne in mind during analysis and programming.

Fourth generation and object-oriented languages

Use of fourth generation languages has been particularly important in shortening the programming time for many applications which run in client/server environments. These languages play an important role in the client/server breakthrough. Various client/server concepts are examined in later chapters in relation to fourth generation languages and relational databases. In addition to fourth generation languages, we are now seeing the arrival of the new concept of object technology.

Network and system management

The implementation of the client/server concept requires a network management capability. An insight into the network's infrastructure must be obtained, and the various network components must be optimally tuned to each other. To support this, diverse management tools are available, including network management tools. In addition to network management, various other kinds of management must be carried out: for example, configuration management, backup and recovery, performance analyses and tuning, version management, printer control and software distribution. Many of these management areas, which fall under the umbrella of system management, are described in greater depth in later chapters.

Client/server concepts

The client/server concept allows applications to be cut up into independent processes. The following divisions are used when discussing the various concepts:

- data management
- application functions
- presentation.

These divisions can be subdivided, and each division and subdivision has its own relationships with networks and management functions.

Analysis and programming within client/server

The introduction of a client/server concept encompasses an entirely new method of developing and building applications and databases. Traditional environments almost always use dumb terminals, and all processes are defined at application level. At present, graphics terminals with graphical user interfaces (GUI) are available, and intelligent databases make it possible to include some logical programming in the database. This change in analysis and programming approach is discussed in greater depth below.

Links to mainframes and minis, and conversion

Existing mini and/or mainframe infrastructures cannot be changed into a client/ server environment overnight. Links to the existing environment will usually remain in use for some time. Often, the mainframe or mini will also remain part of the new infrastructure. These links and conversion can make the implementation of a client/server environment more difficult. On the other hand, new possibilities are appearing, such as transaction monitors on PCs and minis. In the past, this sort of program could be run only on the mainframe.

International standards

The market is exerting more and more pressure on manufacturers to arrive at international standards for operating systems, network protocols, security, management and databases. Much software must be modified if it is to meet international standards. Some examples of these standards are DCE and CORBA.

The organization and client/server

Implementation of a client/server environment can influence the relationships within an organization. This may occur within the automation department, but it may also affect other departments, which have to learn new ways of working. Management support, financial consequences and the way in which the standards defined by the organization are enforced, play a role. The best approach to introducing the client/server concept in an organization, and step-by-step client/server introduction, are both key issues. The organization must learn to work with this new infrastructure, and traditional workflows will change. The organization must set up the standards, and the role of the end user is going to change. Data will not only be held at the central automation department, but will also be available in the entire organization.

As has already been seen in this chapter, a number of developments negatively influence our information systems' quality. Most existing systems are not maintainable or scalable, and they cannot be easily managed or integrated in new technologies. The client/server concept described in this book offers solutions for the creation of high-quality information systems which are able to grow along with future developments.

Client/server architectures

Historically, there has been a logical development from host-based computing to client/server systems.

Host-based computing

One of the first uses of computer technology was host-based computing. This is a method in which all tasks are carried out by a central machine, the host. Users communicate with the machine via dumb terminals, and all application processes are carried out on this central system. Host-based computing usually involves mainframe environments and traditional mini systems.

Master/slave computing

This is a method in which a local system, the slave, does have intelligence, but remains dependent on the central system, the master. Within static, hierarchical organizations, this model may provide an effective method. However, this concept can place a modern organization, which must be able to react quickly to new developments and tendencies, in a straitjacket, because users have so little influence over central processing.

Client/server computing

Client/server became an accepted term for a new automation concept in the mid-1980s. As already mentioned, client/server is more a way of thinking about automation than a technique. At present, it is advanced enough to allow client/server realization without any untoward problems.

The introduction of client/server applications entails the distribution of applications over several systems, in such a way that the user does not notice that the changes have taken place. Good network communication is essential, and to make that possible the software must be modular. The concept contains six basic software layers (Figure 4.2):

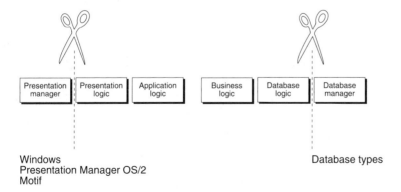

Figure 4.2 Modular construction client/server computing.

- *Presentation manager*
  A presentation manager takes care of the user interface: that is, control of the screens displayed on the user's terminal. Many forms of user interface currently exist: for example, Macintosh, Windows for DOS machines, Presentation Manager from OS/2, and Xwindows with Motif on UNIX systems. The user interface has gone through an enormous evolution in the past few years, and will offer continuously increasing possibilities, such as object orientation and multimedia.

- *Presentation logic*
  This is the application-dependent control. This layer defines the screens displayed for the user, the dialog structure and the fields displayed.

- *Application logic*
  Actual application processing is defined in this layer: for example, batch processing procedures, planning algorithms, authorizations, printer control and communication facilities.

- *Business logic*
  The business logic layer contains the definition of the organization's business rules: for example, employee union regulations, credit limits and inventory management rules.

- *Database logic*
  This layer contains the application's data dictionary: description of the tables, including their columns, data types and their primary and secondary keys.

- *Database manager*
  This is the actual database handler.

Elementary client/server strategies

Client/server applications are usually characterized by the way in which they are split apart. This approach is drastically simplified, but serves well during an introduction to the concept (Figure 4.3).

Five basic concepts are now discussed, and short examples of their application given.

First concept

In one of the first forms of client/server, the presentation manager was run on the client, while all other functions remained on the host (Figure 4.4).

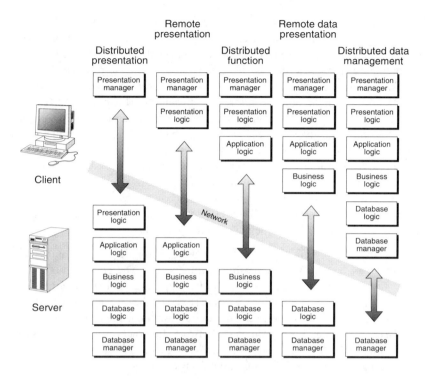

Figure 4.3 Elementary client/server strategies.

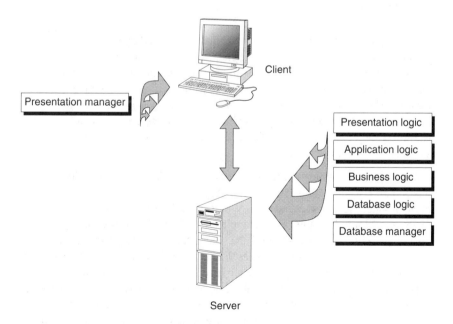

Figure 4.4 First client/server concept.

Terminal processing is handled centrally in a traditional environment. There are also intelligent terminals which take care of part of the presentation locally. This is most apparent in the case of GUIs which work with X-terminals. X-terminals are intelligent graphics terminals connected to a network: for example, Ethernet or Token Ring. The terminal itself has a powerful graphics processor, which is able to display graphic objects on screen very quickly. This makes the terminal very suitable for applications in graphic environments: for example, CAD, display of photos and other images. The great advantage of the X-terminal is that it can execute all kinds of graphics functions, in addition to standard character-based operations. The system can be extremely well secured, since all authorizations can be checked on the server with which the system communicates. The X-terminal, with its own unique address, must be recognized by a given server. These terminals are also inexpensive. They are much quicker at processing graphics applications than PCs, due to their specific graphics characteristics.

The X-terminal's presentation of the user interface is just partially run locally. The other part remains the responsibility of the server. The graphics library, the logic and screen instructions, as well as the other application definitions, are stored on the server. The graphic objects are stored on the server, not on the client. Even movement of objects on screen requires communication with the server. This places a considerable burden on the network. Ethernet is especially sensitive to this kind of burden, and use of the network by dozens of users on a single network segment can result in substantial delays.

Second concept

We have now seen that we can lighten the host's task load by allowing part of the graphics processing to occur via the client. Certain types of application, however, continue to put a heavy burden on the server. We can solve this problem by placing interfaces locally on the client, with their accompanying graphics libraries. The client can be a local PC, a workstation or another graphics server. The graphics server can be used as a client, where work occurs directly with the user interface, or as a server to which X-terminals are linked. This results in the architecture shown in Figure 4.5.

In this concept, the client is much more heavily burdened. First, the local client must be able to provide a GUI, which means that the client must have access to a product such as Windows, Windows NT, Presentation Manager or Xwindows/Motif. In addition, the application's interface-processing programs must be present on the client. Often, the simple fact that a program runs in a window is seen as working with graphics. This, however, has very little to do with graphics. Displaying simple character-based applications is quite easy in a Windows environment. We can speak of graphics work only if we optimally use the specific functionality of a graphics environment and incorporate it into the application architecture. The menu structure of an existing application often has to be totally modified before it can be equipped with a graphical interface.

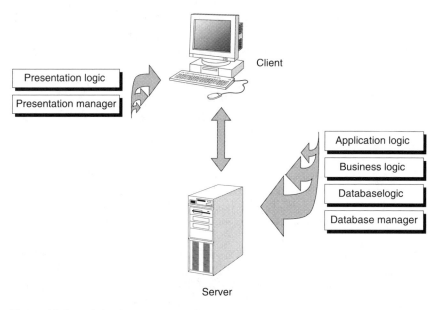

Figure 4.5 Second client/server concept.

Another important point is that optimal use is made of graphics possibilities, such as radio buttons, scroll bars, displaying structure diagrams, drawings and photos. The graphics library supplied with the package is often used to carry out these functions. These graphics applications are then further controlled by an underlying application, but make use of graphic objects specially developed for that purpose.

The advantage of setting the entire user interface on a local system is that the server and network are then unburdened. Running a local user interface, however, does not automatically result in better performance. A local PC will work more slowly with a graphics application than a server or powerful X-terminal specially designed for graphics applications.

This method also results in more complex local management. It also necessitates more powerful clients, expansion of local internal memory, a mathematical co-processor, a graphics adapter card and more intensive management, due to software installation and maintenance of the individual systems. In addition, the PC operating system is not always suitable for controlling large amounts of internal memory or optimally using the processor. However, this concept can be preferable to burdening a server, particularly in cases where infrastructure already exists. In some cases, investments are made under the assumption that enough powerful local machines will be available in the future. Lessening the network's burden can also be a strong argument for choosing this kind of architecture.

Working locally with graphics, with central server support for data storage and for running programs, will become more and more common due to the arrival of multimedia. The more powerful graphics programs run excellently on UNIX systems. Limitations to internal memory are practically non-existent, and RISC processors are more suitable for this work than the processors in today's PCs. Intensive user interface standardization will further increase the role of local systems, and the user interface will begin to exert a great influence on the client/server concept.

Third concept

Once graphics processing is carried out entirely by the client, the next step is to transfer the application routines to the client, resulting in the third concept (see Figure 4.6). The application logic contains the routines which execute the tasks which the program was built to carry out. The logic includes all of the constraints to which the program must conform. In addition, this level takes care of user interface control and maintenance of the data contained in the database. A variety of processes can be stored in an application: the database integrity, transactions, batch jobs, security, authorizations, menus, links to other applications and screen control. Applications in this concept can be built modularly.

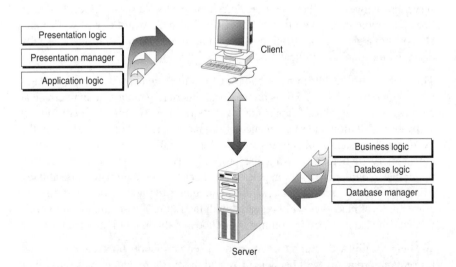

Figure 4.6 Third client/server concept.

Fourth concept

It is also possible to maintain the business rules locally on the client, which results in the architecture shown in Figure 4.7.

Business logic defines a part of the processes and constraints of an organization. It is an important aspect in the choice of a client/server architecture. The rules can be separately defined and stored, if desired, in a library. The application can reference a fixed rule in the library. Take, for example, Mr Clinton, who has a credit limit of $3000. This is not defined in every application which has a relationship with a credit limit, but reference is made to a central procedure where this constraint is stored. This credit limit constraint applies to all of the applications at all times, and is not application but organization dependent. That is why we speak of business logic. A bank branch can refer to centrally stored business rules in all client-related applications. If Mr Clinton is granted a new credit limit, this can be changed easily in a single central operation. Triggers and procedures which monitor the referential integrity of the database can also be centrally maintained.

To apply this form of client/server architecture, the various components must be able to be stored locally, and enough memory must be available to store and run the business logic. The local program then accesses only centrally stored data in

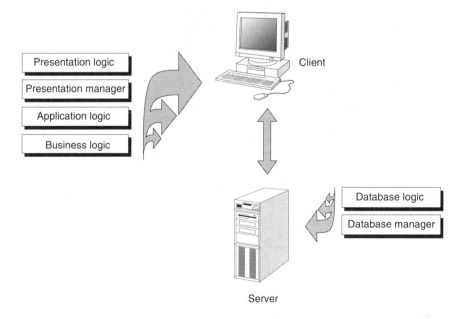

Figure 4.7 Fourth client/server concept.

databases on a central server. This approach can be used in situations in which little or no use is made of centrally stored business rules. This may be the case for applications which execute very specialized tasks, and which do not require central data storage. This method is often used for very technically oriented programs, including optimization routines, complicated calculations and planning and scheduling tasks which are carried out by a limited number of employees. Utilization of this form does mean, however, that all maintenance must be carried out locally.

This concept is suitable for nonstandard applications and for standalone applications. Introduction on multiuser platforms in larger environments has substantial consequences for system management. Management intensity will increase because, in principle, little is standardized. It is, however, a method which considerably unburdens the network, since the network is used only to access the database.

This concept also offers the possibility of running the business logic on a server set up especially for this purpose. This allows various clients to refer to a central server containing the business logic. They are capable of supporting the business logic via a user interface.

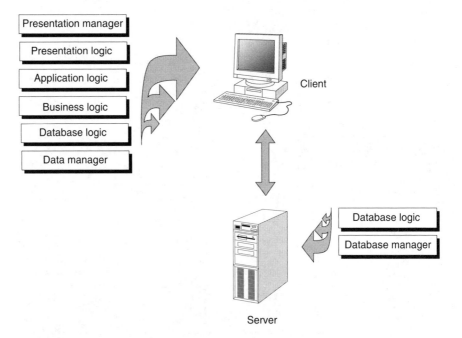

Figure 4.8 Fifth client/server concept.

Fifth concept

The last concept distributes all of an application's functions over several different machines (Figure 4.8). In such cases, we speak of distributed databases. This concept is of such great importance that we have described it separately in the chapter on relational databases.

Application of the concepts

The choice of client/server concept is strongly dependent on the circumstances of an organization. In addition, different forms of client/server can be used simultaneously in a complex environment. In the client/server concept, one program can be run using a client only for the presentation logic, while another program uses the client for both the application and business logic.

In general, we can say that the former concept is the best choice in graphics environments in which centrally stored data is accessed by a group of employees. Allowing the host to carry out graphics support would be senseless. The host is often not suitable for graphics processing, forcing use of the user interface and interface logic for processing.

Each step taken in the direction of program and data distribution must be carefully considered based upon the consequences for application maintenance and the burden placed upon the individual machines and the network. In general, distribution of applications and data increases the maintenance sensitivity of the environment. The burden placed on the servers and the network, on the other hand, decreases. The choice of concept is largely determined by the capacity and possibilities offered by the hardware and software environment, and the servers' and clients' ability to integrate with each other. This choice is determined in part by the available technical infrastructure and, in part by the way in which the organization wants to work with its information.

In conclusion, we can say that software is displaying a clear trend towards modularity (see Figure 4.9). Hard-coded software for all components and definite links with each other are characteristic of 3GL programs. All software was placed on a central server, resulting in the same limitations in the software. The 1980s saw a natural division of software into the presentation, application and database layers. In client/server, this software was further developed and distributed over various systems, enabling optimal execution of tasks. The distribution as it now exists will be further described in the following section.

1960s/1970s

Mainframe

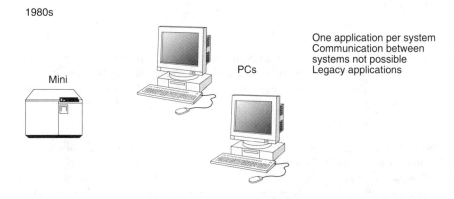

All applications on one system

1980s

One application per system
Communication between
systems not possible
Legacy applications

Mini

PCs

1990s   Mainframe   Client/server

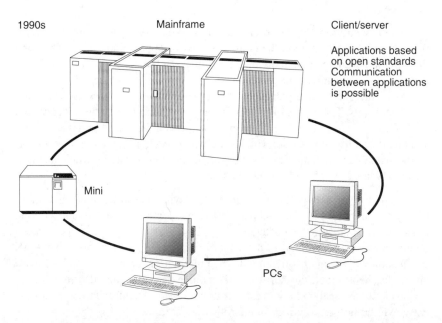

Applications based
on open standards
Communication
between applications
is possible

Mini

PCs

Figure 4.9 Relation between application and hardware architecture.

Distributed processing

We mentioned earlier that applications consist of the following components:

- presentation management

- presentation logic

- application logic

- business logic

- database.

These components can be seen as the various layers of an application. In most client/server publications, client/server is depicted as a concept within which some of these layers run on the server while others run on the client. According to these publications, an important determinant for the structure of the client/server design is the layer in which the delineation between client and server is drawn. This view results in a division into various client/server architectures. This division is, however, very global, and does not do full justice to the practice and concept of client/server as an optimal distribution of tasks over various computers. In principle, all of the tasks mentioned above can be distributed randomly over clients and servers. Today's programs, therefore, are much more modular. This is important to enable implementation of a flexible client/server environment. In a real client/server environment, tasks are systematically assigned to various systems. The following functions can be realized in different reusable software modules:

- security

- authorization

- printer control

- time regulation (synchronization)

- batch procedures

- mathematics or special algorithms

- messages to the operating system or other systems

- standard libraries and regulations.

Two- and three-tiered client/server

Creating an effective client/server environment involves making a lot of decisions about how you want to work with it and what the best solution is for your company. The traditional world is the world of the dumb terminal with the complete application running on the host. This is what is known as a one-tiered architecture.

In the current market we can see that a lot of companies use the two-tiered client/server approach (Figure 4.10). For a lot of organizations this two-tiered architecture is the first step towards client/server, but it is still very often based on a traditional mainframe solution with terminal emulation on the client, or with a simple user interface on the client and the rest of the application with the database running on a server.

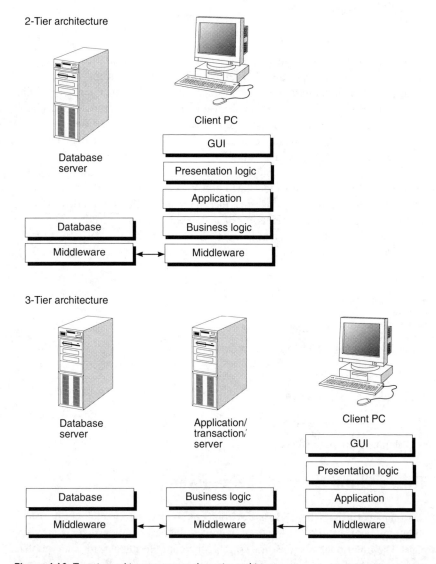

Figure 4.10 Two-tier architecture versus three-tier architecture.

In this two-tiered world we have a database server, and the rest of the application, including the user interface, runs completely on a client (fat client) or the application is also running on the database server (fat server). This architecture can be very useful but also has its limitations – consider, for instance, the networking problems you have and limitations in the software you use. Generally, one uses tools from one specific software vendor, and most organizations prefer open systems because they want to be independent. Organizations want to use the most appropriate platform and software for each business requirement, and not every requirement can be solved using the software products from one vendor alone.

Second generation client/server tools

Organizations can require a different user design per application. Business rules can be set up as an independent system. In this way, if a change is made in the organization, only the business rule requires alteration and not the rest of the application or the user interface. This means dividing the application into three parts. The first part is the user interface with the complete presentation; the second part is the business logic; and the third part is the database. Each part can now run on a different platform. The user interface can run on a personal computer, the business logic can run on UNIX systems, and the database part can run on a mainframe. These three-tiered systems are the so-called second generation client/server tools. In the first generation, software was split in two, with one part running on a client and the rest of the application running on a server. Three-tiered systems usually work with remote procedure calls (RPC) sometimes based on DCE. The advantage of three-tiered systems is greater flexibility in the tools you choose and more vendor independency. Each specific application can work with the graphical front end that you need. Tools like Microsoft Visual Basic, Gupta's SQL Windows and PowerBuilder can be used to develop the front end. For the business rules we can see that some different programming languages are being used such as C or C++ or 4GL languages.

At the database level, we often find relational databases like Oracle, DB2, Sybase and Informix. In this world of the three-tiered systems you are afforded complete interchangeability. When the database is changed, nothing else needs to be affected. Or when the business rules are changed the database and the end user interface are not changed. You are less dependent on the software vendor and you can use the appropriate tools for each application. If an end user needs a specific graphical interface, you can build that on a local client and connect it to an existing server that runs the application, business rules and the database. This three-tiered client server architecture will move towards a multitier environment with many types of software modules that can work together.

What new development will be the mark of this next generation of client/server tools? The answer is object orientation. New generations will be based on object technology. Software will be reusable, and you will be given even more power for rapid development.

Proper organization of these kinds of tasks is of great importance in the client/server environment. To give an impression of the sorts of architectures which can be realized, we now discuss a number of practical examples.

Examples of client/server

In a client/server environment we see many types of architectures and servers. The software modules must work together and are set up once. We start to give some examples on how the various software modules can work together in a client/server environment.

Example 1

We begin with a situation in which PCs are used as clients. The program is split up and runs on various servers. Security runs on a security server. If we log on via the client and try to gain access to one of the programs we arrive at the following example.

The user's PC has only the software necessary to run word processing, spreadsheets and office tools. All client/server programs have to be read into the client's memory from the file server, which ensures that the most up-to-date version of the program is always read into the client's memory. The PC can use a password to log on to a security server. The security server contains a database in which all of the programs are listed, with the programs for which a given user is authorized and the servers to which that user should be linked. The security server authorizes the user to start certain programs via a menu which lists all of the programs for which the user is authorized. Once a program has been chosen, the user is sent through to a file server. At the same time, the necessary files are read into the PC memory from a file server. The PC knows, via the security server, precisely which files have to be read into its memory and on which file server these files are stored. Since the user links to all libraries, including color definitions, keyboard definitions and help message settings are standard throughout the organization.

The user has now read the program into memory via the network and can run the program locally. The database is accessed via a database server. The special business logic is also stored on its own server. The program generates a print command which is accessed via the user's own printer program which runs on the printer server. The program running on the PC calls up the printer program and displays the printer choices.

We see here a distribution of software over various systems which goes much further than the standard client/server architectures which are usually described.

The following components can be run as independent functions on separate systems:

* user interface
* standard libraries and settings

- printer control

- security and authorization

- file serving

- database serving

- 4GL programs with application logic

- communication.

The great advantage of reading program files from a file server into the memory of the client is that local maintenance becomes almost unnecessary, and the user always accesses the latest program version. PC maintenance time shows an enormous decrease, because program files, which regularly change, do not need to be installed locally, and security procedures can also be efficiently implemented. Printers can easily be changed, and the printers which have been deleted or added need only be modified on the printer server. Changes necessitate absolutely no modification to other programs, since one program calls up another. If the number of programs grows, only the database server is more heavily burdened, since the rest of the application is processed locally.

Example 2

In this example we examine a situation in which a user works with an X-terminal. A program is again accessed via the security server. The security server allows the user to access certain programs via a menu listing the programs for which he is authorized. Since the X-terminal's standard libraries are different from the PC's standard libraries, the Example 2 user is sent to other files than the previous user. He starts the program, but files are not read into local memory this time, but rather are started on a processing server. An X-terminal runs locally using only the user interface, while the rest of the program is processed by the server. Since this is a powerful graphics application, this part of the program runs on a server set up especially for graphics applications. The program must regularly access data contained in a database. As this data is spread over the entire organization, a replica of the company-wide database has been created on the department's database server. The user does not have the slightest inkling that this entire procedure has occurred.

Example 3

This example is a description of a situation in which a powerful local workstation is used. A user must carry out all kinds of local planning tasks. The plans are displayed on a system, and they can be modified locally if required. The data for the individual plans is stored on a database server. The mathematical algorithm runs on the local system. The graphical user interface also runs locally. The system checks whether a user is authorized to carry out planning tasks before it starts up one of the planning procedures. The user pulls a replica of the master database into a local database and starts up the algorithm. All plans are stored locally, and the data from the most optimal plans is sent back to the central database system. Data changed in the master database is automatically sent to the replica. In this example, we see the advantage of running a mathematical algorithm on its own server. In addition, parts of the central database can be replicated on a local system, lightening the burden on the central database and allowing the data to be manipulated locally without affecting the integrity of other data.

Example 4

In this example, a distributed database is used which is stored on local servers as well as on the mainframe. The user interface and the 4GL programs are stored locally on the client. The program is sent to the client from a file server after the client has requested the program. The database consists of a local database and a mainframe database. The user can access both databases via DRDA. A gateway to the IMS database also allows the user to request data from the mainframe database via the client. This method allows integration of existing mainframe programs in the client/server environment.

We have now used a few simple examples to illustrate the advantages of client/server. The organization's automation environment can be optimally designed to meet the needs of each individual work area. Modular software allows modification of a given component without affecting the rest of the applications. Modular software and an expanded client/server concept, which can be quickly modified and into which new technologies can be easily integrated, have finally been linked. Software, hardware and management tools can be optimally tuned to each other, resulting in a flexible environment with expanded possibilities.

GOLDEN RULES

- Client/server is meaningful only if you have made the right decisions on your software modules. Be sure that you can use your models more often, and take care that they can work together.

- The choice of your client/server architecture is dependent on your business requirement infrastructure.

- Make sure that your infrastructure is able to support many types of client/server concepts.

- A client/server concept is dependent on your network, your operating systems, your databases and application development tools. All of them are dependent on each other.

- Make sure that you do not have too many options in your organization.

- Client/server can influence your organization; make sure that the end users are involved.

- Client/server introduction is a step-by-step approach.

- Using a three-tiered architecture can be useful if you want to split up your user interfaces from your business rules, and if your business rules take a lot of the load of your system.

- The concepts of client/server are not only software related, but are also dependent on performance, maintenance and demands from end users.

Chapter 5

Networks

Introduction

The client/server revolution now taking place would never have got off the ground if network technology had not undergone such intensive development. The division of labor between computers which dictates the client/server relationship can only function well if computers are able to communicate with each other without problems.

Networks have become faster and faster in the past few years. The burden on networks will become even greater in the near future due to developments that are necessary to accommodate graphical user interfaces and multimedia techniques (for example, audio, film images and photos). All of this information is transported over a network. If organizations in a client/server environment want to communicate with other organizations, they will have to possess countrywide networks which work quickly and safely. These networks must support the transportation of large data files.

We can also expect important developments to follow in the consumer market. The combination of the computer, television and telephone into a single interactive communication medium for consumer services depends upon the existence of data networks with an enormous capacity. At present, general implementation of this sort of service is a dream for the future, but the first experiments in this area are already taking place. In this respect, an important distinction in the area of networks must be made between local area networks (LANs) and wide area networks (WANs).

LAN

A LAN is a network that is used within a limited area, which allows users to send messages with the help of communication protocols. A LAN allows users to share hardware and software with each other. Since the network has become an important tool in most organizations, an increasing number of offices have created the infrastructure necessary to allow network connections in all office areas. All computers, printers and other hardware can be connected to a network, allowing users to communicate with each other (Figure 5.1).

A LAN can have various topologies, such as the bus, the star, and the ring. The choice of one of these topologies largely determines the possible uses of the network within the organization. The speed with which the network operates is also partially dependent on the topology. In addition, it influences the network's security and future growth prospects.

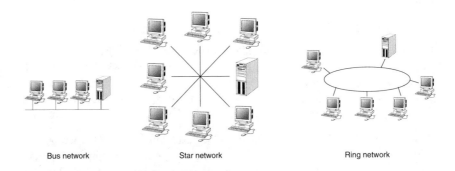

Bus network   Star network   Ring network

Figure 5.1 LAN in an office environment.

WAN

An organization with a network which reaches outside the building possesses a wide area network (WAN). WANs are not only capable of going to another building, but can also maintain international links. A connection between two WANs can be achieved with the help, for example, of public networks, including X.25 (Figure 5.2).

Figure 5.2 A wide area network working with X.25.

Architecture

A network architecture consists of two components: hardware and software.

Hardware is the physical cabling, and all of the equipment such as cards, routers, hubs, gateways and bridges which enable data transmission. Important standards in this area are Ethernet, Token Ring and Fiber Distributed Data Interchange (FDDI).

The software is the network protocols, network management applications and software gateways. Important standards here are IBM's Systems Network Architecture (SNA), the ISO's Open Systems Interconnection (OSI) standards, and the Transmission Control Protocol/Internet Protocol (TCP/IP) suite of protocols.

In this chapter, we cover the most important aspects of the network, beginning with cabling.

Cabling

Coax

Coax cabling is a commonly used form of cabling in Ethernet networks with a bus structure. It consists of a copper core and comes in thick or thin types. The cable guarantees good transmission and is also often used as TV cable. Thin coax can be used for a limited number of users within a maximum distance of 180 meters. If the distance between stations is larger, or if a larger backbone is necessary, thick coax cable with a maximum length of 500 meters must be used.

Unshielded twisted pair

At present, unshielded twisted pair (UTP) is one of the most common network cables for star networks. Two cables twisted around each other give the cable its name. These cables are also used for telephone connections. The two cables are not enclosed in mantles, which is why they are called unshielded. The transmission speed is not very high at present, but this is quickly being improved to 100 Mbit/s (megabits per second). The 100 Mbit/s volume is equivalent to reading approximately ten 250 page novels in a single second.

Shielded twisted pair

This cabling is equivalent to UTP, except that it has a mantel around both cores. This cable's speed can be increased to 100 Mbit/s.

Glass fiber

A relatively new cabling, glass fiber, is rapidly gaining in popularity. The core of the material is not copper, as in coax cable, but consists of glass fiber with a high transmission capacity of approximately 100 Mbit/s. In future, even faster speeds will be possible, up to more than 1000 Mbit/s. The link works with the help of light impulses. The price of this cabling is becoming increasingly attractive, and the chances of a breakdown in networks using fiber optic cabling is very low in comparison to copper. Glass fiber can be used with outstanding results in situations where large quantities of graphics are to be transmitted over a network. The backbone of many organizations is already being implemented using glass fiber because of the medium's capacity and security. In addition, the company can be certain of sufficient future growth potential in the face of increasing network burdens, without having to replace the cabling.

Bridges, routers, hubs, and gateways

Bridge

An organization may possess two networks which are not linked to each other. If it becomes necessary to link such networks, a bridge is usually used. A condition for communication via a bridge is that both LANs use the same protocol: in other words, TCP/IP communicates with TCP/IP. A bridge is often formed by a computer which is linked to both networks via two network cards. Local traffic remains separated from other network traffic: only cross traffic travels over the bridge.

Router

A router is a bridge with expanded network capabilities. Large networks can be set up with the help of routers, which can determine the best route through the network. They know the network's topology and can choose the best path. A router is especially important in complex network topologies to limit network traffic and create alternative routes. A router knows the network addresses of the various systems, so complex network structures can be set up with their help. Ethernet can be linked to Token Ring using a router, and they can be used to link networks which use the same protocol.

Hub

Hubs are used as collection points for all network connections. A hub can be applied in a Token Ring or Ethernet environment. There are also intelligent hubs which can take over the router's function: an intelligent hub possesses management functions allowing the ports and the network traffic using those ports to be monitored.

Gateway

It has already been mentioned that computers must use the same protocol to communicate with one another. Often, however, messages must be sent using networks that use different languages. Gateways are used for this, as they can convert various protocols.

The various types of LAN

In addition to the cabling, a LAN type must be selected to implement communication. At present, there are three types of commonly used LAN protocols.

Ethernet

Ethernet is the most commonly used network protocol worldwide. It can be used with thick and thin coax cable, twisted pair and unshielded twisted pair cables. The topology of a coax Ethernet usually has a bus structure. The other cables, including UTP, are usually used in a star form. Large networks usually have a star topology. Computers are connected to the network via a local connector. With a performance of 10 Mbyte/s (megabytes per second), Ethernet delivers a quick and dependable network for simple traffic in average-sized organizations.

An Ethernet system can be split up into segments, reasonably guaranteeing both security and performance. For implementation in large networks all kinds of tools are available, such as bridges, routers and hubs. The architecture of an Ethernet system allows every user to transport data via the network (multiple access).

The advantages of Ethernet include its price, the ease with which it can be used, and the availability of an enormous range of products from various suppliers. The main disadvantage of Ethernet is that burdens on the system caused by an increase in the number of users can lead to collisions between the messages on the network. At a given load level, network traffic simply stops. Due to the increased demand for graphic applications, the use of X-terminals and the use of multimedia, Ethernet's capacity is too limited for many organizations under present circumstances. However, capacity is currently being increased to 14 times the present limit, to 100 Mbyte/s, so that increased network traffic can be handled. This will prevent Ethernet from disappearing from the market, at least for the near future.

Token Ring

In the 1980s, a new type of IBM network system became popular, the Token Ring network. This network has a physical ring structure instead of the Ethernet bus or star structure. Every connection has its own cables which are routed to a central point, and the ring structure is usually set up in a central unit. This unit is a multiple access unit (MAU), and it functions as a hub. An MAU can be connected to another MAU, enabling all employees to connect to the network and enabling the network to expand as necessary. By laying the ring structure only in the MAU, a star topology can be maintained for the rest of the network.

The principle of Token Ring is that data is carried via a token through the ring network, and is delivered to the computer that needs the data. The network has one-way traffic, as opposed to Ethernet's two-way traffic. The messages are neatly received by the token, which transports them along the ring network to the computer to which they have been sent.

The advantage of Token Ring is the enormous security which it offers. There is no central backbone as in some forms of Ethernet, since each user has his own connection and the cables come together only in a patchbox or a MAU. In addition, the present speed of Token Ring is 16 Mbyte/s, marginally quicker than Ethernet. This enables the connection of more users on a Token Ring segment than is possible on Ethernet. The Token Ring's one-way traffic ensures that every message is received neatly, and practically eliminates the risk of network traffic standing still due to excess traffic.

The disadvantage of Token Ring is that it is more expensive than Ethernet. Use of the IBM cabling system is not cheap, and Token Ring cards are also more expensive than Ethernet cards. There are not as many Token Ring product suppliers, which also helps to keep the price relatively high.

FDDI

The Fiber Distributed Data Interchange (FDDI) is usually used as a backbone standard. It works physically with a double ring structure, which offers greater dependability. If there is a breakdown in the cabling or in a node, a simple bypass still allows the network to continue functioning. The transmission medium usually used is glass fiber. A speed of approximately 100 Mbit/s is standard, and will be further increased in future. FDDI is a highly advanced protocol, regularly used as a backbone, due in part to its dependability. From this environment, users can transfer over to Token Ring or Ethernet environments via the backbone in the local environment.

Network software

To send a computer message, a physical network is first necessary. The real exchange of data occurs via software, which must meet various conditions: integrity of the data upon receipt, for example, must be guaranteed. The communication software must be able to send various types of data: for example, applications, files, electronic mail and graphic images.

In general, messages are too large to send in one piece, which is why files or messages are divided into smaller pieces, each of which contains a header detailing where the pieces are to be sent and how they fit into the total message. Once these packages of information arrive at their destination, the header is removed and the various pieces of information are placed in the correct order: the original message is reconstructed. These activities are executed by the network protocol. A check on whether the messages have been correctly received must take place, and to allow this the communication software must be able to carry out error handling. Software must also be able to trace and solve problems (Figure 5.3).

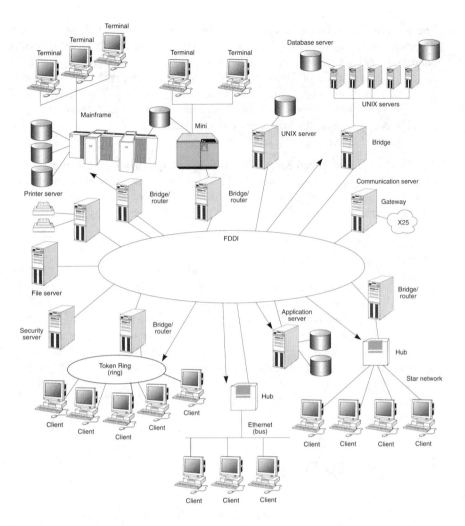

Figure 5.3 Network construction of a typical client/server environment.

Communication software requirements are quite diverse. In addition to sending messages in packages, the software must be able to communicate with bridges, routers and hubs. It must be able to correctly interpret messages from terminals, printers, PCs and other computers, and if the messages are not received correctly, the software must be able to send them again. The software must enable communication, monitoring and network management. Only if all these requirements are met we can communicate correctly with the network. To realize these complex tasks with some degree of organization, the software has a layered structure. A communication model consists of the following layers:

- transmission medium

- data communication functions

- application.

We have just discussed the transmission medium, the network, such as Ethernet or Token Ring. Software, the data communication layer, is able to take care of the exchange of messages, and uses the network to communicate. Both the transmission and data communication layers are necessary to allow applications to communicate with each other. In the past, each layer had to be written separately. If it became necessary to connect a terminal to a host computer, the programmer had to write the communication and application layers himself, which was not only time-consuming, but also extremely maintenance sensitive. This quickly led to a demand for standardization, which in turn led to the existence of an architecture that was constructed in layers, allowing software to be split up into modular units.

SNA

The organization which took the first steps toward standardization in the area of network communication was IBM, which introduced the Systems Network Architecture (SNA) into the market in 1974. SNA has the hierarchical structure shown in Figure 5.4. Each layer has its own function. SNA is applied in IBM environments, and is one of the most commonly used protocols. SNA's architecture is based on the following principles:

- Each layer has its own function, with its own fixed description.

- Each layer provides services for the layer directly above or below it.

- Two systems always communicate via the same SNA layer.

- Changes in a layer usually have no effect on the other layers.

The lowest three layers of SNA form the transport layers. They are:

3   Path control

2   Data link control

1   Physical control.

In these layers, a check is first carried out to determine whether the messages were sent correctly. All elements of the communication process must have an address and all equipment must work. Headers and a trailer are added to the messages during the data link check. Each header contains a number that increases as the transmission progresses, so that the user can see whether everything has been received correctly.

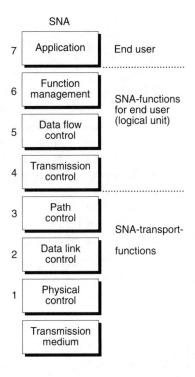

Figure 5.4 Hierarchical construction of the SNA-model.

The other layers, which are now of importance, are grouped together under the name of the logical unit. The logical unit layer consists of the following SNA components:

6   Function management

5   Data flow control

4   Transmission control.

A logical unit is a set of functions available to every user. Every unit has its own address within the SNA network; each station which is connected has an obligatory unique logical unit address. Before starting a session, a logical unit checks whether communication is possible with the other logical unit. Although there were problems with this in the past, in 1983 IBM announced its Logical Unit 6.2 (LU 6.2). This has the capacity to search on other systems which can receive communications for the information required by the user if the system with which the user wanted to communicate is not available. This facilitates advanced peer to peer communication (APPC), which is especially important for transaction processing systems such as Customer Information Control System (CICS) and for distributed computing. This method with LU 6.2 is a form of distributed processing, and will become increasingly important in the future, especially in client/server environments.

OSI

We have now discussed the structure of an SNA network environment. We know, however, that SNA is mainly implemented in IBM environments. There are approximately 40 000 SNA networks worldwide, a large number in an IBM main-frame environment. SNA was the first network architecture to be set up according to the layered model. A disadvantage of SNA is that it is meant mainly for an IBM environment. It cannot be used as easily in multivendor environments (environments within which several suppliers operate). Demand thus arose from the market for a standard network protocol that was suitable for heterogeneous environments. This standard for heterogeneous systems is Open Systems Interconnection (OSI). The OSI model, just as SNA, is constructed in layers and closely resembles the SNA protocol.

The number of OSI implementations currently remains small because the concept is not yet complete. Many organizations, therefore, continue to work in an IBM environment with SNA. At present, international support for OSI seems to be crumbling, certainly now that the US Ministry of Defense has dropped the standard, and TCP/IP is now seen to be more important as the *de facto* standard. The OSI model consists of the following layers:

7   Application layer

6   Presentation layer

5   Session layer

4   Transport layer

3   Network layer

2   Data link layer

1   Physical layer.

The OSI model is similar to the SNA model. Layers 1, 2 and 3 of the OSI model are collectively called the communication-oriented layer, and the upper four layers are known as the application-oriented layer.

DECNet

In addition to IBM, another hardware supplier brought its own network concept on to the market: Digital Equipment Corporation (DEC) with its Digital Network Architecture (DNA). This DEC protocol is open to other suppliers under the principle that multiple operating systems can work with DECnet. DECnet also has many similarities to the OSI model layers, and the product has won a large market share in non-IBM environments during the 1980s. The latest version of DECnet is based on the OSI model.

TCP/IP

At present, there is just one open protocol on the market which enjoys broad acceptance by the various hardware and software suppliers: the Transmission Control Protocol/Internet Protocol (TCP/IP). The spectacular growth of this protocol in the past few years seems due mainly to a broad use of TCP/IP on Ethernet. Both products were introduced in 1973 and are very widely distributed. Another reason for its popularity is that the UNIX market adopted TCP/IP from the very beginning, and has used it ever since to allow UNIX systems to communicate with each other. Both Ethernet and TCP/IP are relatively inexpensive and are much used in the university world. The relationship between UNIX and TCP/IP has remained strong, and this protocol has become increasingly popular due to the recent growth of UNIX. One of the strengths of TCP/IP is the simplicity of the protocol.

Most TCP/IP versions have file transfer, electronic mail and terminal emulation capabilities. At present, almost all the hardware suppliers in the world deliver TCP/IP as a standard protocol with their operating systems. This is valid for both UNIX and non-UNIX systems. The importance of TCP/IP is increasing due to the market's urgent need for an international network protocol which allows heterogeneous systems to communicate with each other. This demand is partially caused by the absence of an OSI market breakthrough. TCP/IP is, then, extremely important for open systems, client/server environments and distributed databases.

LAN protocols

PC LAN market developments have taken place in parallel to other network developments. The NETBIOS protocol, for example, became popular due to the increasing popularity of the PC. Another protocol that has arisen due to the introduction of LANs is NetWare from Novell. This protocol works with SPX/IPX, and each of these protocols covers a part of the OSI layer. Another protocol is AppleTalk from Apple, but this runs only in an Apple environment. This protocol can be used to create a LAN in the world of Macintosh computers, and, just as Novell, it delivers a simple network product that can realize simple file and printer sharing.

Large PC networks require more powerful environments: in some cases, hundreds of thousands of PCs have to be supported and managed in a network. The supplier that brought a product onto the market to accomplish this is Banyan's with the Vines Network Operating System (NOS) protocol. Most suppliers presently have gateways to other protocols, allowing minis and mainframes to communicate with each other independently of the protocol. A new arrival in the market is the Windows NT network product from Microsoft, which has yet to win a place among the existing network product suppliers.

An overview of these protocols and their underlying relationships follows (Figure 5.5).

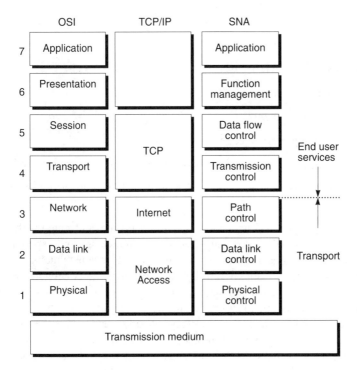

Figure 5.5 The mutual relation between different network protocols.

Client/server and networks

The construction of a network for a client/server environment is a complex undertaking requiring a considerable investment.

In addition to the network capacity, a carefully weighed network protocol choice must be made. Questions with regard to security, network management, and so on, must be answered before the inception of the project in order to avoid being confronted with enormous costs at billing time. The following variables should be borne in mind during the network construction process:

- Where are the clients and servers located?

- What functions will they carry out?

- What is the number of clients and servers?

- What software will be used?

- Will users work with graphics or multimedia?

- Is communication with other networks necessary?

- LAN to WAN or SNA to TCP/IP?

- What are the security requirements?

- Which protocols are necessary?

- Can SNMP be used?

- Which client/server form will be implemented?

- Network management?

- What are the performance requirements?

- What is the infrastructure of the network, including hubs, routers, and so on?

- System management products which are tuned in to client/server environment.

Companies implementing client/server environments are confronted with a veritable forest of standards and products. Extensive knowledge and experience are necessary in order to hack a way through the trees. Problems which seem quite simple at first sight can quickly turn into major headaches. A network card will need to be installed in each computer, for example. The problem here is that not every network card is able to support all the necessary software. This needs to be considered at purchase. In addition, we have already mentioned that each system must have the necessary network protocols in order to communicate with other systems. Each level in the server's communication software must also be present on another system. If TCP/IP is used by the server, TCP/IP must also be used by the client. There are a great number of possibilities with regard to the choice of TCP/IP suppliers, and each supplier offers its own special capabilities and work speed.

Multiprotocol

At present, scores of products which support the multiprotocol principle are being brought onto the market. Take, for example, applications which can run using various different protocols without problems, such as SNA and Ethernet or OSI and Novell. There is a clear trend towards open network environments facilitated by multiprotocol interchange products. A protocol manager recognizes the protocol being used, for example TCP/IP or SPX. A PC with a multiprotocol interchange product can communicate with Novell via SPX, and can communicate, using the same interchange product, with a RISC/UNIX machine with TCP/IP.

Client/server, databases and networks

Working with relational databases and a client/server scheme in networks brings its own special problems. Middleware products, including SQL NET from Oracle, DRDA and database gateways, can offer solutions. Take, for example, a client request from an application to a database on a server. Such a request entails client formulation of an SQL statement which must be executed on the server. This not only means that there is a physical division of the software products into a client section and a server section, but also that these two pieces must be able to recognize each other. Transmission of SQL statements between the two systems is executed by a separate middleware layer such as SQL NET. Working with a single database or a single supplier creates no communication problems. A more heterogeneous environment will encounter more problems, because each supplier has its own SQL NET protocol which cannot usually communicate with other databases. This means that, in cases where the client/server scheme is run via a network, products will be necessary which are optimally tuned to their own database, or multiprotocol products able to access several databases will have to be used in a heterogeneous database environment. Another possibility for heterogeneous database communication is to work with gateways.

Network management

Many networks have a complex architecture which consists of all kinds of network components such as hubs, routers, bridges and gateways, cabling, network protocols and application software. In a client/server environment, all communication occurs via the network, which means that the network structure must be optimal. If the network is down, users cannot access the various servers, and the risk that a large part of the organization cannot work is great. Downtime can be prevented by working with a star network or by laying a double network.

Good network management is, then, of vital importance. Network management can be split into five areas:

- configuration management
- fault management
- performance management
- account management
- security.

A short explanation of these areas follows.

Configuration management

This is the management of the entire network. Remote network management must be possible: if, for example, a terminal in a given building must be disconnected, it should be possible to handle this remotely by configuration management, without necessitating a trip to that building by the network manager.

Fault management

If part of the network goes down, localization and solution of the fault must be possible.

Performance management

Good performance is obviously required for networks. If this is not guaranteed, working with a client/server scheme is a risky business. Network traffic must be measurable and adjustable so that performance remains good.

Account management

The systems linked to the network, and the burden they place on the network, must be recorded. This is especially important in large organizations for internal expense allocations.

Security

Control of passwords, authorizations and access to systems and applications, and so on, all fall under the security function.

Good network management is absolutely essential in a network environment which makes use of the client/server concept. Depending on the size of the network, various software products are available for network management support. In a simple LAN, Novell network management products will suffice. As the network increases in size, and routers, bridges and intelligent hubs are added, professional software products for network management which are able to carry out more functions will become necessary. Some products which can fulfil a larger network's requirements are: Sun with Sun NetManager; Hewlett Packard with HP OpenView; and IBM with NetView. In addition, some well known, independent network suppliers, including SynOptics, Cabletron and Ungermann-Bass, are also active in the market for larger networks. All of these suppliers are able to maintain larger networks with their network management software. These products can manage LANs and WANs, and are able to immediately localize faults and to suggest alternatives.

These network management tools are of vital importance for limiting breakdowns and downtime, and will be increasingly constructed with intelligent software. This will allow the application to independently carry out network management tasks and to suggest alternatives for solving problems. Cabletron, for example, has developed a network management product called Spectrum which it uses to control and manage networks using artificial intelligence techniques.

SNMP and CMIP

As already mentioned, networks will become the nerve centers of organizations. The networks which are now installed in many organizations will certainly not be able to meet the requirements imposed by tomorrow's software if, for example, those organizations want to work with multimedia and graphics applications. To enable the networks to meet these requirements, the near future will see ever increasing demands on network capacity, or bandwidth. There is thus a great need for network management standards. To prepare these sorts of standards, several workgroups were established at the end of the 1980s. This resulted in a short-term solution for network management functions in TCP/IP environments: the Simple Network Management Protocol (SNMP). Another group is working on protocols for future OSI environments; this is the Common Management Information Protocol (CMIP). At present, SNMP is a widely accepted environment, and SNMP2 is already in development. CMIP is becoming more of a guideline to which SNMP largely conforms. More and more important suppliers are working with SNMP, which runs using the Internet Protocol.

Via SNMP, all the necessary information for network management can be found: for example, TCP connections, IP routes, and so on. This allows the user to make the system visual on the monitor, with the help of advanced network management software products, because SNMP is recognized by the software. A network working with SNMP uses:

- SNMP agents,

- a network management station, and

- the SNMP protocol.

The agent is a piece of software that runs on a node such as a PC, workstation, printer, router, hub or server. Each agent possesses a management information base (MIB), which is a database with configuration information. Agents are passive and provide information only if the manager is requested to provide it. A network management application is able to make the network visible via a graphical user interface (GUI). The various network components can be controlled from the user interface. The SNMP protocol exchanges messages between the agents and the manager. Each supplier of SNMP products which work in a network has its own supplier-dependent MIB code, enabling the storage of unique values which allow other applications to gain an insight into the status of the local agent. A disadvantage of earlier versions of SNMP was that these MIB attributes could not be adequately protected. This has been solved in the later versions of SNMP and in SNMP2. Almost all of the well known network management products make use of SNMP. The role of SNMP, then, is clearly of great importance.

Client/server and networking

It is very interesting to see how networking and new IT technology like the client/server environment influence each other. The first networking environments were mostly based on simple Ethernet based on a bus structure. The computers connected to these networks used the network for simple file transfer and terminal emulation. In this kind of environment it was possible to work with many users with no problems. Then came the more powerful personal computer, and file transfer became more important. The end user wanted to share files and printers, so the PC became a networking server and took over the role of the minicomputer. Special networking software like LAN Server and Novell supported the PC world with their software and dominated this area. Workstations, mostly based on UNIX, were also using networking for file transfer for CAD/CAM applications. The files became larger and larger, the numbers of users were increasing and network limitations appeared on the horizon. This led to a few further developments: the first interconnection devices arrived, which were repeaters used for signal regeneration that served to extend the maximum distance a LAN can span. A repeater interconnects two LANs and passes information to the other LAN, regardless of the recipient's location. A repeater does not have enough intelligence to determine when to pass information from one LAN to the other, and this can cause unnecessary traffic and give a degradation of performance. The repeater works at the OSI layer 1, the physical layer.

The next phase was the introduction of a bridge. A bridge learns the location of each device and can connect two LANs using the same protocol. A bridge works at OSI layer 2, does not give you all the protection you need and is rather slow. That was why a new device, called the router, came to the fore. Routers operate at layer 3 of the OSI model. They also provide other services. A router receives packages from each user, and it can send information to the appropriate systems.

Further, the networks were split into segments and the bus structure then became a star structure with hubs. The number of users was limited to a certain acceptable maximum. As soon as the routers arrived they connected all the segments to one complete corporate-wide network. Then the speed increased: Token Ring could now work with 16 Mbit/s instead of 4, and Ethernet increased its speed from 10 to 100 Mbit/s. To support this, different protocols like FDDI and Asynchronous Transfer Mode (ATM) are used (Figure 5.6).

But even with all this new power, we can still see that the number of users connected to a network, the performance, the applications and the cooperation between all the systems is growing quickly, and the capabilities of a network must grow correspondingly. To solve this problem you can split your application by using client/server technology. Then you can store the applications on your client and you are only connected to database servers. This can help, but it also means that you have more maintenance and system management tasks on the client side. The number of users will increase and the demand for power will also grow.

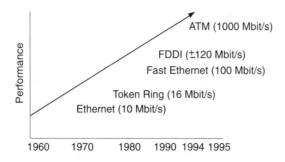

Figure 5.6 Increasing performance of the network.

Networking cost

With the number of users connected to a network growing, we can see the increasing cost of network ownership. At present, maintaining a network and keeping it up and running accounts for approximately 84% of the total network cost (Figure 5.7).

Every end user seeks high availability, and that is also needed for a network. Some research centers concluded that the number of network segments in major organizations in the world has increased over the last five years from 4 to 40. If a network fails the whole organization can go down – and the cost related to network failures is increasing. This means that network security and availability is one of the most important issues in today's computer world.

The world of the client/server concept will never end. Since the arrival of the personal computer we can see that applications are running at the client side and the power needed on a network will only increase. Hospitals will transfer photos of X-rays via networks all over the world; doctors will use special intelligent tools on their desktop to make decisions; multiple media like voice and sound will be used; engineers will use CAD/CAM groupware and will want to work together on the same files despite their geographical differences.

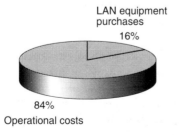

Figure 5.7 Cost of network over the years. *source: Forrester research.

Table 5.1 Bandwidth requirements per active user.

	Raw	Compress	Compressed
Terminal–host	0.8–1kb/s	1:1	0.8–1kb/s
GUI–application	1–2kb/s	1:1	1–2kb/s
Application–RDBMS	1–2kb/s	1:1	1–2kb/s
Database–disk	160–320kb/s	1:1	160–320kb/s
Voice	64kb/s	8:1	8kb/s
Video (full motion)	65Mb/s	20–50:1	1.4–3.2Mb/s
Video (simple)	20Mb/s	20:1	1Mb/s

Everyone will work with object orientation, and end users will work with group-ware products all over the company. Applications will be split up into independent modules and reused by end users, which means an increase in bandwidth. In particular, the use of multimedia and advanced GUIs will result in enormous network traffic. At this moment, compression technology is used to solve this problem, but more bandwidth is still needed (Table 5.1).

We must understand that the first networks were able to do file transfer and printer sharing. The new applications need high-volume bandwidth and advanced network capabilities, and at the moment most network infrastructures do not support this. Network technology also needs to undergo a rapid change. The network must become very flexible, and the cost of changing routers, IP addresses and desktop systems must be brought down.

How can this problem with current networks be solved?

If you are going to work with new client/server applications, several decisions need to be made. Begin by splitting your network into several usable network segments. Place most of the servers near the end users. Where servers must work together, like security and authorization servers connected to file, database and print servers, place them on a high-speed backbone supported by FDDI or ATM. Use high-speed Ethernet in those places where the end user needs it, and use intelligent network management software tools.

Asynchronous transfer mode

The demand for faster networks with more capacity, or wider bandwidth, will continue to increase. At present, many organizations use only Ethernet or Token Ring, but the demand for more powerful networks will increase rapidly. The importance of FDDI will grow substantially, and the widespread use of asynchronous transfer mode (ATM) is imminent. ATM splits messages into small cells and allows the data to be sent much more directly to the correct systems. ATM is a giant step forward, especially for the use of video, multimedia and large giga-bit files. In future, networks will automatically offer multiprotocol support, elim-inating the need for gateways and allowing hubs and routers to grow towards each other. ATM will also permit transmission speeds of 1000 Mbit/s and higher, enabling speech, moving images and data transmission over a single line.

Why is ATM so important for the client/server concept?

The answer is simple. The word 'asynchronous' in asynchronous transfer mode in this case means that the transfer from one system to the other is not bound to a specific time – the transfer stands for the transmission of information. In this case we are referring to the transmission of a constant number of bytes. These bytes are called cells, and we can split them into two parts (Figure 5.8).

The first part is the cell header of five bytes, with the source and target identifi-cation, and the second part is the cell payload of 48 bytes, with the user informa-tion. Together we have a constant cell of 53 bytes. This type of transmission is known as cell relay, and the most used techniques now are packet switching and frame relay. Only the cell relay has standard cell bytes; the other two have a vari-able length. This makes it very usable for transporting video, sound and images. It is powerful enough to transmit gigabytes on a network with no problems. ATM can provide a demand-based bandwidth, which means that each system can get the response that it needs. ATM can be used in star, bus or ring-structured network architectures, making it very flexible. It can work not only on fiber but also on an existing architectures like UTP. ATM will also enable transmission speeds of 1000 Mbit/s and higher, enabling speech, moving images, and data transmission over a single line.

It supports the world of the LAN and the WAN, but it also has the capacity to sup-port it at a home level. People at home can play interactive (two way) games on their television and shop from home.

We can see ATM being used as a backbone environment in large client/server sites. It is also used by organizations who offer multimedia applications where this bandwidth is needed. The only problem with the current ATM world is that we are still at the stage where all the telecommunication standards for ATM are being created by the ATM commitee, which means that it is still not completely standardized.

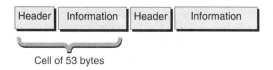

Cell of 53 bytes

Figure 5.8 ATM cell.

The advantages of ATM are as follows:

*   Increased performance at lower cost;

*   Formal ISO standard (emerging);

*   Integration of data-voice-image;

*   Adoption by public carrier services;

*   Networking technology catches up with processor evolution;

*   Increased WAN throughput from the same lines;

*   Fast adoption as corporate LANinterconnect and within 'server farms';

*   Essential for enterprise-wide VirtualLANS (VLANs).

Virtual networking

What is virtual networking? We have just described the need for more bandwidth and the need to have a flexible environment. Until now routers have been able to connect the segments of a network together, but in some cases there has been a serious problem with routers. For instance, a router receives packages from each user with addresses, and it must route it to the system requested. But each package that is sent over the line must be received, filtered and processed. Sometimes a router must also add values like multiprotocol independency and network security to it, and this takes a lot of time. The most important task of a router is to receive a message and send it to the right address. However, if you want to work with multimedia voice and sound at the same time in a network, you can get routing problems. You don't want to work with a router as this is a translator for each package: you need a straightforward connection to the system you require, and nothing in between. Then if you want to send a message to a server you have the server's address and can send it straight to it without any translation or checking.

This can be done with a new technique called the virtual network. This works like a telephone connection. If you dial a phone number you make a connection with another unique phone number. No translation is required – you can have a conversation and nobody else can listen or speak to you during that time. You are completely secure, and if you have finished your conversation you can dial again or dial any other number. This is how a virtual network works. To solve the problem of the router where it is used only as a bridge between segments, you replace the router by an intelligent switch, which can be a switched hub. The connection to the system you require is made without translation, but simply by using switch technology. Within the message you send is contained the address of the other system – like a telephone number. This switch knows where the location is and acts so that you are immediately connected to the receiver of your message. With

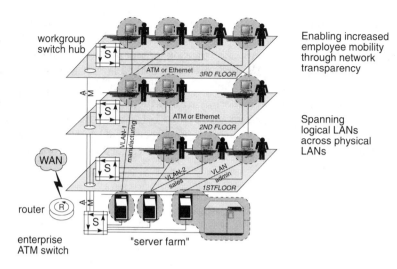

Figure 5.9 Virtual LAN.

this switching technology you can increase your speed many times and make changes very easily as compared with current routers (Figure 5.9).

One of the main operating costs in networking is caused by changing systems to other IP addresses. If a system is moved from one office to another you need to have the funds to support that. This can be solved by using advanced switching technology and virtual networking. In an advanced environment you don't have to change your IP address; the system will automatically find your location. This is made possible by some vendors who use software to support the advanced switching technology. Within the software you find the right address and the switch is connected to this software. Most of the large networking companies like Cisco, Synoptics, IBM and many others like 3Com are turning towards virtual networking. One of the first players in the field was Cabletron. It not only uses the switch technology for virtual networking, but also has intelligent software products (Spectrum) to support not only all the network managment environment, but also the virtual networking.

Wireless connection

One of the new types of client/server connection is the wireless connection. This type of networking is of interest to end users who work in the field and are unable to make a connection to a wired network. This type of client/server is mostly based on a portable system that runs the user interface and the application locally, and has a remote access to the database servers. This type of client/server communication is viable where a lot of data transmission is not required. The connection is mostly based on a radio transmission, or made via a portable telephone for longer distances. The transmission is limited in speed, but for simple file transfer, electronic mail and simple database transactions it can prove very useful for sales reps, engineers, doctors and others people working in the field who need a connection to a computer system but are unable to connect their system to the standard network environment of their organization. Products like Lotus Notes from IBM and Oracle in Motion are designed to work with mobile end users.

Internet

The Internet is one of the fastest growing forms of network connection. The Internet is a worldwide network with thousands of computers and millions of users all working together. In earlier days it was an international medium for electronic mail and information often used by government institutes and universities.

You can make a connection to the Internet using the TCP/IP protocol. One advantage of the Internet is that nobody really owns the Net; it is cheap, the information is mostly free and can be found all over the world. The Internet is country-independent and is the same all over the world. Any user with a personal computer, a modem and some software can make a connection to the internet.

You can send or recieve files using the File Transfer Protocol (FTP) and use the Telnet to log into interactive databases. Furthermore, you have graphical menu systems for finding information, such as the World Wide Web (WWW).

In the last few years we have seen all types of organization using the Internet and World Wide Web as an international data highway. The Internet is not one network but thousands of networks all over the world working together, the concept of which is based on a client/server concept: the client is making a request and a server delivers the answer.

The number of users is growing so quickly that problems now arise in finding the right information. Many server suppliers are using the Net; computer organizations are going to use it for international communication with their customers. Product information, pricing and new releases of software are placed on the Net, and customers are able to retrieve the information using a file transfer. Also, financial organizations are starting to offer their services to customers. With this type of communication we can see that the customer can be located all over the world, and customers are no longer dependent on their local financial organization: the bank can be located anywhere in the world. This type of communication is the beginning of a worldwide data transfer using an international network, and all kind of services can be offered to the Net. If this network is big enough we can transfer all kinds of information, like X-rays for doctors, or multimedia transfers for training all over the world. Database vendors like Oracle are going to connect their database servers to this type of network: end users can use their applications at home and, by using client/server techniques, you can make connections to multimedia or other databases via the Internet. Retail organizations are offering their products to customers all over the world, supported by multimedia applications. The international network will become one of the most important computer connections in the near future, and will influence the way in which organizations will communicate with customers, because the Net has no boundaries and is international.

Chapter 11 considers the Internet in more detail.

GOLDEN RULES

- See what type of applications and software you need now and in the future, and see if your network architecture can support this.

- Choose a wiring system that can also be used in the future.

- At the backbone level you need more bandwidth power than at the segments.

- Take care that you are able to split your network into the proper segments.

- Use intelligent hardware like intelligent hubs at large sites.

- Use routers where needed, but see if a virtual network using switching technology is possible.

- Use network management tools that can support your entire network environment.

- If you have a large site, invest in intelligent network management software that can work with independent system management products.

- Check if your network is secure enough for failures, and set up policies for such failures.

- Make sure that you have enough bandwidth for future developments.

- Multimedia types of communication need a lot of bandwith.

- See if you need a connection between your network management products and your system management products.

Chapter 6

Relational databases and client/server

Introduction

Before taking a closer look at the relational database as such, it may be helpful to consider the role of information in an organization at an abstract level. Information quality as defined in Chapter 1 is extremely important in this connection. An information system is largely a mirror image of a part of the administrative organization. To build and maintain a high quality information system, it is very important that the information is stored in a structured way. Larger organizations usually use an automated database management environment. Database management environment requirements are derivatives of the information quality requirements:

- *Integrity:* the information must be uniquely identified and must conform to the organization's rules and limitations (constraints).

- *Topicality:* the organization's procedures must be designed to ensure that data can be processed on a timely basis and that it is readily available in the database. The database environment must support this.

- *Completeness:* the design of the database must include all relevant aspects of the organization, and it must also be possible to store these aspects in the database environment.

Almost all commercial database systems enable an organization to build an information system which meets these requirements. If, however, we consider the other conditions for high quality information systems, the relational database usually scores higher than network, hierarchical and object-oriented databases.

Relational databases are based on a relatively simple mathematical model which uses data stored in tables. This simplifies data maintenance and enables a simple query language to request information. Relational databases are also easily ported to other hardware platforms. In addition, several good fourth generation languages are now available in relational databases. Growth to a larger system is possible without problems, and the database can also be easily moved to the new system. Specific questions on the use of relational database systems in a client/server environment are discussed later.

The relational database stores data in a table. These tables, in turn, consist of columns (attributes) and contain records. The relational database concept was first described in the 1970s in publications written by E. F. Codd. The concept was further developed by C. J. Date. The relational database is based on insights gained from set theory. Relational algebra provides the possibility of defining new relationships based on old ones. The first relational databases were experimental and very slow. The theory was later enriched with a variety of new concepts and techniques, including foreign keys, indexes and query optimization capabilities. At present, the relational database is one of the fastest database types in the world, resulting in its development into the database of the 1990s. The following are some of the reasons for its success:

- easy setup of the database

- simple modification and maintenance

- easy definition of relations

- simple query language (SQL)

- speed

- flexibility and portability

- support of a great number of hardware platforms

- many 4GL products can work with it

- good connection to modern techniques.

Developments continue. Today's databases are not only used for the storage of administrative data. Digitized documents, texts without a fixed structure and audiovisual data such as photos, film images and audio can all be stored in a relational database. In addition, the database can be used experimentally for object-oriented applications.

From relational database theory, a language grew which was able to easily access the database. This language is the Structured Query Language (SQL). The first version of SQL was quite limited, and many manufacturers introduced their own add-ons. As more independent relational database suppliers arrived on the market, the need for a richer standard became greater. The language is still in development, and although SQL is a fairly rich language, manufacturers continue to add their own elements to the language to meet the demands of ever changing market conditions.

In principle, SQL is a declarative language, which simply means that the language describes what the user wants (declarative), without concerning itself with how the system actually gathers the information (procedural). Most third generation languages are procedural; fourth generation languages are often more declarative.

Some people think that SQL is only a query language, but it is much more than that. One must also be able to produce and maintain databases. SQL is split into the following parts:

- *Data definition language (DDL)*
  This part of the language serves to create the tables in the database, the views (pre-defined partial data collections) and to assign grants or authorizations.

- *Data manipulation language (DML)*
  The data manipulation portion offers the capability of filling tables with records, accessing the records and mutating records.

- *Model language*
  SQL is used within source codes from programming languages such as COBOL. This is called 'embedded' SQL.

Tables within relational databases always receive a unique name. Each table consists of one or more columns, and it must have a unique or primary key that uniquely identifies each of the rows. This is usually done by placing a unique index in each column which determine the uniqueness. The same data can then appear only once in the column or columns. If one tries to input the same data more than once in the same column, the database will refuse to store this data (Figure 6.1).

One of the most important aspects of the relational database is that it allows working with keys, since this makes relationships with other tables possible. There are primary and secondary keys. A combination of one or more key fields which determine the uniqueness of a record from the table is called a primary key. A primary key can encompass more than one column of a table. Each table has a primary key which uniquely identifies the information in the records. The value of a primary key sometimes appears in other tables; we then have a relationship with these tables. We speak of foreign keys in this connection. In this way, various tables come into being, related via key fields. A table can have more than one foreign key originating from other tables. Tables can be added and the structure of existing tables can be modified without having any effect on the rest of the database.

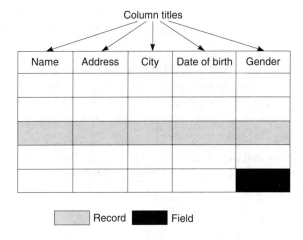

Figure 6.1 Table with rows and columns.

Before going into greater detail on SQL, we need to know more about data analysis. Data ordering techniques which help us to input data in a database are especially important. This process is called 'normalization.' The objective of the 'normalization' process is to mold data into a so-called 'normalized form.' In most cases, only the first three forms are used:

- Normalization provides data which can be stored in a tabular form.

- It prevents data redundancy, and information can be easily found.

- The data can be neatly arranged and stored in the database's data dictionary according to relational model principles.

Normalization is not only a question of efficiency: it results in a stable data model with a minimum of redundancy, and the data is stored as efficiently as possible.

Information is stored only once in a table and can be easily found by the table name and the name of the attribute. Tables can have a relationship with other tables. The dependency of relationships between tables can be easily seen due to the foreign keys. The consequences of changes and additions to, or deletions from, the tables can be easily predicted.

The following example shows how a table can be defined in SQL. We use the data set of suppliers as an example.

Suppliers

- Supplier code   Unique supplier key

- Name

- Address

- City

- Contact person

- Region code   Key from the Region group

Creation of a table in SQL proceeds as follows:

```
CREATE TABLE SUPPLIERS
(SUPPLIER_CODE NUMBER(6)NOT NULL,
NAME CHAR(15)NOT NULL,
ADDRESS CHAR(25)NOT NULL,
CITY CHAR(20)NOT NULL,
CONTACT_PERSON CHAR(30),
REGION_CODE NUMBER(8)NOT NULL)
```

The 'NOT NULL' condition means that the fields cannot be left blank. Fields which belong to the primary key must always contain the 'NOT NULL' condition. The primary key here is 'Supplier code' and the foreign key is 'Region code.' The primary key is created in the Supplier code column.

Data which is stored in a relational database can be easily accessed using SQL's SELECT statement. If, for example, we want to extract data from the supplier data set, we would use the following SQL statement:

```
SELECT SUPPLIER_CODE,NAME,ADDRESS
FROM SUPPLIERS
```

We get these three fields of all records from the database in the 'suppliers' table (Figure 6.2).

When consulting the database, we use the table and column names defined in the database. These names are often technical and difficult to understand for users who are not programmers. It is possible to define synonyms, but that is not always desirable. Simply using understandable table and column names is a much more

Supplier code	Name	Address
1201	Dirksma	Second Ave 102
1208	Gleason	Third Ave 4
1250	Peterson	31Str. 18

Query results

Figure 6.2 The result of a query.

obvious solution, and it is important to make fixed agreements on this sort of detail during the database's design stages. This is advantageous for both the programmer and the user, who must be able to consult the database using all kinds of modern query tools in SQL. Unclear table and column names are a potential source of misunderstanding, and unclear naming conventions limit the power of the database. During the creation of the database, a number of rules must be taken into consideration:

• Make sure that the same language is used as consistently as possible for naming columns and tables.

• If users regularly consult the database, involve them in the naming process to ensure that recognizable names are used.

• Avoid strange abbreviations and codes.

• Try to keep names short.

• Try to keep the number of key fields limited, preferably to one column.

• Indicate which date is meant when naming important date fields (for example, purchase date, sale date).

Special relational capacities

We have now discussed some of the basic aspects of the relational database. In the past few years, however, other characteristics of the relational database related to processing in the client/server environment have begun to attract more attention. We shall discuss the more important components here. They must be analyzed thoroughly during the design and implementation of a client/server environment. Particularly important in this connection are:

• joins and query optimization

• database integrity

• stored procedures

• data dictionary

• commit and rollback.

Joins and query optimization

Information which is spread over more than one table often has to be extracted from a relational database. These tables are usually linked to each other using foreign keys. In our example, the 'Region' table is related to the 'Suppliers' table. We would like to obtain an overview containing the supplier's name and the associated region codes. We now need to link two tables via SQL. A query like this one, involving more than one table, is called a join in SQL.

REGION

– Region code   Unique Region key

– Region name

SUPPLIERS

– Supplier code   Unique Supplier key

– Name

– Address

– City

– Contact person

– Region code   Key from the region group

The SQL statement coupling the two tables is:

```
SELECT REGION.REGION_CODE,SUPPLIERS.NAME

FROM REGION,SUPPLIERS

WHERE REGION.REGION_CODE = SUPPLIERS.REGION_CODE
```

The above statements link the relationship over the columns which appear in both tables. A join enables record requests (select statement), record additions (insert statement), record modifications (update statement) and record deletions (delete statement) over more than one table.

A join can cost an inordinate amount of processing time, which makes it a very important issue during the database design stage. As our example has shown, relational databases allow extremely easy access to data. How and where the data is stored is sorted out by the database itself. We specify only the name of the table and the columns, and the database quickly generates the results. This freedom also has disadvantages, however. Say that we want to access two related tables, A and B. Table A has 100 000 records and table B has just 400. Access can occur in two ways: we can look at each record in table A and then combine it with the relevant information in table B. If we did that we would have to access the database 100 000 times. We can, however, also switch the process around: first examine each record in table B, then find the relevant information in table A. In that case we need to access the database just 400 times. Although both strategies generate the same effect, the second method is in many cases a great deal more efficient. This example shows how important query optimization is. The burden placed on network traffic by queries on distributed data is another important reason for query optimization.

In many databases, until not long ago the programmer had to optimize queries by hand. This has now changed. Every good relational database now has query optimization. The database itself maintains a log file which contains statistics on how a record from the same table is consulted. An incoming query is analyzed, and with the help of the statistical data the optimal strategy is devised for execution of the query. This allows the database itself to choose the quickest means of processing data, which can result in an enormous increase in speed, and the programmer no longer has to worry about this kind of task.

Query optimization is very important in client/server applications that make use of distributed databases. For optimization reasons, tables are often copied to various servers. Tables in such environments are often distributed over several servers. System performance and the network burden are dependent on the optimal execution of queries, so extra attention must be given to these aspects during the design of client/server systems. Optimal distribution of tables over the various servers is extremely important.

End users nowadays have the opinion of working with query tools to create their own joins. This will have an impact on database design. Alternatively, it is necessary to set up a specific query environment, such as a main warehouse.

Database integrity

A database is worthless if the information it contains is not trustworthy. Database integrity is an essential aspect of database implementation which requires extra attention in a client/server environment.

What exactly does database integrity mean? The most important point is that the database must continue to conform, under all conditions, to the constraints set out in the database design. The constraints are a description of all of the rules and limitations to which the organization's data must conform, and the number of constraints may be unlimited. Two examples are: each order must be identified by a unique number; and only article numbers which appear in the article file may be used. Before every modification to the database, we must analyze the consequences that modification may have on database integrity. The three types of modifications are:

• inserts

• updates

• deletes.

The foreign key relationships are especially important during changes to the database. Changes to a table can have direct effects on other tables related to the table to be changed. Figure 6.3 shows the foreign key relationship between two tables. A patient can have more than one dossier, but each dossier must contain

Patient information

Patient no.	Name	Address	City
06897	Johnson	Park Lane	Amsterdam
06898	Jones	Bill Street	New York
06899	Quincy	Hyde Park	London

Foreign key

File

File no.	Patient no.	Doctor	Department
688	06898	Frost	XY
689	06890	Smith	XY
690	06891	King	AB

Figure 6.3 An example of a foreign key relation.

the patient number. What happens if we change the patient number, or if we discard the patient information? There are three strategies for processing update and delete operations:

- *Cascade*
  If a table's primary key is changed (deleted), and that primary key appears in another table as a foreign key, then all of the records contained in the second file, which also contains this key, must also be changed (deleted) (Figure 6.4).

- *Restricted*
  A primary key may not be changed (deleted) if it also appears in another file.

- *Nullify*
  If we change a primary key that also appears in a second file as a foreign key, the foreign key in the second file must be replaced with zero values for all records tagged with that foreign key (Figure 6.5).

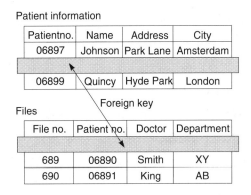

Patient information

Patientno.	Name	Address	City
06897	Johnson	Park Lane	Amsterdam
06899	Quincy	Hyde Park	London

Foreign key

Files

File no.	Patient no.	Doctor	Department
689	06890	Smith	XY
690	06891	King	AB

Figure 6.4 The result after a delete cascade.

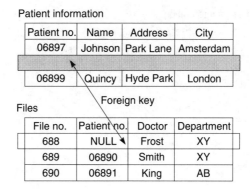

Patient information

Patient no.	Name	Address	City
06897	Johnson	Park Lane	Amsterdam
06899	Quincy	Hyde Park	London

Foreign key

Files

File no.	Patient no.	Doctor	Department
688	NULL	Frost	XY
689	06890	Smith	XY
690	06891	King	AB

Figure 6.5 The result after a delete nullify.

In the recent past, the capability to automatically monitor relational database integrity did not exist, but database suppliers are now able to automatically ensure database integrity. We still see, however, instances where integrity monitoring is separately programmed in the application. This means that identical integrity rules must be programmed for each application that makes use of the same tables. Each change in the rules leads to corresponding changes in all of the applications. The basic relational database constraints are defined by:

- inclusion of the primary and foreign keys in a database;

- the cascade, restricted and nullify constraints.

Definition of this sort of constraint in SQL occurs as follows:

```
CREATE TABLE SUPPLIERS
(SUPPLIER_CODE NUMBER(6) PRIMARY KEY,
NAME CHAR(15)NOT NULL,
ADDRESS CHAR(25)NOT NULL,
CITY CHAR(20)NOT NULL,
CONTACT_PERSON CHAR(30),
REGION_CODE NUMBER(8)
        CONSTRAINT FOREIGN-REGION_CODE
        REFERENCES REGION(REGION_CODE)
        ON DELETE CASCADE)
```

In the above example, we see that the primary keys and constraints are immediately defined during table creation.

Creation of a cascade constraint with the name Foreign-region code allows database integrity to be managed centrally. This eliminates the need for the programmer to program database integrity each time into the application. It does mean, however, that, when developing new applications, the analyst and programmer must be aware of the structure and relationships within the existing database, as maintained by the database manager.

Stored procedures and intelligent databases

Keys and the cascade, delete and nullify constraints account for just a small number of the constraints which we want to impose on the database. The past few years have seen the arrival of the possibility to program those processes which are executed in an organization directly in the database instead of at a higher level in the application. In the past, all procedures had to be programmed separately in the application for relational databases. It is, however, far more efficient to store certain procedures centrally, which can result in performance improvements. This method is usually applied to business rules.

In an inventory system, for example, within which mutations in the records can be generated from various applications, inventory levels must be constantly monitored. Using a procedure, the programmer can decide to check whether the inventory levels are sufficient after every inventory table mutation. To ensure that monitoring takes place after every mutation, a condition is defined in the database which gives the warehouse manager a signal if orders must be placed to refill depleted inventories.

This kind of condition, also called a constraint, can be programmed into the database using a procedural language or SQL. In some databases, conditions are split up into triggers and procedures.

Triggers are defined immediately during table creation. A trigger can be set off by:

- inserts

- updates

- deletes.

Referential integrity can also be monitored using triggers, and a trigger can also call up other procedures. Procedures which are separately called up are called stored procedures. These are called up only upon specific request. Procedures always receive unique names and are, in turn, able to call up other procedures. This allows all kinds of vital control mechanisms to be built into the database. In addition, the constraints offer added efficiency, since certain constraints need only be programmed once. Another example of the definition of a constraint follows:

CREATE TABLE INVENTORY

(ARTICLE_QUANTITY NUMBER(4)**CONSTRAINT PKEYINVENTORY**
PRIMARY KEY,

ARTICLE_DESCRIPTION CHAR(15)

QUANTITY NUMBER(3)

CONSTRAINT CHECK (QUANTITY > 3))

We now have two constraints:

PKEYINVENTORY This is the primary key of the inventory table.

CHECK   This ensures that the quantity is greater than 3.

Help texts can also be sent to a program and other programs can be activated via
constraints, which results in intelligent databases. These are normal relational
databases which have received an extra level of database possibilities due to the
insertion of constraints at the database level. The database then becomes more
than just a storage area for records. Parts of an application can then be
programmed at the database level instead of at a higher level, in the application.
It is self-apparent that maintenance of constraints and monitoring of database
integrity is even more complex in a client/server environment, where applications
and databases can be distributed over various systems. Good design of stored
procedures and triggers is very important in such situations.

Data dictionary

To maintain a good overview of all the tables and the underlying relationships
and constraints, the database administrator needs an outline in which all of this
information can be found. This outline is the data dictionary, which must contain
the following information:

•   table names

•   column names

•   data type (Char, Number, Date, Time, and so on)

•   length of the field

•   Not Null fields

•   primary key fields

•   foreign key fields

•   foreign key tables

•   indexes

- integrity rules

  - cascade

  - restricted

  - nullify

- stored procedures.

Without this information, the database administrator has no control over his databases. The importance of the data dictionary is frequently underestimated, but only a good data dictionary gives an insight into the design of a database. The consequences of changes to the database for the database structure as a whole can only be determined based on the data dictionary.

Certain database products also provide insight into the number of records per table, the relationship of tables to applications, read, write and update authorizations, security, authorizations and management information. Such products allow optimal database management.

In a distributed environment, the data dictionary becomes even more important, since it becomes necessary to see not only the foreign key relationships, but also the physical machine locations of the various tables and their dependencies.

Figure 6.6 is an overview of a number of normalized tables from a simple data dictionary.

Table Supplier

Supplier code:	number 6 not null primary key	
Name:	char. 15 not null	
Address:	char. 25 not null	
City:	char. 20 not null	
Contactperson:	char: 30 not null	
Region code:	number 8 not null	foreign key table Region

Table Item

Item code:	number 8 not null primary key
Description:	char. 25 not null

Table Order Line

Item code:	number 8 not null primary key	foreign key table Item
Order number:	number 6 not null primary key	foreign key table Order
Quantity:	number 6 not null primary key	

Figure 6.6 Simple data dictionary.

Commit and rollback

Commitment of transactions is an important aspect of the client/server concept. Transactions are processed in an application, and the records which have been input via a screen are stored in a database. Once all the data has been stored, the commitment procedure is carried out. At that time, the records are stored and the constraints are checked. If all data conforms to the conditions it is stored in the database. Only after completion of the commitment procedure is the data definitively stored. However, during constraint checking, the user sometimes notices that the transaction cannot be carried out because completion of the transaction would endanger the database integrity. The user can also decide to call a given transaction back, in which case the entire transaction must be cancelled. A rollback mechanism has been introduced for this: the rollback command can be used in cases where the user does not want to complete certain transactions, as it returns the database to its original state. The complexity of transactions on a single database already makes the correct implementation of the rollback command difficult. Rollback implementation in a distributed system is even more problematic, so this also requires close attention during database implementation in a client/server environment.

We have now examined the most important aspects of designing relational databases. In this chapter, we have looked at only a few new techniques and the implementation of a single database on a machine. Use of relational databases in a client/server environment is, however, far more complex. In a client/server environment, several databases on different servers can be used, these databases can originate from different suppliers, and several applications can use the same database. An application can also use several databases simultaneously. In a large client/server environment, copies of tables are maintained on other servers to ensure optimal data accessibility. The design and maintenance of this kind of complex information system requires very careful consideration.

The relational database plays an especially crucial role in this respect. This database can today be utilized in a variety of ways, and it can also be distributed. A distributed database is a database which is split up over several servers, while the database manifests itself to the user as a single entity.

We shall explain this further using a simple example. We have a large organization with a variety of independent departments responsible for their own finances. Each department needs a database in support of local activities. Both department-dependent data and organization-dependent data exist. A new price list and the assignment of new product codes can, for example, be seen as organization-dependent data. This data is sent to all of the database servers in the departments from a central system. In addition, all of the departments must be able to request data from the other departments. If one department, for example, lacks a given raw material, it must be able to access the other departments' inventory system to see whether one of the other departments has the raw material in stock. The automation system is constructed so that local autonomy is protected, but the departments are still able to communicate with the rest of the system and to share corporate data with other departments. To automate this, we must distribute the databases over the various departments. A modern relational database is able to distribute the tables over various servers. Such databases are called distributed databases.

Rules for distributed database management

Date drew up 12 rules for working with distributed databases in 1987. These rules form a good introduction to the issues involved in working with distributed databases. Date's rules are now generally accepted as the basis of distributed database technology. They are:

1   Local autonomy

2   Central server independent

3   Continuously available

4   Data location independent

5   Data fragmentation independent

6   Data replication independent

7   Distributed query processing

8   Distributed transaction management

9   Hardware independent

10   Operating system independent

11   Network independent

12   Database independent

An explanation of these rules follows.

Local autonomy

The first rule is that in a real distributed database, each local database is completely independent. Each local database completes its own processes and has its own separate database. Each database monitors its own security, data integrity, recovery and consistency.

Central server independent

This rule follows from the first rule. There is no central machine on which the databases depend: a master database does not exist.

Continuously available

The services supported by the database must always be available. A database may never be unavailable due to downtime.

Data location independent

The data location may not have an effect on application processing. Although the user never has to know where the data is actually stored, he must always be able to access the data.

Data fragmentation independent

With the help of snapshots and replicas, parts of tables can be copied over to another server. If the copy is of part of the table, it is called 'fragmented data.' This data must be placed in an independent table on the local server, accessible to the user.

Data replication independent

Replicated database tables must be accessible as independent tables on the local server. These tables must, however, be able to update the replicated records, and to further check and maintain them so that integrity remains guaranteed. This has consequences for each replica's locking mechanism, since replicas must be locked during table updates.

Distributed query processing

It must be possible to request data located on various machines in a single query, without sacrificing performance. This is possible only if the database supports an intelligent form of query optimization.

Distributed transaction management

This rule includes issues such as two phase commit and commit and rollback transactions.

Hardware independent

Distributed databases must be able to run on various hardware platforms.

Operating system independent

This rule means that the databases must not be dependent on a specific sort of operating system. This is really a plea from Date for open systems. There are too many databases which are dependent on a certain operating system (for example, the AS/400 database).

Network independent

A distributed environment must be transparent for the various network environments.

Database independent

An organization should be able to support several databases or several suppliers. This is extremely complex given the fact that standards for SQL dialects, and locking and trigger mechanisms, are few and far between. Procedures and gateways to other databases are another problem.

Client/server environment with distributed databases

We will discuss a number of transactions and methods which are especially important in a client/server environment with distributed databases.

Two phase commit

In a client/server environment, the commit and rollback transactions are of great importance in monitoring the integrity of the database. Distributed databases may also involve extra complications, especially if an application on a client uses a database which is distributed over two servers. We can explain this with the help of an example.

A bank application makes use of a client's information table stored on server A, while the credit information is stored on server B. To request credit information on a given client the two tables have to be joined. If changes are made, the client data has to be written to server A, while the credit data has to be written to server B.

It is quite clear that things could go wrong here. For example, if server B goes down shortly after the information is written to the server, the information will not be consistent. Server A contains new data, while server B contains the old data. To prevent this type of situation the two phase commit was introduced. The two phase commit ensures that the transaction succeeds as a whole, or does not succeed at all. Half completed transactions are impossible.

This occurs as follows: the data is first written to both tables A and B, and a report of these transactions is maintained in a log file. A message is subsequently sent to both servers. Once both servers have reported that there were no problems with the execution of the first phase of the transaction, a commit is issued which makes both parts of the transaction definitive. If, however, one or both of the systems report a problem, the transaction is cancelled on both systems via the rollback mechanism. The rollback brings both databases back to their original state and eliminates the danger of inconsistency in the database (Figure 6.7).

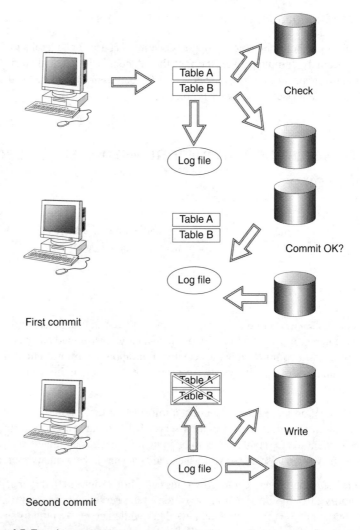

Figure 6.7 Two phase commit.

Areas of attention for two phase commit

Application of two phase commit makes the system particularly sensitive to a breakdown of one of the servers. Tables which have a relationship with each other can be placed on different servers. The check on the execution of the two phase commit is carried out with the help of a management system which controls all of the queries, and registers whether or not the commit can be executed. The speed with which a two phase commit is executed largely determines the performance of the system. If a single system goes down, a rollback must be carried out and users cannot continue working until the rollback has been completed. A distributed database is sometimes chosen so as to spread the risk of downtime, but two phase commit partially undoes this advantage. This type of disadvantage can be partially eliminated by applying database replication.

Query optimization

Optimization is more important in a distributed environment because a number of complications can occur in this environment. If, for example, we execute a join on a table with 100 000 records, and a table on another server with just 100 records, and the table with 100 000 records is dumped into the smaller table via the network, the burden on the network would be substantial. If many users execute this sort of transaction simultaneously, the chance of the network or certain systems becoming overburdened increases enormously. To solve this potential problem, good databases possess various optimization options.

A query optimizer determines the most optimal relationship between the tables. Only the table with the fewest number of records will be transported over the network, and queries which have already been executed several times are executed by the query optimizer in such a way that the database is accessed as efficiently as possible.

Snapshots

If certain tables are accessed often (for example, referential tables), the table or a part of the table can be copied over to another server.

Take, for example, an organization with a large number of branches throughout the country which sells articles with exactly the same codes and related article descriptions. The codes and descriptions are issued by the head office. To automatically display an article description on screen in a branch after filling in the code, the user must be connected to the central database where this information is stored. This means that the branch has to maintain contact with the head office all day long, which leads to high network costs. The central system must also be

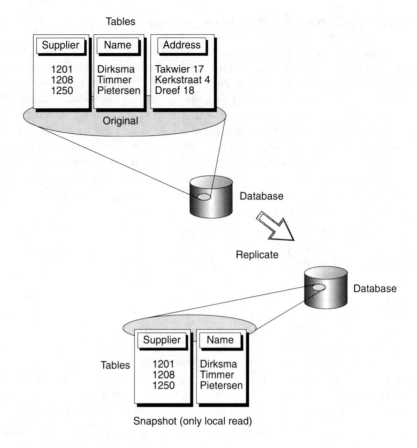

Figure 6.8 An example of a snapshot.

available at all times. To solve this problem, the head office decides to implement snapshots. This is a table or a part of a table which is copied to a local server (Figure 6.8).

Usually, snapshots are used only with tables that are accessed solely to retrieve information. Referential tables which do not change very often, for example, are very well suited to snapshot use. Referential tables on the central system which are changed can be copied automatically to the other servers using a special procedure. Snapshots are used to access and view data, not to input or change data on the local database server. A snapshot offers the following advantages:

- It prevents unnecessary network traffic.

- It makes the local application server less dependent on the central server.

- It provides greater data availability.

- It gives better performance.

Replicas

Replication is a more far-reaching distribution concept. Not all relational databases can use replicas, as their use requires a database able to work with distributed management. Replication, which consists of the copying of one or more tables from the central server, is one of the most interesting of distributed database technology concepts, but also one of the most complex (Figure 6.9).

While snapshots were used in cases in which the user needed only to access and view the data, replication is used when the user also needs the ability to decentrally modify tables. This does mean, however, that the same record on all of the other servers must also be changed. The complexity lies in the maintenance of data integrity, since the database manager must be able to see where the replicas are, and must ensure integrity for all of the tables. The database administrator must possess an excellent insight into the data dictionary of each server. The advantages of replicas are:

- less dependency on central database;

- more local possibilities;

- decentral processing with less network burden;

- more possibilities for local tools, such as query tools;

- more possibilities to distribute applications throughout the organization;

- data stays closer to the user.

The use of database replication offers a solution to the problems which can be encountered in the two phase commit when a server goes down. In addition, replication offers an organization the possibility to continue working, even in the case of server fall out, and guarantees high performance.

Replication is literally copying tables, including the records and procedure constraints, to another server. This means not only that the data can be accessed on several database servers, but that it can also be updated, in contrast to a snapshot, which is used to request data that cannot be updated. The way in which a table is replicated depends upon the requirements and the integrity levels to which the data must conform. One or more tables can be copied to various database servers, located in other departments or in other parts of the world even. Data replication is applied where the performance, availability and dependability factors are critical. This may be the case, for example, when banks copy a part of their client data to bank branches in another country.

In all cases where the aforementioned critical database factors play an important role, replication can offer solutions. A replicator copies, according to the organization's requirements, the data of a master to a target database. This can be done at a given point in time, but it can also be carried out at the moment at which the records are modified in the master. Replication allows users continuous access to

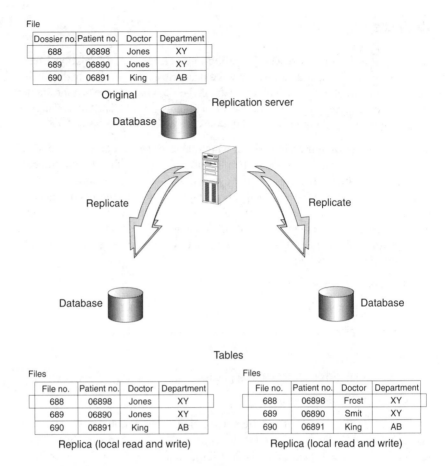

File

Dossier no.	Patient no.	Doctor	Department
688	06898	Jones	XY
689	06890	Jones	XY
690	06891	King	AB

Original
Database

Replication server

Replicate

Replicate

Database

Database

Tables

Files

File no.	Patient no.	Doctor	Department
688	06898	Jones	XY
689	06890	Jones	XY
690	06891	King	AB

Replica (local read and write)

Files

File no.	Patient no.	Doctor	Department
688	06898	Frost	XY
689	06890	Smit	XY
690	06891	King	AB

Replica (local read and write)

Figure 6.9 Example of replication.

the databases: if a system goes down, the user can log on to another server, which takes over the first server's tasks. Replication can also unburden the network by placing the data as close as possible to the user. All data that is modified is immediately copied to the other databases. Usually there is a master database, which sends modified data directly to the replicator. The replicator knows the database servers to which the data must be copied. If a database is not available, the data remains on the replicator, and as soon as the system becomes available the data is brought up to date. It is vital that the data to be copied is always synchronous over a great deal of the organization. The data integrity must be 100%, and to achieve this the replicator must meet certain requirements. The master database can use a trigger to indicate the conditions to which the data of the other databases must conform. If the data does not conform to the trigger values, this is reported. For example, during an update on the system, a user can stipulate 'Update data where last record is updated at 9 November time 10.15 am'. If the database sees that the last record was modified at another time, a warning notice can be generated that a discrepancy exists between the master and the target database. A rollback can then be executed or the transaction can be allowed to proceed.

Forms of replication

One form of replication applies to the master–slave relationship, a relationship which always works via a master. This means that only the master may be updated, for example during the modification of price lists in branches. Usually, the target database must also be modified, in which case we speak of a master–master situation. The data is then sent via the replicator from one master to the other (Figure 6.10).

This means that all updates can be done via the master only. This is time consuming, and when the master database is not available, updates cannot be made. Another situation involves temporary masters. Certain data from countrywide organizations, for example, can be sent to provincial organizations, which add their own data, before being distributed to local organizations. In this case we speak of 'dynamic replication masters.' These transactions can be executed if only the administration of the system is capable of carrying out extremely strict checks. This method eliminates dependence on a single system, making the system less vulnerable (Figure 6.11).

Flexible support of databases, at the right moments, and high performance result from replication, as well as high levels of data integrity. Another result of replication is that processes can be carried out using several systems. There is also the possibility that the table is owned by two master databases. If one table is updated

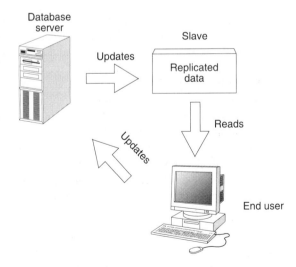

Figure 6.10 Master–slave replication.

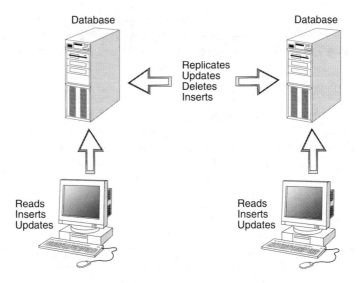

Figure 6.11 Master master replication.

the replicator must take care that the record in the other database is updated as well. We use the asynchronous mechanism for this transaction. This means that if one system fails, the other database continues and is waiting before the failed database is up again. Update conflicts will be detected and can be resolved by selecting the most recent of the updates, or using other rules. Obviously, it is of great importance that there is a very good database administration to support this type of replication.

The current replicators can be viewed as having one of two main capabilities: synchronous or asynchronous. What is the difference between asynchronous and synchronous replication? In the world of synchronous communication, if we want to update one database it is necessary at the same time to commit on the other database. This update is one single transaction. This transaction uses the two phase commit procedure to support this synchronous communication. If the database receiving the copy is not able to commit, then the complete transaction is rolled back. This synchronous transaction can be used in a multiple database environment where you always need exactly the same data as on the original database. This can take place in banking or reservation systems, where a form of high availability is needed in the database. However, this synchronous communication means that both systems must be available, and that the infrastructure allows the synchronous transaction to take place in an acceptable time frame.

Asynchronous connection is much easier to handle. In this case, we replicate data from the master database to the other database in a separate transaction. This transaction can take place after the commit has taken place in the master database, which can be one second or several hours later. It can also take place when the connectivity is available or when the transaction costs are at their lowest. If the remote database is not available, then the data that must be copied to the target database stays in a queue and waits for propagation. This means that there is no problem in the performance of the master database because it does not have to wait for a two phase commit transaction. This form of replication can be used in a data warehouse situation, or in situations where the new data is sent to target databases only once a day.

Replication in a multivendor world

In a data warehouse in particular you will find a number of applications, and in each application you might find different names for entities and attributes. In the data warehouse there is only one name per entity. This means that you can repli-cate this information on a target database with table names and attributes with names different than those on the master database. It might also be important to send it to a target database other than the master database. Where your mainframe is working with DB/2 and your warehouse is an Oracle or Sybase database run-ning on a UNIX system, you will need a multidatabase vendor replicator. Some new replicators are now on the market which support these functionalities, such as the IBM data propagator.

Replication on PCs

In some cases we can see the need for local databases at the personal computer level. This will increase as more people work at home or travel internationally and want to do some local transactions on their PC. Data may be needed locally for decision support; sales professionals will need to have the latest information (such as prices) of products. Most of the relational databases offer portability to PCs, and now replicators can send data to these databases on the PC. Many data-base vendors are now offering replication to PCs.

Messaging – another method of replication

In addition to database replicators there is one other form of replicator. The soft-ware in question is the message and queueing mechanism. This type of replication can copy database information, and it can also copy all files and mail between systems.

The messaging software can be installed on clients and servers of any type, and it works like independent middleware for message exchange between client and servers. All the communication problems and operating system dependencies are handled by the program itself. It offers an application programming interface (API) and any software that can work with this API can use this middleware mechanism.

This type of replication also uses the asynchronous replication method and is very powerful in many cases. A client sends a message, such as a file, to a server via a queue. An address will be connected so that the message knows the direction of the server. The server finds a message in its queue and it can send a reply

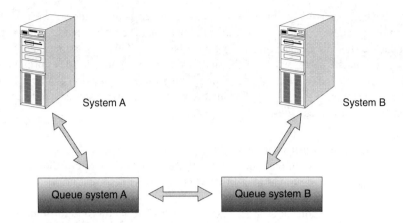

Figure 6.12 Message queuing.

acknowledging receipt of the message; the server sends this reply to the client's queue (Figure 6.12).

Messaging is very flexible, cheap and can be used corporate-wide. Messaging and queuing work like an email function; a message and the receiving system is alerted when something has arrived. Mainframes, minisystems, LAN servers and personal computers can work with messaging. Most messaging products are operating system independent, which means they can work on many hardware systems and with many types of software, so that changes in the environment will not have too much of an impact.

Forms of distributed processing

Databases in a distributed environment communicate with each other via the network. Take an application which runs on a client and uses two tables located on different servers. The client must know exactly where the tables are located when executing a transaction on the database. If a request is sent from the client to the server, the server must know exactly which client must receive the data. The addresses of the tables must be stored, and be accessible to both the client and server. We discuss three concepts in this regard:

- central architecture (star concept)

- decentral architecture (synonym concept)

- distribution at client level.

Central architecture (star concept)

The first distributed techniques solution is the star concept, which involves the use of a server that acts as a buffer between the client and server. The addresses of the tables and the database with which an application communicates are contained on the star server. The star server contains a complete overview of the various addresses. All clients are linked to the star server, and all user access to the database goes through the star server.

This can be explained using a simple example. An application has a table called 'Articles' and a table called 'Orders.' 'Articles' is stored on server A and 'Orders' on server B. All of the clients are linked to the star server and search for the address of the database servers for each SQL statement. Each client sees that 'Orders' is stored on server B and 'Articles' on server A via the data dictionary on the star server (Figure 6.13).

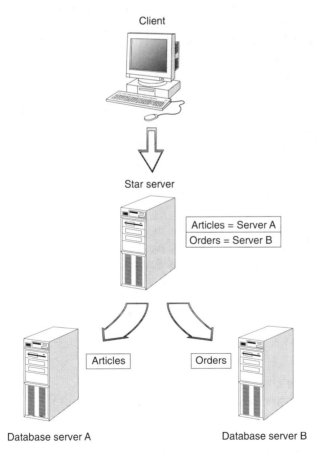

Client

Star server

Articles = Server A
Orders = Server B

Articles

Orders

Database server A

Database server B

Figure 6.13 Star concept.

If a new application is added or a table is transferred from one table to the other, the server merely has to be informed. This simplifies and speeds up maintenance.

The fact that all clients are directed to a star server can be an enormous burden on this star server and on the network segment to which this server is linked. In addition, users are extremely vulnerable to star server breakdowns. In such cases we talk of a single point of failure. To get around these problems, several star servers can be installed. This allows the distribution of client links over various star servers, more efficient distribution of network traffic and decreased downtime risk.

Working with a star server frees the user from the necessity of having to program all kinds of communication. The intelligence is contained on the star server, which also contains a repository with all the addresses. Two phase commits must also be executed via the star server.

If a commit to three tables, which are stored on three different servers, has to be carried out, the star server carries out a check with the three servers. Only after the star server has received the go-ahead from each database server can the records actually be stored on the three independent database servers. If a signal that the commit cannot be carried out is sent by just one of the servers, the star server carries out a rollback.

If several tables on several servers are accessed, and the number of records per table differs considerably, the query optimizer must also be set in motion. These components are automatically driven, resulting in a powerful instrument with many capabilities.

The advantage is simple maintenance, since a star server need only be maintained if a database table is transferred to another server. A star server can be installed in each department, for example, and if users make very little use of servers in other departments, the star server can be adjusted to reflect this. The user then has no need for an exact copy of each star server in each department.

We need to pay consistent attention to the performance and vulnerability of a central star server when using this model. It should be clear that several star servers are necessary if a large number of users are linked to the system. In some cases, the star server may actually have to be installed locally on the client. This means that the simplicity of maintenance will, to some extent, be nullified. This can be partially solved, however, by distributing the latest server addresses to the star servers on the clients from a central star server. Despite its problems, the star server offers excellent database distribution over several servers. Distribution via a star server is used by CA Ingres, which delivers the star server as a separate product capable of enabling distributed database use.

Decentral architecture (synonym concept)

Another distributed database technology concept works with synonyms. This concept is entirely different from the star concept. Each client is linked to a database server which contains a data dictionary of all tables on the site, including the tables located on other servers. Take an application which runs on a client

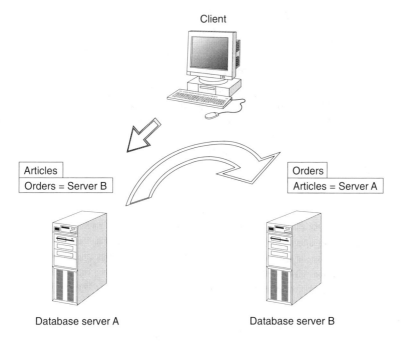

Figure 6.14   The synonym concept.

and requests information from a server. The application needs information from two different tables via a join. We again use the 'Articles' and 'Orders' tables as examples. The 'Articles' table is located on server A and 'Orders' is located on server B. The client's standard link is to server A, which contains the 'Articles' table. The client requests the data from the database server, which searches its data dictionary for the 'Articles' table, finds it, and subsequently searches for the 'Orders' table, but cannot find it. The server does, however, find a reference to a server address where the table is located. This reference is a synonym: the table name 'Orders' is stored in the data dictionary, but with the correct server address (Figure 6.14).

In the data dictionary on Server A, we see the following:

Articles

Orders @ B

The use of synonyms allows users to find tables from each client linked to a server. The location of the tables becomes unimportant, as the user is always sent to the correct server via references. This means that users are not dependent on a single server containing the tables or references. Each server possesses a data dictionary with the correct addresses, which means that addresses no longer need to be placed in tables located on the client. The advantage is that each server is able to function as a distribution channel, eliminating the possibility of a single point of failure. Speed can also be positively affected. Users always work on the database to which they are linked first, and only if the table is not found there does the system start searching for a synonym and refer the user automatically to the correct server.

This system of synonyms also offers the possibility of working with a query optimizer. For each join executed, the query optimizer first examines the number of records each table contains, and only after this step has been completed does the system decide how the query should be executed. If the query has already been carried out a few times, the database automatically knows what the most efficient processing is. The two phase commit is also used here during transactions to ensure database integrity.

This method involves not just a client/server transaction, but also a server/server transaction. An important consideration when working with this method is that, during transfer of tables from one server to another, the synonyms on all the servers must be updated. A system must also be implemented to take care of placing the new table names and synonyms on all of the servers. Correct construction allows users to log in anywhere in the system, and to always arrive at the correct database server. This use of synonyms is presently used in Oracle database version 7.

Distribution at client level

We have now discussed two client/server methods; the first method requires a star server, and the second method works with synonyms on the database server. The third method involves providing the application with an exact reference on the client as to where the correct database server is located. If the application runs on an application server, the address of the database server must also be located there. This method is used, for example, by Sybase. By placing all of the references in a separate file with all of the addresses, the method offers a central overview of all of the database servers. Placing this data on the client allows users to work in the most direct way possible, as application refers users directly to the correct database (Figure 6.15).

As is true of all distributed database environments in which table addresses often change, this method requires intensive repository maintenance. Data which is hard coded on the clients will need a correspondingly large amount of maintenance as the number of clients increases. Since there are almost always more clients in an organization than servers, modifying the data on a server is often easier than modifying data on clients. The maintenance of references on clients does, however, often offer performance advantages. To avoid manual changes to the software on all of the clients, software can be centrally distributed to the clients from a file server, which ensures that clients always have the latest version of table addresses. This method has also proven itself. We thus have three methods of working with distributed databases, each with its own specific, valuable contribution to the concept. Each type also has its own approach to security, optimization and authorization.

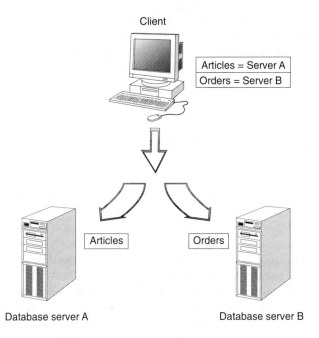

Figure 6.15 Distribution on client level.

That less maintenance is necessary for a central repository, in a reasonably unchanging application environment with fairly stable tables containing all of the table addressess, is true for all three of these concepts. This means that an organization can go further and further to improve performance. Working in a distributed database environment which is still in development produces noticeable exploitation efforts. A distributed environment requires extra insight into the database structure of an organization. A great deal of attention must be paid to the manner in which the database is distributed, which data is organization-dependent, and what limits should be imposed on local data. In addition, the organization must determine whether it would be useful to copy referential tables via snapshots to other servers, and whether the network is not too heavily burdened because data is spread over the entire organization. We must bear in mind that users also want to use query tools and other office tools in distributed databases. It is presently doubtful whether these tools can communicate with distributed databases, since they are not always able to work with the correct network protocols. The concept becomes more complex as various additional databases are introduced in an organization.

All large database suppliers have their own implementation strategy for distributed databases, and these cannot easily be combined. Simultaneous use of Oracle, Ingres and Sybase on a distributed platform causes technical problems which require extremely complex solutions. The issues become more difficult as triggers and procedures at database level are used more intensively.

A heterogeneous database environment with distributed databases usually requires one database product to be seen as the master. The other products are controlled by the software in the master database, which usually means that gateways to these products must be implemented, or that software, such as Uniface, must be chosen which is able to work with heterogeneous databases without using gateways.

Transaction processing

A computer is able to process large quantities of data. One of the ways in which it does that is via batch-oriented processing. This means that the data is input in the system and temporarily stored for processing at a given moment or after a certain command is issued. The related transactions are then checked and executed, and the data is stored in the correct files. This method of batch processing is used just about everywhere, but it is not really suitable for many applications. It is especially unsuitable for applications in which hundreds of thousands of users continuously use the computer, and all of the systems must immediately contain the latest data. This can be the case at banks, insurance companies, large organizations with inventory on hand, and many other organizations in which data depends upon timely processing. It is very attractive, for example, for a travel agent to be able to see whether there is still room for a client, and if that is the case, to immediately book the client's trip.

Direct transaction processing is much more efficient, as organizations can react more effectively to transactions which must immediately be processed. Take a bank application, for example. We have a client who wants to draw money from his account. Before the transaction can be booked at the local bank branch, several on-line transactions must be executed by the computer. First, the system has to check whether the client's balance is sufficient; then his withdrawal has to be immediately subtracted from his account. Finally, a receipt is generated, and the system is given directions to prepare the client's bank statement. If this client goes to another branch to withdraw money, this branch must have access to the very latest balance information, otherwise the client would be able to withdraw money, in excess of his actual balance, at all of the branches.

In this environment, batch processing is out of the question, and on-line transaction processing (OLTP) is usually used. At present, OLTP is one of the cornerstones of many organizations, many of which would not be able to carry on their business in the way in which they now do without OLTP. Partially due to the increase in decentralized processing and client/server use, OLTP will continue to gain in importance. Most 4GL and relational database environments are focused on decision support environments, in which the data in the database is usually only accessed for viewing. Decision support systems are not presently suitable for thousands of users who must be able to access and update large on-line files simultaneously. OLTP usually uses several servers which communicate with each other and work in a distributed environment. Traditionally, this form of OLTP is usually run on large mainframes. One of the most often used transaction processing monitors is IBM's Customer Information Control System (CICS). There are tens of thousands of users of applications built with CICS, applications that are usually built using 3GL languages, but which can now also be built with 4GL languages.

Most transaction-oriented systems offer various types of standard preprogrammed libraries: queue management, security, locking, file handling, recovery, connectivity, administration, and so on. An application written with CICS usually runs under a mainframe operating system such as MVS, but can presently be obtained on AS/400 and UNIX systems as well.

Transactions

What exactly are OLTP transactions? Transactions are preprogrammed actions executed at the moment at which they are called up by an application. These transactions can be executed on systems other than the system on which the application runs.

Certain conditions must be met during transaction processing. These conditions are known under the acronym of ACID: Atomicity, Consistency, Isolation, Durability:

- *Atomicity:* the change induced in the system by a transaction is atomic, which means that it is not composed of parts. Either the entire transaction succeeds or the entire transaction does not occur.

- *Consistency:* if the transaction is executed on a consistent system, the result is also a consistent system. A transaction must not destroy the consistency of the system.

- *Isolation:* transaction A can have an effect on transaction B only if it is processed completely. Transactions which are executed simultaneously are completely independent of each other prior to completion of the processing.

- *Durability:* once a transaction is completed, the change to the system becomes permanent. The transaction is not lost even if the system breaks down.

In the case of related transactions, the user must know whether a given transaction has been accepted of not. This is recorded by a transaction manager. Several systems which communicate with each other can be connected to a transaction manager. In transactions where an action is executed that is dependent on another action, the transaction manager is able to execute a two phase commit or a rollback. This allows excellent OLTP implementation in a distributed environment, enabling the OLTP method to be easily linked to the client/server model.

Until the start of the 1990s, the world of OLTP was primarily a mainframe one. CICS from IBM is the absolute world leader in the area of transaction monitoring. It is obvious that environments in which thousands of users work impose rather heavy requirements on the network protocol. This protocol must also be able to communicate with all of the systems connected to the environment. If one system goes down, users must still be able to send messages to another computer, using another system. This was made possible partly by IBM's flexible network protocol LU 6.2/APPC used in the SNA environment. This network protocol enabled users to send transactions over networks, to execute transactions on various different systems, and to move over to another system if a system went down.

Until a few years ago there was a definite dividing line between OLTP systems and decision support systems. OLTP systems are optimized for a predefined set of transactions, which is one of the reasons why such systems perform so well. Decision support systems, on the other hand, usually use relational databases in combination with a multifunctional query environment. Users can request all information present in the underlying databases on-line. Obviously, such environments are more difficult to optimize. Still, suppliers have succeeded in realizing forms of query optimization that make even this type of database suitable for applications which, in the past, could only be realized using OLTP.

Mainframes and client/server

The mainframe plays a dual role in the client/server concept. Many organizations are currently busy with down-sizing and the inherent decrease in the role of the mainframe which is an intrinsic part of that concept. These organizations are usually busy setting up a new infrastructure and intend to transfer the files which run on the mainframe over to the new environment. Other organizations are using the client/server concept within the existing mainframe environment. The organizations which implement this concept plan to hold on to their mainframe environment, but also want the advantages of the client/server concept. Usually, these organizations have an existing mainframe database and they want to use PCs as a client environment, or they want to implement local database servers which are constantly linked to the mainframe.

Client/server communication with mainframes

An issue which should not be underestimated during down-sizing is the existence of relationships between the existing applications on a mainframe and in the new environment which can have far-reaching effects on the concept. The applications on the mainframe must continue running, in some cases, until the very last application is implemented in the client/server environment.

This can mean that data must be input in two systems, with the great risk that the new environment possesses a completely different database structure with completely different data types. The complexity increases as more applications with critical time limitations are run on the mainframe. It increases even more if the mainframe must not go down, or if its databases are accessed by several applications simultaneously. This implies that mainframe data integrity requirements also affect the new client/server environment.

To solve this problem, an exact copy of the common data must be stored on both systems. In such a situation, the user must know which database can be modified and where the responsibility for database integrity lies. Data entered on a UNIX server must be simultaneously input in the database on the mainframe. This simultaneous data input often has to be carried out on-line, since batch processing is not possible because of integrity considerations.

Links to a mainframe are a separate dimension within the client/server concept. In a client/server environment a relational database is usually used. If a relational database communicates with a hierarchical database, the concept is more difficult than if two relational databases were to communicate with each other. A relational database can communicate with other relational databases via SQL. Translating an SQL request to a hierarchical database is, however, more difficult. Two phase commits between the two systems executed to guarantee database integrity on both systems will generally have to be programmed by the user.

Links to the various databases

In a client/server environment it is possible to link various databases. The most common forms are links between relational and hierarchical databases and the communication between relational databases. We shall examine these links in greater detail.

Links between relational and hierarchical databases

If the system includes a client/server environment running with a relational database and a mainframe with a hierarchical database, the following components must be examined in some depth:

- Do the databases communicate on-line or via batch?

- How large are the interrelationships?

- What are the database integrity requirements?

- Are critical applications located on one or both systems?

Depending on the communication requirements, there are various standard possibilities which can be used to link relational and hierarchical databases. There are five relatively good communication alternatives allowing new client/server environments to communicate with a mainframe with a hierarchical database:

- gateways;
- file transfer, possibly via message queuing;
- replicator;
- TP monitors;
- RPCs.

Gateways

To enable communication with a mainframe, many relational database suppliers have brought special software onto the market which is able to span a bridge between their products and the hierarchical database on the mainframe. The connectivity between the systems usually occurs via a gateway. SQL statements can be issued from the relational database in the direction of the mainframe's hierarchical database, including the Select, Insert, Update and Delete statements. The SQL statements are translated into a language understood by the hierarchical database via the gateway. In addition, many gateways also include the addresses of data in the hierarchical database. An SQL Select statement is translated in the gateway, processed on the mainframe, and the data which was stored on the mainframe is returned to the client/server environment.

There is currently a wide variety of gateways, including gateways which automatically translate from SQL to an IMS database. Many gateways can execute only Select statements (reads), but there are also gateways which can also execute updates, or writes, in the hierarchical database. There is, however, usually only one-way traffic via the gateway. The transaction is arranged by the client/server environment and sent to the mainframe. No action can take place from the mainframe to the client/server environment, unless it is separately programmed.

File transfer

Communication with a hierarchical database can take place in a variety of ways. The file transfer is an example of traditional communication: messages are usually transformed into ASCII code and read in via a batch procedure. This method is naturally not new; there are, however, variants which offer greater possibilities, for example, message queuing. The user indicates which messages must be sent from one machine to another. Files are sent via the user's mailbox to the mailbox of the addressee. Files sent to another system always arrive at that system. This method does not guarantee data integrity, but it does offer quick and secure file transmission over the various systems. This method is not meant for the exchange of large database files, but works mainly as a mailbox function for various messages, including file transfer. The advantages are that users can link several databases with one and the same product, and that the data is portable over several platforms.

Replicator

Another method that enables communication and which offers two-way traffic is replication. As already mentioned, data replication can be applied to copy data to various systems. The master of certain data must be known, as it is responsible for sending a new copy of the data to the database server each time the data is modified. In our gateway example earlier in the chapter, we saw an SQL statement go from a local database server to a mainframe. This SQL statement is translated via the gateway and the data requested from the mainframe is sent back via the gateway to the client environment.

This is, however, one-way traffic and it offers limited possibilities. If two-way data transmission is required, data must always be available on several systems, including a local database server and a mainframe. This allows the use of a replicator, and is possible using both hierarchical and relational databases. Use of a replicator allows data transmission to several different systems, while the only condition is an indication of which database is the master.

Today we also have replicators that can replicate from a nonrelational to a relational database. This is important because there are still a lot of IMS databases and file systems on mainframes. Relational database replicators must also be able to replicate to relational databases from other vendors. Replication is very important in data warehousing concepts and is very often used there.

TP monitors

The fourth method involves communication between applications that run on a mainframe and applications that run in a client/server environment with the help of TP monitors like CICS. The CICS application layer enables various systems to communicate with each other. In addition, the CICS software layer can currently be transported to several platforms, allowing each platform to possess its own database. Using CICS, the client/server environment can run with a UNIX server with a relational database and the mainframe can run with a hierarchical database.

RPC

A library of self-written procedures defining the translation from one database to another can be called up by an application via remote procedures. The conversion must usually be manually programmed, and exactly which procedures are called up by the application must be known. Creating links via remote procedure calls

(RPCs) is quite time-consuming because the entire transaction must be manually programmed, while a gateway often carries out these functions, at least in part, automatically.

Communication between relational databases

We now go further with our concept and abandon the hierarchical database on the mainframe. The client/server environment is still running with a relational database server and will now start seeking communication with a mainframe which also contains a relational database. This environment opens the door to some new possibilities. All the methods discussed above can also be applied within a relational database environment; a relational database environment can also make use of file transfers, gateways, replication and CICS as communication tools. In addition, databases can be acquired from the larger database suppliers which run on the local servers and the mainframe, with preprogrammed solutions to all possible SQL variances, allowing users to start work immediately with distributed database processing. This offers many advantages, as besides the consistency of SQL, more possibilities are offered by triggers and procedures that are written in a single language. Management also becomes easier.

An organization can choose to run a single supplier's database in all local departments and on the mainframe. This is, however, not usually feasible. Usually, an existing relational database must communicate with relational databases from another supplier. To achieve some degree of consistency in the various environments, a concept is being introduced to enable various relational databases to communicate directly with each other (Figure 6.16).

DRDA

This concept is meant to allow the various types of database supplied by IBM to communicate optimally with each other, but it also allows other database suppliers to work with the concept. The Distributed Relational Database Architecture (DRDA) enables various relational database management systems to communicate with each other. DRDA is a component of the Systems Application Architecture (SAA). IBM allows applications to run on several IBM platforms throughout its entire hardware line using SAA. DRDA also supports IBM's UNIX line, and the concept is also open to non-IBM relational database suppliers. Some of the larger database suppliers have already developed a driver that allows them to communicate in an IBM environment via DRDA, thus eliminating the necessity of gateways and finally making the database environment completely transparent.

IBM has its own database on each hardware platform: on the mainframe, DB/2 and SQL/DS; on the AS400, the OS400 DBMS; on the UNIX line, DB/2 6000; and on the OS/2 platform, the OS/2 database. SAA SQL, IBM's variant of the language, is usually used on IBM hardware platforms. DRDA allows just about any database

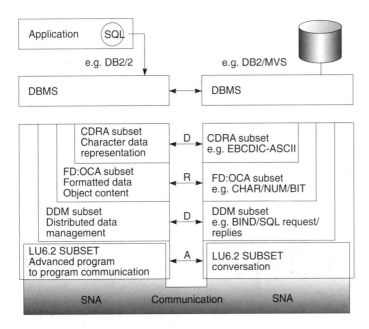

Figure 6.16 The use of DRDA.

to be placed on any hardware system, though the systems must communicate with each other via the LU 6.2 network protocol.

The principle is based on:

- application requester functions
- application server functions
- database server functions.

A request in the form of an SQL statement is sent from an application to a server. The request is then sent through to the correct database. Once it has arrived at the correct server it collects the information and is sent back to the client. Systems can communicate with each other in various ways.

DRDA ensures that each difference in an SQL dialect is translated, including the various data types which may exist in the different databases. The translation of EBCDIC to ASCII also occurs via DRDA (Figure 6.17).

Both normal SQL (dynamic) and compiled SQL (static) can be used, leading to improvements in performance. The first version of DRDA does not yet work in the form of distributed requests, which enable users to work with distributed databases and to do multiple database joins. The system itself executes the most favorable query optimization over the various databases and the various types of networks.

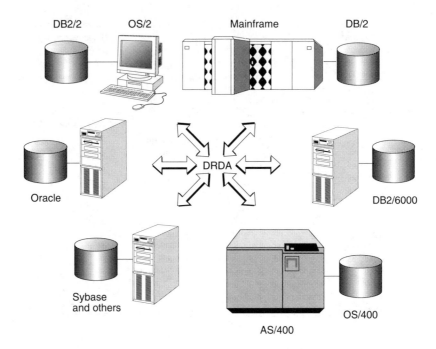

Figure 6.17 Database communication via DRDA.

DRDA creates an open IBM environment for IBM's entire hardware line, and makes continued investment in existing systems viable. In addition, the concept will become really attractive once the large independent database suppliers, including Oracle, Ingres and Sybase, have completed their DRDA communications software, and once DRDA can work fully in a distributed environment. These developments lead to new, open heterogeneous database techniques for client/server environments and distributed databases. Existing investments can then be depreciated over a longer period of time, and communication between mainframes and client/server environments is simplified.

There are currently countless products on the market which enable communication between mainframe and client/server environments. Many gateways enable only one-way traffic. In some cases, an SQL read option can be applied to various hierarchical and relational databases. In addition to gateways which are able to execute a read option (select), gateways are also available which can perform write options on the mainframe.

If a two-way database is necessary, the simplest method to achieve this is to implement a single supplier's database, which can work as a standard distributed database throughout the organization. However, if a large database is already installed, this option will seldom be possible, which makes DRDA quite important. Options such as file transfer, message queuing and replication also enable two-way traffic. These options also contribute to the improved role of the main-frame in the client/server concept.

Various new products, including DRDA, have made it simpler to incorporate existing applications into a client/server environment. This is an excellent development, especially for organizations already possessing large databases. On the other hand, the switch over to new environments from old environments frequently leads to difficult price issues. If both an existing mainframe and a new client/server environment have to be financed during a down-sizing operation, the expected short-term expense decrease will be nullified by the expense associated with supporting the mainframe during the client/server implementation process, especially if support for the mainframe has to be continued until the last application is up and running in the client/server environment.

Data warehouse

Many organizations try to get information from their systems to support their business. All too often it happens that after considerable investment in networks, hardware and software, one is still not able to use the data in the company at a strategic level. Decision makers desperately need access to the data to make informed and effective decisions. To solve this problem you can set up a data warehouse.

What is a data warehouse and why do you need it? The answer lies in the history of database technology, and in the current possibilities of a client/server environment.

In the 1960s companies mostly worked on batch-oriented computer tasks. The 1970s and 1980s saw the growth of on-line transactions. Users were allowed to enter their data in real time into a multiuser database. Thousands of users could enter their information for day-to-day business. These applications were typically built for high speed, large numbers of users and single transactions on one or two records. Clearly, when running a company, information from your database is needed. In most of the environments at that time, management was getting only a small part of the data for their analyses.

Even now, in most of the traditional worlds this data is fragmented and spread over the entire organization. It can come from different files anywhere in the organization, and there is great difficulty in keeping control over such files. Some are lost or the data is very old. Until recently, it was very expensive for the available hardware and software to provide cost-effective access to enterprise data. In today's business one of the keys to success is the ability to make the right decisions based on the correct information. If the information is in the database and can't be accessed because the end user has to struggle with file systems and other technology problems, alternatives will need to be sought.

With the introduction of new techniques, end users began to play a role. Using powerful desktop systems, they wanted access to their data to carry out decision support. End users wanted to have access not to the on-line system, but to databases for trend analysis and decision support. In the late 1980s, to solve the problem of the information gap for managers, IBM started to develop the Information Warehouse. This is a concept supported by modern hardware and software products to overcome difficulties in accessing data across the entire organization.

What is a data warehouse? A data warehouse provides a solid foundation of integrated, corporate-wide historical data to carry out decision support. The data is stored in such a way that we can do trend analysis over a long period of time.

In most organizations there are two types of databases. One is the operational database, where we find the operational data. This environment is for running day-to-day, unintegrated business applications supported with on-line systems. Operational data is extremely detailed, uses a large number of applications and is not designed for strategic decision making. It is stored in a complex way and is often dispersed over multiple systems. The same data element founded in several applications very often has a different meaning. Operational data is not filled with historical data – it is designed for day-to-day business.

The operational data store (ODS) is built seperately and apart from the data warehouse. The data warehouse is a resource in which the data is structured so that it is immediately available in the form needed for decision support. A data warehouse is:

- *Subject oriented:* the operational world is built around applications. You have an application for purchasing or stock. While the data warehouse is organized by company name, a part's name or an employee name, the data in the warehouse is organized so that it contains only information for decision support, while the operational data may contain information that is not useful for decision support (Figure 6.18).

- *Integrated:* in operational data, several applications are run. Developers make decisions as to how an application should be built. Thus, in each application you may find different names for the same entities. The coding of the

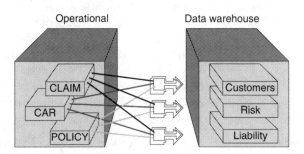

Figure 6.18 A data warehouse is subject-oriented.

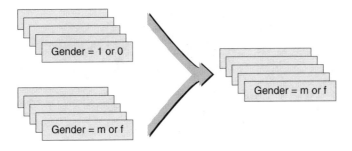

Figure 6.19 A data warehouse is integrated.

names might be different, and you may also find differences in keys and other characteristics. In a data warehouse you must integrate this information and make it consistent (Figure 6.19).

• *Time variant:* in each data warehouse the data must be time dependent. The data contains information collected over time. If you want to do analyses you must have an element of time connected to the information. The data in a warehouse will never be updated, so you need a time stamp to see when the data was updated in the operational environment (Figure 6.20).

• Nonvolatile: data in a data warehouse is never updated or changed. Once the data is in the warehouse it can only be loaded from the operational data and accessed by the end user, so the data warehouse is only loaded and accessed, while the operational data can be updated, deleted or changed (Figure 6.21).

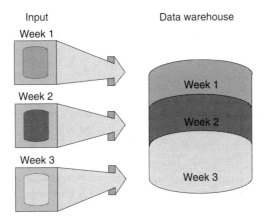

Figure 6.20 A data warehouse is time variant.

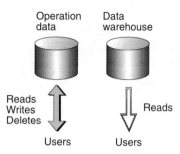

Figure 6.21 A data warehouse is nonvolatile.

Metadata

In this concept we have the operational database and the data warehouse. If we want to set up a data warehouse we will always need another database. This is known as metadata. It gives us information on:

- what data exists;
- where is it located;
- what format it is in;
- how it is related to other data;
- who the data is from and who is reponsible for it;
- when is it updated and by who.

Metadata is a critical component. The first place to look for information is in metadata, where you will find the data exists. Metadata is data about the data, and it is a kind of data management. It will give you the data definitions and the sources.

If you set up a data warehouse you will need a metadata tool that controls all this type of information.

The role of the end user

The most important reason for setting up a data warehouse is to support the needs of the end user. Setting up a data warehouse is the first step toward accessing the underlying information you may need. Clearly, when you store all your important information in a warehouse, this database can grow to enormous proportions. When a lot of departments are using the data warehouse you can distribute it over the entire company in datamarts. The next issue is ensuring that the end user has the proper tools to gain entry to the data warehouse. There are several tools which support the end user – these are query tools, statistical analysis tools, executive information systems (EIS), and data mining (Figure 6.22).

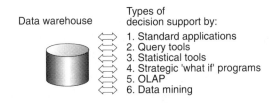

Data warehouse

Types of
decision support by:
1. Standard applications
2. Query tools
3. Statistical tools
4. Strategic 'what if' programs
5. OLAP
6. Data mining

Figure 6.22 End user tools.

Query and trend analysis tools and OLAP

The role of the end user tool is now very important. With advanced windowing and query/analysis tools on their desktop machines, users are connected to the database servers and are able to undertake decision support. The management of the company should be able to make the right decisions based on accurate and correct data.

Some of these queries are standard queries built into specific applications, or queries developed by query products. With query products the end user may develop queries himself at any time. One of the problems is that end users can create joins over many tables; this can place a tremendous burden on the processor, and it can take a long time before they receive the answers. For that reason, we can see that some end users only get access to views of some database tables.

When working with millions of records with query tools, you will probably have to work with parallel database servers and with multiprocessing machines. The end user can create queries without any index, and to do queries in this way can cause a lot of network and hardware performance difficulties.

Parallel management is very attractive because it splits the SQL statements up over several processors and adds power almost linearly.

You can also use in-depth query tools as On Line Analytical Processing (OLAP). This is very useful for very detailed questions on a specific part of your database. You have to design your own environment in OLAP on a multidimensional database.

Data mining

What is data mining? It is all about the extraction of knowledge from data. In this context, knowledge means relations and patterns between data elements. Besides the query and analysis tools, we also find a new and exciting technology for business strategy in the form of data mining. Data mining is a technology that automatically finds hidden relationships in the database. With the outcome we can make predictions. Data mining is using the data in the warehouse, and with modern techniques like neural networking and machine learning algorithms you can compare the records within a database. This algorithm can find hidden patterns within the records that we normally can't find ourselves with standard query and statistical tools. Data mining can compare millions of records with each other, and it can take a long time before we have any answer. If you are going to work with millions of records, you need a powerful multiprocessing machine.

What is the difference between data mining and a normal query environment? What can a data mining tool do that cannot be realized using SQL? Firstly, it is important to know that query tools and data mining tools are complementary: a data mining tool does not replace a query tool, it just gives the user a lot of additional possibilities. Suppose you have a large file with millions of records describing the purchase data of your customers over the last 10 years. There is a wealth of potential useful knowledge in such a file. Most of this knowledge can be found by firing normal queries at your database: who bought which product on what date; what is the average turnover in certain sales region in July, and so on. There is, however, knowledge hidden in your database that is much harder to find using SQL. Examples would be questions like: What is an optimal segmentation of my clients (for instance, how do I find the most important different customer profiles)? or what are the most important trends in customer behavior? Of course, these questions could be answered using SQL. You could try to find some defining criteria for customer profiles and query the database to see whether they work or not. In a process of trial and error one could gradually develop intuition about what the important distinguishing attributes are. Proceeding in such a way, it would take months or years to find an optimal segmentation for a large database, while a machine-learning algorithm like a neural network or a genetic algorithm could find the answer in minutes or a couple of hours at most. Once the data mining tool has found a segmentation, you can again use your query environment to query and analyze the profiles found. If you have a large database, one could say that there are three forms of information stored:

- surface information that can be easily found using a query language;

- hidden information that can be traced using pattern analysis or machine learning routines;

- deep information that cannot effectively be traced without any clues.

An example of deep information would be an encrypted message stored in a database. As for the other two possibilities, one could say: If you know exactly what you are looking for, use SQL; if you know only roughly what you are looking for, turn to data mining (Figure 6.23).

It is clear that data mining is not an activity that stands on its own. A good foundation in terms of a data warehouse is a necessary condition. Noise or dirty data and incomplete data, legal and privacy issues all form important problems. One must pay attention to the process of cleaning the data: remove double records, typos in strings, add missing information, and so on. In data mining, too, the old 'garbage-in-garbage-out' rule still holds. Implementing data mining in an organization is starting a process of permanent refinement and detailing of data. The real aim should be to create a self-learning organization.

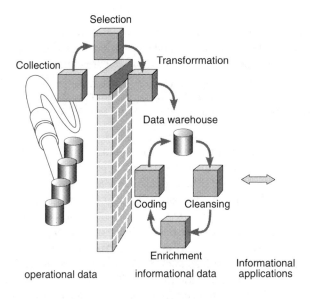

Figure 6.23 Process from operational data to data warehouse.

Building a data warehouse

Over recent years, some experience has been amassed in how to set up a data warehouse. Building a warehouse is a step-by-step project; you do not have to build it in one big step. The following checklist should be helpful:

- Check what type of information the end users really need.
- Locate where the information is coming from and how this data is related to the rest of the data.
- Analyze this information and find out what type of business processes are related to this data.
- See how you can send this information to the data warehouse.
- Set up the client/server architecture for the data warehouse with a network, replicators, database type, and so on.
- Analyze the data you need, and determine whether the data is correct and clean.
- Set up the metadata with descriptions of transformation.
- Create the data warehouse.
- Fill the data warehouse.
- Create the end user applications.
- Set up a database managment environment to control the system.

If you are going to build a data warehouse you should place the end users in a central position – they are the ones who have to make decisions on the data. If you decide to transfer some data from the operational data to the data warehouse you have to identify the end user demands. If you are going to transform the data descriptions to one common data type in the data warehouse, you have to come up with names for tables and attributes that are familiar to the end user. Finally, you have to give him the appropriate end user tools so that he can make the correct decisions.

Setting up a warehouse will take some time. Not only do table names change, but also the structure of your database. In a data warehouse you must pay attention to the fact that you have a lot of data, and that query tools and end users can ask any type of question. This means that any index can change, and the data must be placed in a different way than the source from which it emanates. The reason is that you must optimize the new database for only asking a query or for data mining. In this update you will not make any updates but you must optimize it for queries. In some cases you must first load a lot of data into your computer system before you can start asking for information from it. This can take many hours, and for that reason we will work with many departmental datamarts with local databases that are optimized for the end user tasks. A good warehouse is designed for this specific task and is supported by advanced products.

Top down and bottom up: solutions for data warehousing

There are two main techniques to choose from when building a data warehouse. The first is known as the 'top down' approach. In this case, you begin by setting up an enterprise warehouse and locating all the end user information in this corporate database. All the information of the organization is stored in this warehouse, and if a specific type of end user or a department requires some information, this data can be copied from the central warehouse into a smaller local warehouse. This local warehouse is an extract of the original warehouse, and is usually referred to as a 'datamart.' This datamart enables the end user to work on the data that he needs; to load it on parallel machines in his department; to do On-line Analytical Processing (OLAP); or to work with query tools or other, more advanced data mining techniques (Figure 6.24). Employing the top down approach in setting up a complete data warehouse affords you greater control of your warehouse; however, developing such a warehouse is a lengthy process. If your central data warehouse is very large, it will take a long time before building it is completed and an end user can work with it. For this reason, another design option for a warehouse is needed, and this option is called the 'bottom up' approach. The starting point of this type of warehouse is the construction of a small warehouse

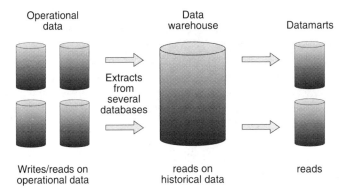

Figure 6.24

for each department or group of end users. When these have been built, the corporate warehouse can then be generated out of these datamarts. This means that a local warehouse can very easily be built in a short space of time.

In most cases, the datamart can be managed on a departmental level and can be very useful for setting up the corporate warehouse. At a departmental level, end users will generally have specific requirements and your data warehouse can be optimized for particular tasks accordingly. But in many cases, the integrated warehouse is needed as well. If you have a lot of operational data you must make and maintain a connection with each datamart. This connection to all kinds of separate data systems and the increasing cost of maintenance will ultimately prove very expensive. It is important to bear in mind that, whereas a datamart is primarily used at a departmental level, senior management requires information regarding the entire organization, and needs the data of all the departments.

Choosing the right data warehouse depends upon an understanding of the time scale involved, the number of systems you intend to connect and the needs and demands of the end users.

Data warehousing and client/server

The need for a data warehouse is the key to decision support systems and can improve the productivity of the business. Companies who want to respond very quickly to the market need such an information system. When you want to set up a data warehouse you need a lot of products: hardware and software, a network, databases, end user tools, replicators and many other products, and a good architecture for the warehouse itself.

With client/server technology it is much easier to set up this kind of environment. In a warehouse you will find several databases, and data must be transferred from one database to another. This can be done with replicators. Some new replicators are able to do the transformation from the OLTP environment to the data warehouse. Most of the time there are several database servers involved, most of which can work with parallel technology. Modern databases do support this type of transaction. On the client side we see desktops working with standard applications for trend analysis or end users with advanced query tools. We need database administrator and system management tools to control this environment. Companies like IBM have a complete range of hardware and software products to support an information warehouse, but other companies like Oracle, Computer Associates, Informix and Sybase also offer a lot of tools to set up a data warehouse. All kinds of end users will be connected to data warehousing, and they can create their own systems to ask for the information they need.

Working in a distributed database environment and system management

If you are setting up a data warehouse or any other type of distributed environment, you must look not only to the database products but also to the system management tasks. End users need access to many types of databases so they need security passwords, connection and routing to many types of servers. The authorization must be controlled and the systems must be set up in such a way that there is maximum flexibility. For example, end users can move to other parts in the organization. The network, the servers, printing at many places and many other items like version control and change management in the databases are important; all of these items are sometimes forgotten in setting up a distributed environment, and they are part of the infrastructure of your warehouse.

Middleware

As already mentioned, the client/server concept is based on a client which sends a request to a server. In the case of the server, we speak of a backend system, while the client is called the frontend system. To take care of communication between the backend and frontend, a separate layer, called middleware, is necessary (Figure 6.25).

Middleware takes care of the link between the two systems. The client packages its request in the direction of the server and sends it on the local middleware. The local middleware sends the request to the middleware on the server, which in turn passes it on to the software on the server. Once the request arrives at the server,

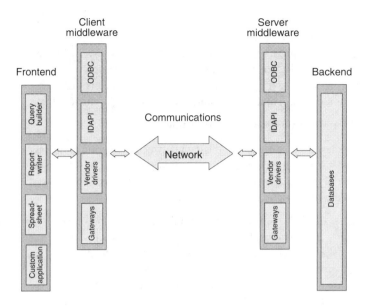

Figure 6.25 Client/server through middleware.

it is processed and the answer is packaged and travels back to the client via the middleware. We usually encounter middleware in network environments and as gateways to SQL type databases.

The principle works as a remote procedure call which is called up from the client. The requirements imposed on middleware have changed rapidly over the last few years. The Oracle product SQL* Net allows a 4GL Oracle product, located on a client, such as SQL Forms, to communicate with an Oracle database on a server. SQL calls in the direction of the database are generated from SQL Forms and transported via SQL* Net. SQL* Net can also be viewed as middleware.

At present, the requirements which middleware is expected to meet are much higher. Users want to be able to access various SQL dialects from a middleware product and not just a single type of database, as is the case with SQL* Net. Middleware products are currently being introduced which can access various types of relational database. The ODBC product, for example, offers an SQL interface to various types of relational database in a Windows environment on a PC. Good middleware allows users to work with a limited number of products in a heterogeneous environment. Many modern middleware products can access several types of database from the client, and can process the entire query and data conversion process.

A lot of confusion surrounds the term 'middleware', and it is often inconsistently used by the industry. We see it as any software glue that lies between the back-end and the frontend. Middleware is very often an independent product layer, and in most cases it is able to support many types of operating systems and can run on a number of different computer systems. DRDA from IBM, SQL* Net from Oracle and Open Client from Sybase are all middleware products. In addition, message queuing products and ODBC from Microsoft also lie between the back-end and the frontend. Remember that middleware products are function specific, with each product having a different purpose. This means that there are several types of middleware, and each product offers different functionalities.

Several types of middleware can be distinguished:

*   Middleware that transports the data between the applications on a client and the database on the server. Here we find products like SQL* Net, Ingres Net and Polyserver that support communication between the 4GL at the frontend and the relational database at the backend.

*   There are SQL gateways. This middleware is a kind of SQL translator like ODBC from Microsoft, whereby the client needs an ODBC driver. It is able to make contact with many types of relational databases. There are other SQL translators like EDA SQL from Informationbuilder, OMNI SQL from Sybase or Datajoiner from IBM. All these products provide access to relational databases, and some like Datajoiner can also communicate to nonrelational databases.

*   The gateways to various types of database also play a role here. A request is sent to the server from a client. Gateways execute translations to the various types of databases which all have their own dialects. Products such as Omni SQL from Sybase with an MDI gateway to DB2, IMS and Oracle facilitate this process. In an IBM environment, the DRDA middleware product allows us to carry out client/server functions in a heterogeneous database environment.

*   Messaging products like message queueing are able to transfer data from one application to another.

*   Object middleware products like the Object request broker from the OMG group.

*   Groupware middleware like Lotus Notes.

*   Transaction monitor products like Tuxedo and CICS.

All of these products offer a different function, and in a client/server environment you will find many types of such products.

In a client/server environment it is important to pay due attention to the middleware products because they are the glue between all your products. Not every middleware product can work in a multivendor database environment. This means that, for every type of database you run, there is an equivalent number of middleware products. Each middleware product and version can be different. Middleware products like SQL Net are able to make the connection between the client and the server or between the server and any other servers.

This type of middleware controls authorization and access to all the clients and all types of servers. Furthermore, with a good middleware product you can make a connection with DCE. Middleware can transport records in a number of ways, and can thus influence the speed of your performance.

If you have a variety of middleware products you will have several avenues of access to your environment. This gives rise to a lot of maintenance and version control. Middleware is pivotal in a client/server environment as it is always connected to other products. It is therefore vital that you understand its relationship with other products, both individually and in association, so that the total impact of combining access, authorization, connection to DCE, independence and database connections can be anticipated.

The functions supported by the various middleware products can differ quite dramatically from each other. The power of such products is that changes can be executed with little or no programming, and that these changes can be carried out on the client or server side without changing communications. Far-reaching standardization of software dialects will also increase the importance of middleware, and could lead to a significant decrease in maintenance.

GOLDEN RULES

- Relational databases are very useful in a client/server environment.

- In a client/server environment you need optimization tools for your database.

- Use replication techniques if you work with the same data on many places in your organization.

- Use messaging techniques for other methods of replication.

- If you work in a multivendor database environment, make sure that you have the proper middleware products or gateways to connect them with each other.

- Set up a data dictionary for your complete organization.

- The metadata and data dictionary are very important in controlling your database.

- Data warehousing is becoming more important to support the end user.

- Besides query tools and OLAP servers you can use data mining.

- You can use data mining techniques for finding hidden patterns in the database.

- Database triggers and stored procedures are vendor dependent; you can use them if you are working with just a few databases.

- Make sure that you have good database management tools to support your client/server site.

- Relational databases will be used from personal computer to mainframe. Make sure that your infrastructure is able to support this. This means that you should have a relation with system management tools that control version control and security and changes in the database.

- Middleware is very important because it connects many type of software products and can influence your connection with many systems.

- Working with distributed databases and data warehouses is related to a very well organized managment environment. You will need metadata and database management tools to control it.

- A data warehouse is optimized for the queries or data mining questions of the end user, and it must be designed for this task.

- In a distributed environment you must pay attention to system management tasks like version control, security, authorization and data management.

Chapter 7

Development of client/server systems

Introduction

Client/server is a form of corporate computing in which:

- Modular software functions can be optimally distributed over the different cooperating computer systems.

- The data can be spread over the entire organization.

- There is a strong focus on the needs and support of the user.

There are two trends at the organizational level which affect the implementation of client/server environments. The first trend is stricter organizational information system requirements with regard to data flexibility, scalability and interchangeability. In addition, user support requirements with regard to modern applications in the workplace are becoming increasingly important. Today, the user employs word processors and spreadsheets, but also wants access to databases to carry out local calculations, or to send queries to the database. Office tools are also becoming increasingly popular. New products require integration in the existing infrastructure. Local requirements are high and the new techniques support the employee at the workplace better than traditional methods, leading to noticeable increases in employee productivity.

Business process re-engineering

The implementation of client/server systems is part of a larger project in many organizations, a project aimed at the redesign of procedures and tools. The goals of such projects are cost reductions and increases in service levels. This kind of project is called business process re-engineering (BPR). As the name implies, BPR is strongly focused on business processes. The organization must carry out its business processes as effectively and efficiently as possible. The BPR project often leads to a streamlining of existing procedures; superfluous process steps can be eliminated or process steps can be executed simultaneously instead of sequentially.

In addition to examining the business processes, BPR also looks at the processing resources available within the organization, such as employees, computers and networks. Tools can be introduced to allow the processes to work more efficiently, examples of which include workflow management tools, communication tools, spreadsheets and client/server systems.

Client/server systems ensure better local support, which can facilitate more efficient business processes. That is why these systems receive so much attention during BPR project planning, and why many BPR projects include the implementation of the client/server concept.

Successful implementations

It is vital that organizations considering the implementation of a client/server architecture explicitly formulate their objectives prior to investments in planning, software and hardware. Automation's goal is to contribute to the realization of the objectives of the organization as a whole. Fundamental changes in the structure of the automation system must always be evaluated within an organizational context.

Cost reductions are often mentioned as a reason for switching over to client/server architecture. Although it is certainly true that the implementation of a client/server concept leads to long-term cost reductions, organizations must not expect dramatic results within too short a time period. Client/server has such sweeping effects that organizations should actually count on cost increases in the beginning. It is true that sites which are confronted with a drastic decision, for example the expansion or replacement of the mainframe, can avoid a large lump sum investment by gradually implementing client/server. Aside from the cost aspects, there are usually other reasons to switch over to client/server, for example:

- better local user support;
- implementation of workflow management linked to BPR;

- flexibility;

- shorter cycle time IT changes;

- independent data and application management by business units, without risks for the infrastructural information facilities;

- easy introduction of new technologies, for example multimedia, document management and so on;

- integration or linking of independent databases managed by various divisions;

- lower maintenance costs.

Without a clear objective, client/server implementation is a 'shot in the dark.' One of the advantages of the client/server approach is that it can easily be implemented in phases. The environment can gradually be constructed around the existing infrastructure. The old systems can then be successively replaced by new systems or permanently integrated within the client/server environment.

Many organizations start up their first client/server implementations themselves, but not all of them are successful. A successful implementation of the client/server concept needs a consistent approach. After many years of setting up large client/server projects, with all kind of products, we have set up a global procedure for companies. The following guidelines cover essential stages in the implementation process, and should make a significant difference and ensure a successful implementation.

Inventory of information system demands

Before setting up large client/server projects within your organization, it is essential to identify precisely what it is that you wish your information system to do. Ask yourself how you want to use your new information system to respond to changes in the market and the demands in the company, and within what time frame you want to respond. Identify the type of end users you have, and the ways in which an information system can support them. Take care that not only are the wishes of the IT department involved, but also that you focus yourself increasingly on the end user.

Too many client/server implementations are far too technology driven. A good client/server solution will improve the efficiency and productivity of the company and the end user, who can be a manager or secretary who needs this information system for their business. If they can respond earlier or with better or more complete information to the market, then your information system becomes a strategic product.

The requirements of the IT department can be completely different. They can come up with requests for cheaper and faster computer systems, improved networking, reduction of maintenance costs of hardware and software or the supply of better system management products to the information system. The result of this exercise should be a comprehensive list of end user requirements, and a second list which itemizes the needs of the IT department and identifies the proper architecture to support the business.

List of current information system components

Make a list of your current information system components. This should include the applications you use. Consider the software you use, your network and your hardware including all personal computers and printers. Include all items such as security and service levels and your overall system management procedures. You can use this list to see if the current information system is able to support a client/server environment.

List of system requirements

If you have made a complete inventory that includes the demands for efficiency improvements, user-friendly systems, maintenance, interoperability, availability, performance, and so on, you can then create a list of requirements which relates to hardware, software and network products.

If you want to introduce a client/server environment, make some clear statements identifying where you expect to see improvements for the organization. Draw up a list of the improvements for the company and the end users, and highlight new ease of access to the right data. Be sure to have a clear picture of the step-by-step progression of the project you are proposing. It is vital that you can present and measure the benefits involved, and that you can say when the project will be ready. Remember that installing a client/server system is not the objective itself; the objective is to identify the demands of the organization and use the client/server concept to meet them.

Workflow and client/server

See if your current information system is related to your business strategies. Is your workflow within the organization related to the business processes in your information system? It can happen that, during your workflow analysis, you will find some inefficient procedures in your organization; this is a problem for older companies in particular, where antiquated practices are updated without a corresponding modernization of software. You may have to change your business flow and use client/server techniques to support you. Client/server itself will not help you to change your company, but it will help to give you a technical architecture to support your organization get information at the right time, in the right place, and keep your information system as flexible as it can be.

If the workflow is not related to your information system, you will have to set up a new workflow where you can identify three major items:

- the process flow;

- the data related to that flow;

- the users – that is, departments, business units or others who are involved with these processes.

Workflow processes and procedures

Often business processes will be subject to frequent change. In this case, you need to identify these changes and make a decision as to whether you want to work with stored procedures in a database, with a three-tiered architecture or a two-tiered architecture, or whether you wish to write a special procedure within your application.

Client/server relationship

At this point you will face one of the most important tasks – choosing products to correspond with your requirements. Always remember that in a client/server environment your complete information system involves a dependent relationship between your hardware, software, network and management products. This means that, when choosing a database product, you must also ask how it relates to the middleware, the network, the network protocol, the user interfaces, the 3 or 4GLs, the world of standards like DCE, support of the network, system management products, and so on. Establish in what way your existing world is connected to the new world. Perhaps you need specific tools like gateways for network and database connections, query tools for a multivendor database, specific middleware like DRDA and many other products like conversion tools.

Take care that all your products can work together. This is important because any product that you use can influence other products as well.

If you go to a hardware or software vendor at this stage and buy something based on marketing jargon from sales people, you run a serious risk of making a poor choice. To get the appropriate information from them, you need to ask the right questions. Unfortunately, in a lot of cases you will find that most of your IT people, who may have worked for years for you in your traditional world, are not always able to come up with all the right questions. It is possible that their previous work would not have required or involved a knowledge of all the relationships between the products or of their full capabilities – for a lot of them, this is a completely new world.

Setting up a pilot project or training scheme is helpful. The support of some experienced, independent consultants at this stage in the proceedings is very useful and saves a lot of time.

Architecture

The next step is to complete the client/server architecture. Setting up a client/server environment is like building a house – you need a clear design. Therefore, you need to make decisions on network architecture, the levels of client/server modules like the user interface, business logic, databases, security and authorization. Decide on the structure of the integration between network, databases, applications and user interfaces. Establish the location of the clients, the servers and the network products like hubs and routers. Finally, you need to make decisions about how end users are to be connected to the architecture, and how the existing world should be integrated. All the decisions you make are based on the requirements of the organization. Ensure that your products can support the architecture.

Network and system management functions

Once your architecture is created and you have made decisions on several products like development tools, databases and end user tools, you come to a second important phase of your project. In this phase you need to make decisions on your network and system management tools. These tools are essential – without them you can expect growing maintenance and operations costs.

How do you make the right decision for these tools? In your architecture you have a blueprint of your client/server world. You know exactly what hardware, software and network you have. You know the relationships between the products and the service level you have to deliver. Find out if your operations department can deliver the service levels to the organization with the support of these products. Come up with a list of function requirements of these tools, and ensure that you understand the relationship between these products, because any action taken can influence other products or services.

Make a workflow of your operations department and set up the processes of the departments who control the site. In this workflow you can see how any action will influence other parts of your system management. For instance, software distribution can influence your version control. If you want to control all the operating systems on the several clients and servers, check if your product is able to do this, and to what level. All these requirements must be coordinated before you buy a product. Make a list with required functionalities and service levels which you have to support and see if your network and system management vendors can offer you the appropriate product.

Standards

At this point, you have installed the hardware and software and your networking products are running; all your training is completed and it is time to build your first application. This is the third part of your project and is obviously extremely important. There will be a lot of pressure on you to do this very well. To be successful in any large client/server site you have to understand that all the products interact and therefore rely on standards. Proprietary systems delivered some standards, but they may not be useful to you. In the open world you are able to make tailor-made standards for your own organization. Without standards, controlling your site will prove impossible. For example, you need standardized security management on each platform. Obviously, any individual deviation would cause havoc, so this must be an absolute standard. If you wish to be successful, you will have to develop your own set of standards and policies. A short example of where standards and policies are needed follows.

- *Network standards*
  You need to come up with the right names of all your devices and IP addresses. You have to take care of the security and availability, the backup and restoration of network devices, setup of the event values and thresholds and setup standards for performance and trend analysis. Further, you have to split up the network into the 'user' segments of a LAN backbone and WAN backbone, preferably using switches or multiprotocol routers.

- *Operating system standards*
  Your operating systems, including your PCs, must use standard file names, security, protection, backup procedures, names of directories, connections to other systems and mounting procedures.

- *Database standards*
  In a database world, you have to make decisions regarding standards for names of tables and columns; authorizations; replicators; distribution; constraints; stored procedures; indexes; grants; backups; table spaces; file systems; connectivity to a warehouse.

- *Application standards*
  You need standard libraries for stored procedures, remote procedures, connection to databases and user interfaces and file names.

- *User interface standards*
  Find standards for keyboard functions, colors, windowing, setting up libraries, security connection to file servers or other servers and integration with other products.

- *Software module standard*
  You have to develop reusable software standards such as printing, security, business rules and authorizations, and you must design a dictionary for your developer's: a kind of metadata environment, where they see what has been developed and know where they can find it.

This is just a small list, but it gives you an idea of how much is involved and what you have to do if you want to be successful. Be sure that these standards are used by everybody and that nobody can create standards without management approval.

In all cases, you will find that standards and policies are important. Without them you cannot make the connectivity that is needed. Everything is connected to each other – file names, devices, IP addresses, and so on, are used to connect the hardware and software. After you have done this procedure you will understand the need for standards like DCE or your own company standards, and that this is the basis of your network and system management. If you have created standards, you can start to write policies for your operations department and they can program these rules into the network and system management products.

Client/server problems

With this approach both authors have set up large client/server sites very successfully, and have done a lot of research at other sites where client/server implementations failed or were not very successful. One of the conclusions reached is that you have to create standards and policies and set up a proper system management environment. On many sites we saw that there were no policies in place, and that everybody had started to build his specific part without the necessary overall knowledge of the relationship between the products. As an example, we saw that developers were controlling the operating systems of servers without any knowledge of the rest of the infrastructure. They were building security for an operating system but forgot about the security of a database because they were not familiar with it. As a result, every file name they used was unknown by other operators. In each application we saw different user interfaces with different keyboard layouts. Many end users complained about the integration of the products. Connectivity was impossible in this environment; end users were not properly involved; many developers developed the same system applications many times and connections to other systems failed. In addition to the lack of standards and proper system management, another important reason why in many places the cost increased or the project failed was that there was conflict between the necessity of departments or business units working together and each department manager wanting to develop all standards himself. This led to procedures being set up several times and in different ways, and to poor connectivity between units. In many of the cases where these projects failed, it was clear that the introduction of a client/server environment was not well prepared. Many traditional IT departments were unable to adapt their organization. They did not have the necessary experience to work with end users, to develop special graphical user interfaces, to oversee the total concept and to dispense with traditional responsibilities which had become obsolete. If faced with this situation, the support of management, consultants and good training can be very helpful.

With the client/server concept you are turning away from the traditional mainframe world, but to install a successful client/server site you must have mainframe knowledge in order to understand and control it. If everybody in your organization sets up his own rules and standards, your costs will increase without any improvement for the organization or end user. Prepare yourself well and use the guidelines which we have set out. A well prepared client/server implementation can always be successful.

Project method

Implementation of client/server environments requires a project approach different to that which is traditional. The traditional project approach is usually based on the construction of the information system to fit the existing organization, which means that it always trails behind new developments. Client/server, on the other hand, can be used to create a flexible environment which anticipates the implementation of new techniques. The new project approach must more fully include the necessary integration of the various products, including user interfaces, applications, databases and networks, the new internal standards, management tasks and the role of the user.

The organization will have to pay much more attention to management tasks in a client/server environment. In addition, during the development phase of client/server, prototyping can be used more intensively. Diverse products currently enable the parallel development of databases and related programs. The development of standard screens, for example, can occur simultaneously with the development of the several algorithms used in database creation. The components can be further improved step by step. Testing can also occur during the development phase, instead of waiting until an application has been built. Such a development process will seldom involve the construction of a monolithic application, but will involve instead the intensive application of modules. In addition, the environment will remain permanently in maintenance, and will gradually and dynamically evolve based on the changing requirements of the organization.

This is quite different from many existing project methods, based on milestones in which fixed blocks must be completed before going further. This is often called the 'waterfall model,' and it is usually a very time-consuming and expensive development method. Client/server environments can be developed far more easily according to a 'cyclical model.' The application environment is continuously enriched, as it were. Components can be constructed more quickly, but far more attention has to be paid to the underlying relationships between products, libraries and procedures. This can be detailed in a well formulated project plan.

As already mentioned, standardization can be implemented at all levels, and this must also actually be done as much as possible. A user interface, for example, must conform to certain ergonomic requirements. The right user interface structure allows the user to quickly learn to work with various applications, because it is the same on every system. Performance can then be guaranteed, and maintenance simplified. The same is true for the application and the database. Far-reaching standardization will considerably ease introduction, and will substantially shorten the learning curve.

As the client/server concept makes use of various heterogeneous products, standards must be defined early on, product lines must be optimally matched, and agreements must be reached within the organization. If this is not done, the organization can expect problems in the areas of version management, general management and connectivity, and the costs will rocket.

Project team

Traditional environments often display stiffly hierarchical project organization. The client/server environment, however, requires a completely different method. Once standards have been defined, programmers often work very closely with the analysts. The use of Case tools also certainly contributes to the disappearance of hierarchies. The differences between the analyst and the programmer are becoming ever smaller.

In addition, the project manager must be acquainted with the various technical dependencies of the concept. In the past, knowledge of a single platform was usually enough. In a client/server environment, knowledge of PCs, minis, mainframes, user interfaces and networks is essential. Complexity is increasing as organizations are increasingly working in more heterogeneous environments. The project teams must be well organized: in general, small project teams with a flat structure produce the best results in a client/server environment.

Analysis

During the analysis, insight into the information streams and procedures executed must be obtained. Activities, rules, conditions, location and necessary data can be mapped out. The analysis brings the relationships between the various departments into view, allowing the central model to be constructed. The database components needed in each department or unit can be determined based on the process structure. This also gives an insight into which tables are used in which departments, enabling the database to be distributed, or parts of the database to be copied via snapshots or database replication.

In the analysis, the processes and data model components must remain traceable. We will discuss these briefly.

Processes

The process description can be used to check whether specific constraints should be used. The constraints can be programmed in the application, or at the database level, or they can be stored on a separate constraint server. Certain processes are executed regularly and are not dependent on the program being built: they are used by various programs. In that case, a trigger can be built, or a fixed procedure can be programmed, which can be called up by the application. These are called 'business rules.'

We must make a distinction between regularly changing and fixed rules. The analysis can then be used to determine which components are appropriate as objects in the form of procedures.

Data model

A relational database can be distributed over the entire organization using data tables. Certain tables can be of specific importance to given departments, while other database components may be of interest to the entire organization. The distribution of data must be carefully arranged and agreed upon. The importance of the individual user becomes especially apparent at this stage. Due to the implementation of various query tools, a user can access the database. If data-naming conventions have not been agreed upon and the database does not contain meaningful names, the user has a problem. That is why object-naming conventions must meet the following requirements:

- clear table names

- no usage of codes

- short and concise descriptions

- consistent language.

Database design is a dynamic discipline. During testing, for example, the performance of a database may prove to be less than optimal, and a change in the data model may be necessary. Key fields, indexes and tables may be modified. If the database model is used throughout the organization, agreements must be made detailing who may use which tables and who may modify the tables. These issues can be determined during the analysis.

Processes in relation to the database

If triggers and procedures are used which have a relationship with the database, the relationship must be known during the design of the data model. If an analyst uses a table which is already used within other programs, he must be acquainted with the triggers and procedures linked to this table at the inception of the analysis. A table with a trigger could start a process, using the update or delete function, which would be undesirable within the new program on which the analyst is working at that particular moment. That could mean that triggers and procedures will have to be modified. This is why the development of a data model without insight into the triggers and procedures of the new database model can be risky.

Rapid application development

As is true of the implementation of every new technique, the question of which analysis technique to use for the development of applications also arises during the introduction of a client/server environment. Usually, traditional techniques are used to construct a new environment. This is quite strange considering the fact that client/server applications make use of new insights which usually require a completely different development cycle.

Many traditional techniques required the full completion of a phase before continuing to the referential phase (the waterfall model). The software was often completely integrated, requiring a stiffly structured approach. The client/server environment, however, allows much more development in cooperation with the user. User interfaces and extremely rapid prototypes can be displayed on screen. This often requires special analysis techniques in order to gain an insight into the processes to be programmed for each screen. Object-oriented approaches offer great programming ease and flexibility.

The client/server concept allows the completion of components independently of one another. The development of a user interface can partially be seen apart from the development of the application and design of the database and screens. Of course, fields can be placed on a screen only if they are stored in a database. If database design is carried out in parallel to the diverse components, modifications in one component can be even more quickly carried out than in another component, due to the enormous flexibility of the several software products. One of the advantages of using new development techniques is rapid application development (RAD).

Organizations are able to respond very quickly to the market with this technique, which allows you to work very closely with end users. The end user can comment on the applications during development. In most cases, we see 4GL languages like Oracle, Uniface and PowerBuilder as products that allow you to undertake RAD. Nowadays, new techniques like object-oriented development are also used. Products like Visual Age from IBM and SmallTalk are able to build object-oriented programs in a very short period of time. But RAD means that you must also set up a dictionary with your standard tools.

Joint application development (JAD) requires some extra attention. In a client/server environment it is important that you are going to work with the existing libraries. If you are going to work with business rules you need a library and a dictionary of all your existing rules. Developers must be made aware of this dictionary. They should work only with the standard libraries and with the standards, as we have discussed.

Development of user interfaces

At present, working with graphical user interfaces (GUI) is very popular in many organizations. This is logical, given the fact that working with a user interface considerably extends the capabilities of applications. The user can link scheduling facilities, drawings and other objects to an application, and if necessary store them in a database. This is a considerable expansion in comparison with a simple terminal, which can only request data or input it. There are many user interfaces, such as Windows from Microsoft, Presentation Manager from OS/2, the Macintosh interface and Xwindows/Motif under UNIX. This software represents the presentation layer of the user interface. New products like Netscape and other Internet browsers are coming up with a complete independent GUI platform environment with full mutimedia capabilities.

The development of a GUI requires far-reaching knowledge of screen commands and user interface techniques. A user interface can support standard applications, including applications built in 4GLs. These are usually portable to several user interfaces. An application, however, which uses various specific GUI techniques must meet high ergonomic standards in the areas of user friendliness, performance and system memory use.

The development of a user interface is quite complex: knowledge of user requirements has to be combined with knowledge and experience in interface links to the application and the database. If applications are to be run in a user interface, standard settings for keyboards, security, colors, logon procedures and objects can be very useful, as they make maintenance easier and eliminate the need to continuously program these components. The portability of the standard settings must be carefully checked before introduction.

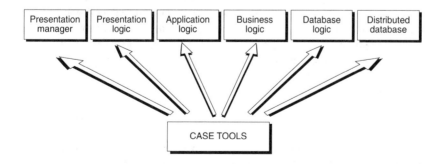

Figure 7.1 Which aspects of the client/server concept are covered by a case tool?

In addition, various Case tools support the development process. Case tools can store and immediately process libraries in applications. Many Case tools are able only to set up database models. Since today's databases carry part of the intelligence in them, working with Case tools which do not offer insight into this intelligence (stored in triggers and procedures) is not very sensible. Use of a Case tool which is also able to create a part of the user interface and application is preferable (Figure 7.1).

Development of applications

The development of an application is also bound by strict requirements. If the requirements which the system must meet are known, standard libraries can be used, as in the case of the user interface. Applications can be split into application requirements and organization requirements, using the business rules. An application must make a link with the user interface and the database. Various components which have an effect on the performance must be examined and, as far as possible, standardized: for example, referential integrity rules, indexes, SQL statements, batches and printer commands. Various questions must be carefully considered: Will security and authorizations be programmed in the application or recorded in a separate menu environment, or will this regulated at database level? Will the application be installed on an application server or on the client/server. Applications can also possess various libraries, and these must be easily changeable if modification of the application becomes necessary. Optimal implementation of an application requires insight into the processes which occur in the organization. The delineation of business logic and application logic is of importance in this connection.

Development of the database

Database development must involve all departments if corporate data is used in all departments. If the client/server environment includes department tables, these can be stored and maintained locally. If, however, several departments or business units have to use the tables, decisions must be made with regard to the responsibility for table creation, maintenance and deletion. Dynamic environments in particular require an in-depth knowledge of the existing database structure and all database structure rules, including database integrity aspects, triggers and procedures. Good maintenance can be executed only if the possible effects can be predicted with some certainty.

Many of the questions worked out in standards must be examined before the acceptance of a database. What does the application do precisely? How often is the database accessed? Must security be regulated at database level? What backup procedures are to be used? What requirements must performance meet? Which tables will be used by other applications?

A database is an important performance determinant. Take, for example, not only the unique indexes which identify the primary keys, but also the indexes which identify the secondary keys, or the creation of views, working with query optimizers, and the placing of database tables on the correct server, or working with snapshots in the case of distributed databases. During database development, the tables already used by existing applications must also be known, as well as the number of records expected to be used, as this can also have an effect on system performance. A database in a client/server environment is not only a storage location for tables, but can also be an active part of the programs. This requires extra attention during the design stage.

Testing

In a client/server environment, testing must naturally be carried out before the programs are put into use. A test environment in the client/server environment is of importance, since an application can be run on PCs, minis and mainframes, even though it is often developed on a PC. In a test environment, networks, gateways and distributed databases can be encountered.

This often means that not every component can be tested in the development environment. If programs are developed in test environments independent of the production environment, extra test phases must be built into the production environment. Given the fact that a client/server environment can have a relationship with a great diversity of hardware and software, fixed testing procedures must be carefully mapped out during the test phase. Programs are usually developed in a separate development environment. After a functionality test in this development environment, the programs are tested again later in the production environment.

Implementation in the production environment

In addition to the test phase in the production environment, during which the management plays a large role, extra attention must also be paid to the implementation of the new system in the existing client/server architecture. This phase involves the following steps.

Modification of existing tables, triggers, procedures

Once a program is placed in production, tables are created in the database. If the same tables are also used by other applications, these tables may have to be modified to conform to the requirements imposed by the new application. Columns, for example, can be added or modified. To do this, the database manager must write a script. If more than one server contains this table, for example, in the case of snapshots or replicas, scripts must be written for all of the tables.

Modification of existing programs

Changes to tables can have an effect on the programs in the production environment which also use these tables. It is actually quite probable that the existing programs will have to be modified and compiled due to changes to the tables. Modification of a table can cause a chain reaction. Implementation, for example, of a new program can have an immediate effect on existing programs. Triggers may have to be modified, and during execution of this maintenance certain tables and programs cannot be active.

Modification of the distributed environment

Another aspect of new table implementation in a distributed database environment is that new table locations on the server must be clearly documented. The star server of the server where the synonyms are located must be modified if new tables are added.

Modification of the network and system management

Software placed in production must be identified according to fixed version number conventions. The version numbers must be input in the version management database.

In a new client/server environment it is important to set aside time to train yourself with new equipment and various types of software. In the beginning it is very helpful to start with a pilot site and get familiar with all the products. If you have set up an architecture, you must be able to test the product in such a way that, before you install it in your operational site, you have detailed information of the complete installation. Testing involves installing the product and all your standards and connecting it to all the related systems like the network, databases and other products. For an effective test, it is necessary to make a checklist that covers all the issues:

- network
- databases
- programs
- user interface
- standards
- middleware
- gateways
- connections to other products
- backup
- security and authorization

- printing

- relationship with systems management tools such as version control software distribution, and so on.

After the testing period you should start the change management procedure. You need to describe the influence of the new system on your environment. All the relationships within your new environment must be fully described and defined in the configuration and change management database in your system management products.

End users often begin their training at this point as they get familiar with the products.

Building a client/server application means building with software modules. You need the right modules and you have to find out how you want to implement them within your application. During the implementation you must make decisions on where to place all the modules. Take care that you have a reference where you can find all the existing information on your software. See where you have stored your triggers and your rules, and give the location of the servers and clients where you stored your software. Use your system management products to control this information.

GOLDEN RULES

- Make a complete list of the components of your information system.

- Identify where your workflow is not supported by your information system.

- Make a complete list of your new requirements.

- Establish the cost benefits for your company.

- Quantify efficiency improvements for end users.

- Design the architecture.

- Match the architecture with the products.

- Ensure that all the products can work together.

- Create software modules.

- Create standards and policies.

- Adapt the company structure to ensure achievable service levels.

- Adapt network and system management.

Chapter 8

Network and system management

Introduction

Negative indicators of failing client/server projects
90% show a lack of adequate systems management structure

(adapted from Jeremy Frank, Gartner)

The management of a client/server environment is a specialism in itself. In a mainframe environment, all kinds of products and services are necessary to keep the system running. The same is true of a client/server environment. The environment often consists of heterogeneous hardware and software products, imposing extra demands on management. As the number of components making up the environment increases, management of the environment becomes more complex.

In a mainframe environment, the software is optimally matched to the hardware and the consequences of changes are easily predicted. Compared to a client/server environment, the mainframe is relatively easy to manage: everything can be controlled centrally (Figure 8.1).

A client/server environment may contain innumerable PCs, servers and a mainframe (Figure 8.2). The client/server environment has a layered construction: the first layer is the network, which is the foundation for the entire environment; the next layer of importance contains the various operating systems. The databases run above the operating systems, supporting the various applications. This

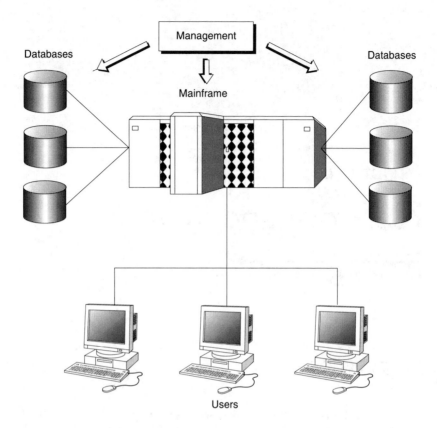

Figure 8.1 Traditional mainframe environment.

complicated structure must manifest itself to the user as a single transparent system, which means that management also has to be integrated over these layers. More and more products are being introduced on the market to ensure good management of client/server, and these can be split up into three general divisions:

- network management

- system management

- application management.

These areas cannot be evaluated separately. If something goes wrong in a client/server environment, the user notices in principle only that his system does not work. There can, however, be various underlying reasons. An application may, for example, no longer function due to a bug, but the database may also be dysfunctional. A dysfunctional database may in turn be caused by a breakdown at system level: for example, insufficient memory, or a hardware breakdown. The

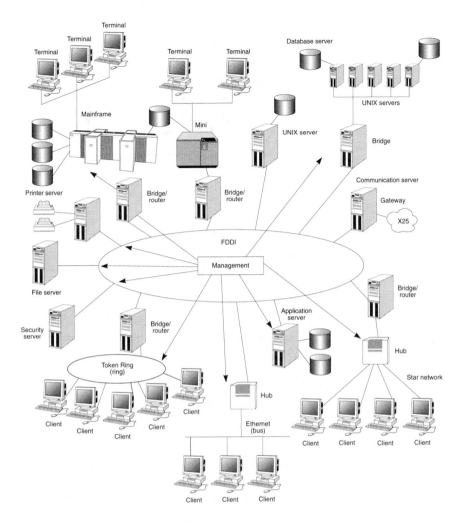

Figure 8.2 Management of client/server.

network itself can also be at fault: for example, because it is overloaded or because a router or hub has gone down. In the latest version of network and system management products there is a move toward enterprise management: all the products can work together, and most of them are using object-oriented technology to support it (Figure 8.3).

The manager of a client/server system who is confronted with an error situation cannot limit himself to an analysis of just the application, just the database, just the operating system or just the network. He must examine all of these components in combination. If the management tools do not allow this, responsible management of the site is impossible.

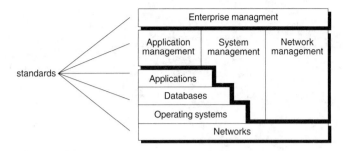

Figure 8.3 Integrated management approach.

Network management

The network is vital to every client/server environment, which of course means that management of this network is of the utmost importance. The network can be based on Ethernet or Token Ring with bridges, routers and hubs linking various computer systems, including PCs, servers, mainframes and printers. A good network management system can make the network visible on screen. Systems can be managed remotely. All system data can be read in and stored in a database on a network which works with SNMP. All parts of the network can be made visible on screen, and they can also be accessed remotely. The operator can, for example, look into a hub to see what data traffic is traveling over the network. Network performance can often be measured using these tools. The networks may be small, but they can also take on enormous proportions, exceeding national borders. With the help of network management products, the entire environment can still be managed from one or more central points. Some important network management products include HP Openview, NetView from IBM, Sun Netmanager and Spectrum from Cabletron.

Modern companies cannot work without a network. Networking is the glue between clients and servers and brings them together. But networking is also one of the most important elements of a client/server environment. Some investigations into networking costs have been done, and one of the key issues is clearly the cost of labor. If you have a network you can undertake a huge variey of tasks like measurement of the network load, error handling, adding new devices like computers or routers to the network, switching, authorizations and many others. But how can a device be controlled when it is in another building, and how can all your network traffic be measured and your error messages controlled? This can be done with network management software, now mostly based on the SNMP protocol and the management information base (MIB). There is some confusion about the term 'network management,' which stems from the world of PC LAN servers. In that world network management is also used to describe management

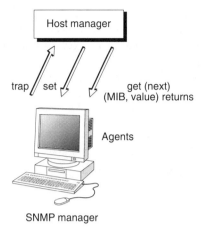

Figure 8.4 SNMP communication between agent and manager.

of the file server, but network management is only the control of the network infrastructure including hubs, routers and bridges, but not file servers. The control of a file system that runs with an operating system is managed by system management tools.

If you want to manage your devices with network management tools, the device would have to support an SNMP agent. The associated MIB has to be loaded onto the network management system for the correct MIB OIDs (object ID, representing a manageable parameter on the device) to be used. The management software on the management system will use the MIB to communicate with the agent on the device using SNMP.

SNMP stands for Simple Network Management Protocol, and that is what it is. It was built for current network management tasks and is easy to work with. The SNMP protocol is simple in structure because of its limited capabilities and ease of implementation, which were two of the primary design goals. The drawback of this design is that the network manager will have to understand the meaning of all the device-specific OIDs and their possible values. This means that network management software must be able to represent the requested SNMP OID in a uniquely interpretable way.

At present, only four operations are available on the SNMP protocol (Figure 8.4):

*   *GET:* retrieves specific management information like the value of an object.

*   *GET next*: used to retrieve information from the next managed object in the MIB.

*   *Set*: used to manipulate information on the device using the SNMP agent of this device.

*   *Trap*: used to report extraordinary events to the manager, such as a cold start or a link down. SNMP events are limited.

SNMP is based on a community of agents and a manager. The agent is installed and the related MIB is loaded into the management software. Each agent is uniquely identified on a device, and the manager can take actions using the available operations like GET. SNMP is a connectionless protocol based on the TCP/IP User Datagram Protocol (UDP). There are no ongoing connections maintained between a manager and its agent; each exchange is a separate action supported by the polling mechanism.

There are two types of management: management by polling, when you ask for the value of the agent; and management by interrupt, when you receive a trap.

The manager sends a GET request to the agent and the agent gives the GET response. If that occurs, the name and the value is returned to the manager. This information is requested by the manager; this manager takes the action and it can read the returned codes. This polling mechanism with SNMP between the manager and the agent causes some overhead, depending on the number of devices in the network.

The world of SNMP is still growing, and is growing faster than CMIP or any other network management protocol. The expectation is that SNMP2 will become more important in the near future, and then CMIP, because there is already a large installed base of SNMP and it is anticipated that it will become very easy to migrate to SNMP2. At the moment, SNMP is the most widely installed protocol for network management, because it is easy to use, open and well accepted in the TCP/IP world.

One of the problems with MIB is that not every hardware and software product has an MIB, so you cannot monitor your environment completely. In a client/server world, not only the hardware devices but also the software devices need to be monitored. At this stage, software vendors like Oracle, Sybase and IBM are coming up with standard MIBs for database functions like datafiles, tablespaces and many other database-specific MIBs. In the past only hardware devices like routers, hubs, printers and computers were able to work with MIBs, but now we can also get information on software products.

One of the main problems with SNMP is that the agent is not intelligent: it cannot take any action itself, and so is still a very simple environment. The agents can only give a GET response or a trap to the manager, and the manager is the only one that can take action. SNMP is also unreliable because SNMP messages are unacknowledged: an agent cannot be sure that it reaches the managing station.

What one would like to see is that, if something occurs on a local agent, it is not only sent to and monitored by the manager, but that some local action could be taken and the problem solved automatically. At present, the only thing SNMP can do is send information to a manager.

One other problem which arises in large client/server sites is that, when working with a large number of servers in a distributed environment and manager-to-manager communication at the SNMP level is needed, SNMP can support only a basic mechanism between a manager. However, we expect that this will also change in part for SNMP2. Furthermore, SNMP is more a monitoring tool than anything else, and the security level of the product is low, but this is also changing in SNMP2.

A lot of research into this area has been undertaken, and one of the solutions for the future is working with object-oriented network products. Managers will be able to communicate with managers and agents will be able to take actions because objects installed on local agents are intelligent. This is what the next generation of network management will become. Until then, SNMP and SNMP2 will become more and more popular.

An example of how network management tools function follows. Take, for example, a complex graphics application such as a CAD/CAM system. A number of designers are linked to this system via the network. At a given moment, several alerts are sent via the management tool to the manager: several systems are no longer accessible to the users. Using the network tool, the manager can execute a number of checks: Are the hubs functioning correctly? In which segment is the breakdown? What is the network burden in this segment? This allows the manager to pinpoint the exact location of the breakdown. An in-depth analysis requires more information, however: Which system caused the network overload? What kind of processes run there? To acquire this information, the manager must resort to remote system management tools.

System management

Many tasks cannot be executed with network management products: for example, system tasks at operating system level such as making backups, controlling printers, installing and checking databases. All tasks involved in managing the systems and keeping them up and running fall under the heading of system management. One of the most important aspects of setting up a new client/server project within a company is the installation and tuning of system management tools.

Over the last few years we have seen that the labor cost related to the client/server environment is higher compared with traditional systems. While this is true, it is a fact which must be viewed in context. High labor costs result directly from increased labor time. This can, in the main, be accounted for by the learning curve for the new environment.

The end users are far more involved than in the past, and they are the key users in this new world. They need better information and have to be trained how to work with all these new tools. We see also a learning curve for the new hardware, software and networking infrastructure. In a client/server environment you will find many dependencies between hardware and software products, and to manage this is extremely difficult.

You have to create new policies and standards within your organization, and it is hard in the beginning to see what relationships there are between the products. To overcome this problem we can use management tools. To solve network problems, network management is one of the main solutions. Most of the other labor costs beside the end user cost can be solved with system management.

System management controls and manages the client/server hardware and software environment. The network and all the devices are controlled by the network management, but every company has procedures such as user and password names, what to do if a printer fails, the time to do a backup, the help desk functions, what to do with new versions of software, the distribution of software, control over the databases and operating systems. All these rules and actions related to hardware and software products and the applications within the company have to be established, and have to be as fully automated as possible. System management is well understood in the mainframe world, but is relatively new in the world of client/server computing. It is of great importance. In our overview of cost justification we emphasized that the installation of network and system management is a must. Only a good architecture and standards in combination with the use of the correct management tools can minimize your labor costs.

System management in a client/server site is of great importance because there are so many relationships between all your products that you have to put tools in place to provide support. If you have a new version of an operating system on your mainframe, you have the difficult task of installing it, and before doing so you have to do a lot of preparation. In a client/server site the installation of a new operating system version can influence not only one but a number of servers. All the products on these servers and all the software on hundreds or thousands of clients can be affected, and in some case they have also to be updated. Without good quality control in your configuration management and without the support of software distribution tools and version control tools, this action will result in tremendous labor cost.

More system management tasks are required in a client/server site than in a mainframe site. This can be dealt with by using the right system management tools. To choose the right management tools there are several guidelines to bear in mind. Be very careful with the quality of these tools. Some tools are related to network management products; others can be connected to these products. Client/server sites do need such tools, but not every tool is suitable for each client/server site. A lot of these tools don't have any real intelligence, and intelligence is what you need if you want to control your site. Always remember that any action taken by one tool may result in action from another tool. If these tools can't work together you will need to write your own connection and maintain that for each new version. Most existing tools are still related to the mainframe world, and can't support a real distributed environment. Alternatively, you will have to write a lot of code yourself. Some tools are good in supporting traditional environments and others like Tivoli are very good in supporting distributed enviroments.

Some other tools are used in the PC LAN world, but they are unable to control a sophisticated client/server environment with intelligent hubs, routers, numerous devices and operating systems. They are more networking tools then system management tools. Also, the hardware and operating systems that most of these tools support is limited. There are some players in the system management market like HP's Openview, Sun Net and Solstice, Computer Associates with Unicenter, Tivoli, and IBM with their System View products (now implemented in the Tivoli framework after the take over of Tivoli by IBM). Most of these tools are turning toward an object-oriented environment. Tivoli was the first object-oriented product based upon the DCE and DME descriptions.

This distributed support and the need for local knowledge in the software is moving system management vendors to a world of open systems and object orientation. If we really want to work with objects we have to develop an architecture in which all the products can work together. One of the problems that we now face is that all the different system management products are unable to work together or need a specific vendor-dependent connection.

This problem is solved if we are going to use international standards like CORBA and if most of the system management tool suppliers have committed themselves to this standard.

In future, we will see network, system and application management working closely together, and then we will be able to talk about enterprise management.

Application management

Application management can be divided into the following components:

- databases
- applications
- business rules
- user interfaces.

Database management includes creating and checking data dictionaries, and maintaining tables and their relationships with the applications. Maintenance on the tables cannot be carried out unless the exact consequences for all applications using these tables is known. The relationship between development environment and database must facilitate the evaluation of possible consequences.

Once the application has been developed, it must be introduced in the production environment. Fixed standards must be defined for the production environment, and standards must be set for communication between the applications, allowing easier maintenance. Fixed agreements must also be made for business rules: Where are they to be recorded, in the databases or in the applications, central or decentral? how is maintenance to be carried out? and so on. In addition, central agreements must be made with regard to the structure of user interfaces. These can be stored in central libraries.

We now use an example to illustrate the importance of application management and its integration with database management. In large organizations there is usually a computer network in which a number of systems are set up as a database server. In many cases, up to 100 servers may be involved, which are used to run relational database management systems from various suppliers (for example Oracle, Ingres, Sybase and DB2). Several machines from various suppliers are also integrated in this network, such as UNIX systems from IBM, Sun, HP, DEC and others, or mainframes and non-UNIX minis, such as the AS/400. The machines are often located in geographically distant locations. The database servers are used by hundreds of applications, often using overlapping parts of the data sets. Additional requirements for such an environment are that certain applications may not go down, that data consistency must be guaranteed, and that performance must be adequate in all circumstances. Some application vendors, such as SAP and BAAN, are coming up with technologies to support their applications with management tools. Some vendors are going to develop application MIBs for this.

Clearly, only very large organizations will possess this sort of system. All over the world systems of this complexity are already being set up for banks, airline companies, government institutions such as the income tax authority, and so on. In general, the management aspects of this sort of site are grossly underestimated, even by experienced database administrators from the mainframe world. The past few years have made it clear that, without adequate management tools, this sort of environment can simply not be managed stably. The following points are important in this respect.

Remote management

Remote management of databases is necessary due to geographic distribution.

Technical differences between relational database management systems

The management of a database from a single supplier requires great specialized knowledge. Training of a database administrator takes about six months, for example, and this increases almost linearly as the number of different types of databases used within the organization increases.

Version management and application development

Due to the geographic spreading of the systems and their complexity, it is impossible to maintain a complete image of the architecture of the system using traditional methods. The local servers are usually managed by local divisions which can themselves develop applications that make use of the databases. This leads to an enormous maintenance problem. If, for example, application A and application B make use of the same database, maintenance on application A also has an effect on application B. This problem, which is known as a version management problem, leads to a situation within which conceptual database designs are never stable. In this kind of complex system, changes to the data model will occur two or three times a week, on average. Each application in the system can be affected by such changes.

Given this situation, the ability to carry out various management tasks is essential. These tasks include:

Technical database management

- the creation of new databases

- tuning databases

- making backups, and so on

Management of database contents

- monitoring consistency, completeness and topicality of the data stored in the database.

A good database management tool in a client/server environment must possess the following functional characteristics:

- A database administrator must be able to carry out the majority of these tasks from a single control station in the network.

- The tool uses a graphical user interface, which details the database, the network, the contents of the databases, and so on, schematically. The database administrator can easily execute commands using point and shoot interfaces.

How does such a tool actually work? Take a client/server environment within which a new application will be implemented. The new application is based on a relational database and makes use of a number of standard tables. The information found in these tables may already be available somewhere else in the system because it is used by other applications. In that case, we would want to link the existing tables to those of the new system. We may have to change some table definitions to accomplish this, but that can only be done if the changes will not affect other existing systems. We must be able to use a tool to request the relationship between existing applications and their tables. The tool must also be able to change table definitions, and must be able to provide an insight into the constraints defined for the tables. One important tool in the market for database management is IBM's Datahub, which allows you to control many types of relational databases like DB2/6000, Oracle, Sybase and other databases in an intelligent way. In addition, existing servers may be overloaded by the introduction of a new application on the system. We can unburden them by maintaining centrally defined and monitored snapshots on other servers (Figure 8.5).

System management is a very important part of the management of client/server environments. To enable effective monitoring in the client/server environment, many components must be standardized. Before we install system management tools, it is especially important that all of the computer systems are set up, in as far as possible, to meet certain standards. The following components must receive attention (Figure 8.6):

- operating system

- directory structure

- security

- naming conventions for directories and files

- communication protocols

- fixed structure of the various software products.

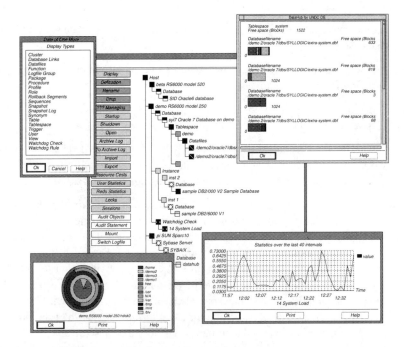

Figure 8.5 Database Management Product: DataHub for UNIX.

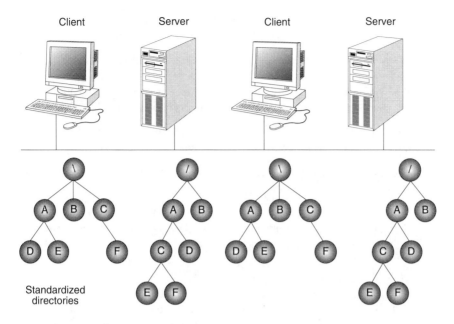

Figure 8.6 The standardized structure for system management.

The directories can be standardized by giving them carefully delineated names. If applications are to be placed in a directory, they can be linked to version numbers and the directories can be secured to prevent damage to the programs by unauthorized users.

Files which form an application are placed together, which facilitates the formation of a homogeneous entity for security, software distribution and version management. Management is simplified and becomes technically feasible. Security functions can also be more easily executed if the system is standardized, and management tools can be better matched to their environment. A single database server can be fitted with a standard setup and each of the other servers can copy this setup.

The setup of PCs deserves extra attention. Client/server software stored on the hard disk of a PC must be stored in a precisely identified location on that disk, in the directories meant for that software. This is necessary for the execution of management tasks. Since users are able to enter the operating system of the PC, they are able to access and change files, including not only the files of the client/server environment, but also the autoexec.bat and config.sys files, which may contain data with regard to the client/server environment (for example, the authorization names for other servers and the software which runs on those servers). This demonstrates that the security of the PC is extremely limited. Inadequate security can lead to difficult management and monitoring problems in the client/server environment.

There are several solutions which enable the organization to retain control over PC security:

- Not every user needs a PC with hard disk and disk drives; employees can work with diskless PCs or with X-terminals at some workstations.

- PC users with a hard drive must load client/server software as much as possible from a file server. The PC user has access to the client/receiver environment only via a security server, where the user is checked and authorized to copy the software via the file server and the network into the PC memory.

- Software which has an effect on infrastructure functioning must be written to special segments/directories of the PC which are protected from the user.

- The use of products such as NFS and network communication must be shielded from users as much as possible.

The principle of standard settings is valid for most components in the client/server concept. It encourages simplicity and provides enormous savings during implementation and maintenance.

Naming conventions and aliases

Many of the hardware and software products in a client/server environment are interrelated. To enable underlying communication, most products use unique names. Servers, for example, can be described via a unique IP address or other code. Certain software products, including network products and distributed databases, usually refer directly to these unique codes. This is dangerous, however, because if a database is placed on another server, each software product which uses the unique code must be modified.

This extra maintenance can be prevented using intermediary files with aliases and location-independent naming conventions. The relationship between the unique name, the physical location and the system is eliminated. We instead use an interface with an intermediary file containing both the alias and the real reference. If the database is now placed on another server, access to the intermediary file is sufficient to find the alias, which in turn provides the real reference and the new address. All other software products simply continue referring to the alias. We usually use the location independence mechanism in dynamic client/server environments in which optimal flexibility must be realized. Aliases can easily be defined after you have set up the architecture.

After you have set up all your standards, you can start to work with system management tools. A description of the most used and most important tools within the system management family is given below (Figure 8.7).

Configuration management

After you have defined your architecture, naming conventions and standards, you can start to implement your system management.

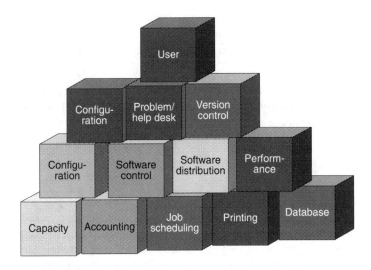

Figure 8.7 Management areas

A central issue to start with is configuration management, which is the function that ensures that the organization retainscontrol over all of the systems. A database contains all relevant data on the PCs, servers, network products, software and other components. This includes information with regard to the configuration and other data necessary for management of the system.

Configuration management gives you information about the location of your products; it shows you the relationship with the end users and the version numbers they use. It also gives you detailed information about your systems, and configuration management can be used as a kind of metadata of all your devices. To do configuration management you must put this information in a database. Some examples of the configuration attributes are:

- identification code

- serial number

- category

- status

- version

- model and type

- location

- responsible owner

- supplier.

All these objects are stored in a configuration database, and any change within the organization must be executed within this database. The information in the database can be used by management to determine the size and the growth of the IT infrastructure.

Configuration management is also the basis for change management, the help desk and version management, as it is important to tune all products to each other. The version numbers, which are stored in a central database, can be requested.

Software distribution

In many organizations, the application software is not directly located on the client. When a client starts an application, the applicable files are picked up from the file server. In principle, only the central file server need be used during the distribution of new software or loading of updates of existing software, but in some cases it may be useful to maintain certain application software on the client. In such cases, special measures must be taken for effective software distribution. Software distribution is the distribution of software from a given file server, via the network, to other systems. System management distribution of software to the clients on an ad hoc basis is called 'software distribution.' The situation in which clients pick up their software themselves from a file server is called 'file transfer.' Before distributing your software, you must have a complete overview of your products, your version numbers and the locations of the software. You must have a complete inventory of the software before you distribute it, information which should be stored in the configuration database and which should include all the items mentioned such as version number, location of software and type of operating system. It is also necessary to check on related products in advance, as not every software product with a specific version number is able to communicate with other products. Software distribution relates not only to application software, but also to operating systems, databases and other files. Software distribution is necessary in the following cases:

- *During the installation of new software.* Software can be manually installed on a local system by loading disks, but this can be quite time-consuming in situations with many users. The software can also be sent automatically to the user systems via a distribution/file server.

- *During updates of existing software.* During updates of existing systems, automatized distribution is preferable.

- *During the distribution of drivers and scripts.* The distribution of application files is often insufficient. In many cases, drivers and scripts must also be installed.

Certain conditions must be met before software can be distributed:

- The network addresses of each system to which software is sent must be available.

- The directory location at each system on which software must be placed must be known, which is why standardization is an absolute necessity.

- Authorization must be obtained for access to each system to be updated.

- The exact composition of each product being distributed must be known. Many applications are built up out of several files which together form a program. The system manager must know exactly which files belong together and exactly where they must be placed.

- The system manager must know exactly how long it takes to distribute software over the network, and what the consequences of distribution are for the network.

- Distribution methods must be consistent and fixed. If a computer is not turned on, software cannot be distributed to it. The time at which software is sent to local systems must be fixed. This can occur when the user logs on or when the user specifically asks for a given program via the server. Another method is the use of a batch program which automatically runs through a list of systems.

- Checking mechanisms must be available, which signal that all local software has arrived correctly at the local client.

Version management

With the help of network management or special software distribution products, the exact systems to which software must be distributed can be indicated. Through the use of software distribution, the system manager can guarantee that the latest version of the necessary software is available.

Version management is necessary because the organization must have an insight into the version numbers of the following components:

- version number of the operating system,

- version number of the user interfaces,

- version number of the applications,

- version number of the database,

- version number of the development software,

- version number of various network software products.

Version management determines whether products can communicate with each other. The following example demonstrates the consequences of a lack of good version management.

The version of an operating system largely determines the software products with which this operating system can communicate. The version of an operating system, for example, can determine whether that system can work with a 4GL, a database, a user interface and other products. This is also true of other software.

Working with a 4GL imposes requirements with regard to the version number of the database and the version number of the user interface. Version management largely determines whether new releases of software products can be introduced.

An example is an organization which works in a client/server environment with various operating systems, including DOS, OS/2 and a number of UNIX systems. The organization has PCs which work with DOS version 4.0 and PCs which work with DOS version 5.0. In addition, a limited number of PCs work with OS/2 version 2.0. In addition to the PCs, UNIX database servers are used which work with a Sun system with Solaris 2.0, an IBM system which works with AIX version 3.2 and an IBM system which works with AIX version 4.1. On the PCs, a user interface is also used, including Windows version 3.0 and version 3.1.

In this environment, X-terminals and PCs are used as clients. On the PCs and application servers, to which the X-terminals are connected, 4GL applications are run. The 4GL can, due to the high user interface requirements, no longer work with Windows version 3.0, but can work with version 3.1. The 4GL, however, has a new release.

All versions of the 4GL must be the same because they are all perfectly tuned to the underlying database. The user can now no longer work with AIX version 3.2, but he can work with AIX version 4.1 because this corresponds to the version which also works with Windows 3.1. Users can continue working on the Solaris operating system of the Sun. If the organization begins working with a new 4GL release, the underlying database must be modified.

We now discover, however, that the database with which the organization communicates does not yet have a version available for the Sun with Solaris, but that it does for version 4.1 of AIX. This makes the importance of version management very clear. We now have applications which run with the new 4GL and applications which, for the time being at least, cannot be transferred over to the new environment due to the version policy of the various suppliers. To prevent the organization from losing control over version management, the organization must know precisely which version numbers of the software are available for each system.

Before distributing the new 4GL software, the Windows version must be upgraded from version 3.0 to version 3.1. The same is true of the IBM UNIX line, since only version 4.1 can be used in place of version 3.2 of AIX. This means that version management must not only provide an insight into the versions available, but must also take dependencies between versions into account.

The PCs which work with DOS can also have tools for users which query the database, but the new database which must be installed is not yet supported. A single new release can affect all of the software in the organization.

Version management involves not only the version numbers of the products from software suppliers, but also the development environment. Developed applications can consist of a single executable file or of a series of files which belong together. A program can have a file which controls the user interfaces, a file with the application logic, a file with printer controls, and a file which regulates communication with the database. Applications often consist of a variety of files which together form a single programming system. Upon initial development, the combined files making up the program receive a version number of 1.0. The program developer must be able to combine a set of files and provide the resulting program with a version number. This set of files must then be seen as an entity which belongs together. Even if just a single file must be modified (e.g. due to a change in only the user interface), version management must decide whether to give the set of files a new version number. The files related to application logic and the database links remain unchanged in this case, but unchanged files can also receive a new version number due to changes in their relationship with other files.

This example demonstrates that version management is a question of making underlying agreements. Again, an increase in the heterogeneity of the environment leads to an increase in the number of management tasks.

Version management and software distribution

We have now examined the issues involved in version management and software distribution. Once a determination has been made of the products and files to be distributed, version management must be able to check and manage the version numbers of the various software products.

Take a set of files which together form an application. These files must be distributed in compiled form to the clients, and to achieve this the distribution product must know exactly which files it must send to those clients. All of the versions of the various products on the PC must then be tuned to each other. There are two types of version management: management of products developed within the organization and management of standard software products. Again, the underlying dependencies must be carefully examined before introducing new software products, in order to prevent communication problems between the various products (Figure 8.8).

An interesting method of combining version management, client security and software distribution is the installation of all applications on an application or file server. The PCs establish a link with an application/file server via NFS. A product like NFS allows the establishment of communications with files on other computers, and allows the manipulation of the data as if the data were locally stored (Figure 8.9).

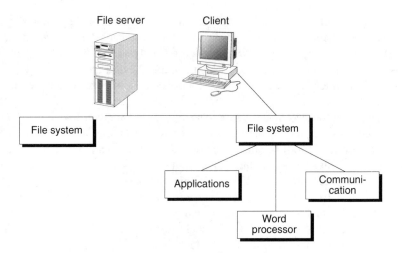

Figure 8.8 Local applications on client.

If NFS is installed on a PC and linked to files on the application server, the application can be started on the PC as if the files were stored locally. This software link eliminates the need to install application software on the PC. The latest versions of the software need only be placed on the application servers. When the PC is started up, the user is always connected to the application server, which ensures that the latest version of the software is used. This eliminates the need to automatically install application software on the hard disk of the PC via software distribution. The software can be distributed solely to the application servers. The security is taken care of by providing the user with read-only access to the

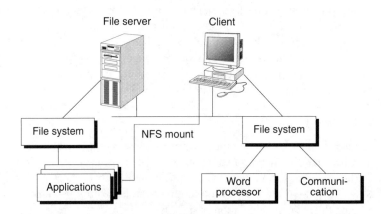

Figure 8.9 The installation of NFS to a PC.

applications on the application server, which limits the amount of security precautions needed at local levels on the PC (Figure 8.10).

The user can receive authorizations via a security server for applications on an application server. This allows management tasks such as security, software distribution and version management to be related to each other, and offers various possibilities which can simplify system management.

Change management

Change management's task is to record system modification procedures, which of course requires the effective registration of all components. A new release, for example, will give rise to a number of consequences. All dependencies must be described and all changes must immediately be registered. The modification of the PC's operating system, as in version management, can lead to considerable change management procedures.

If we migrate to version 5.0 of DOS, the new release must be recorded in the configuration database, but at the same time we must determine whether the new release has an effect on the other software products with which this operating system works. If problems arise, the changes which were made can be seen in the database. Take the following situation: network management facilities are used to distribute software to the PCs where it is subsequently installed. Once the software has been distributed, the configuration database can automatically be modified to reflect the latest changes as required. The relationship between change management, configuration management and other management tasks is quite clear in this situation.

Within change management you can control any change in your IT infrastructure. Only well qualified plans and authorized changes can be executed.

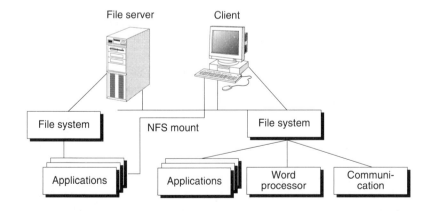

Figure 8.10 Software distribution.

Help desk/problem management

Another component of system management is the help desk function. Help desk personnel must be able to analyze complaints received with the help of network management facilities which allow them to access the local system from where the complaint came. The help desk personnel can find the cause of the problem by reading various parameters with the help of system tools such as performance management, which display active functions or generate help messages, 'trouble tickets' or network and system management messages. Certain products are able to provide suggestions for problem solutions. In a help desk application the problems can be examined for an optimal solution, as the help desk database contains similar problems encountered in the past. These problems and their solutions can also be examined to help in solving the problem at hand.

Information registered in a help desk environment consists of:

- person making the complaint;
- person who received the complaint, time complaint was received, description of complaint;
- action to be taken;
- person or organizations to be contacted;
- dependencies which may be encountered during problem solution;
- change management functions activated;
- activities which have been executed;
- status of the problem;
- classification of the problem;
- reporting of the problems.

The help desk possesses the specialized information required to solve hardware problems, such as the persons and organizations to be contacted. Help desk personnel also know how to react to extremely critical system crashes, ensuring that the systems are again operational as quickly as possible, and can also activate various monitoring functions. The help desk function is especially important for larger organizations.

Printer management

Client/server environments often include a number of printers controlled by central printer servers. Printer management ensures that all print jobs are distributed to the correct locations in the organization, and that each application possesses adequate print facilities. Printer management includes the following functions:

- *Configuration of local and remote printers.* To make a printer, matched to a certain machine, approachable for users of a different machine, a remote printer queue has to be defined. In a large network the configuration of printer queues can be a complicated task.

- *Allocation of printers to users and/or clients.* To execute a print command in a large printer network on the nearest printer, a mapping is needed from the PC or workstation to the printer. It is also possible to define, on behalf of the user, to which printer his output has to be sent.

- *Rerouting of print jobs.* If certain printers are temporarily out of order, for example in the case of a breakdown, it has to be possible to send the print jobs to another printer.

Although printer configuration, printer queues, routing definitions, and so on can be stored in the configuration database, additional printer management tools can be of great help. In addition to printer management, management cover print design, typography, logos etc.

User management

User management is closely related to security management. In the case of security management, the rights of a user to a system or database are defined. User management is the management area including:

- defining users;

- administration of user information, such as name, location, telephone number, address, and so on;

- authorization on various platforms;

- discarding users which take no longer part in the process.

There are tools which give the opportunity to carry out user management tasks for a certain platform, but integrated solutions for several platforms, like UNIX, AS/400 and Novell, would be very useful.

Performance management

An often heard complaint from an end user is that the system operates too slowly. To make objective remarks and to undertake the correct actions, the following tasks have to be performed in relation to performance management on a continuous basis:

- *Gathering of information concerning system performance.* Time needed for certain processes, free disk space, fragmentation degree of tables in a table space, length of a print queue, and so on.

- *Data processing in statistics.* For example, average CPU load, number of read and write operations to disk, number of print jobs, number of paging operations (page in, page out), and so on.

- *Observation of trends and possible bottlenecks.*

- *Monitoring of systems and taking action where problems arise (problem management).* Keep an eye on which processes require a lot of CPU time.

- *Optimization of performance through fine tuning of systems and databases.*

A close match to problem management can, for example, lead to the reporting of problems which are a result of bad performance.

Client management

In a client/server environment the operations department must pay a lot of attention to the use of the clients like PCs and workstations. To realize proper management of these machines, it is important to define standards for their configuration and installation. Different configuration and installation that will not be supported should be not allowed. To support the clients you need specific software that runs on these clients, and you have to establish backup and restore management, as PCs require a special backup procedure. If fileservers and database servers are used, one can even decide not to make backups from PCs, as the backup procedures from the servers protect against loss of data. As PCs and workstations are running at end users' desks, remote management is needed. For good client management we need a multitasking operating system on the client site so that we are able to control the current status of the client while he is working.

Accounting

The organization often requires cost allocation calculations in a client/server environment to obtain a good overview of the costs of, for example, a given user in comparison to the total system. This can only be achieved through the implementation of a good accounting system.

The accounting system must provide answers to the following questions:

- Which users make use of the system?

- What kind of tasks do they carry out?

- What kind of system burden does that generate (disk I/O, CPU, network, database)?

- What are the price agreements of using the systems?

Security

Security is a broad concept involving the security of hardware and software and the operational continuity requirements with regard to hardware and software. It also involves preventive tasks such as making backups. The checks carried out during user logons to applications and databases also fall under the security remit. Procedures for calamities are also important security issues: if a system goes down, certain procedures must be followed. Security levels are dependent on the budget available, and the requirements imposed on hardware and software operational continuity.

The great number of security issues can be globally divided into the following categories:

- Hardware security:
  - PCs
  - servers
  - mainframe
  - X-terminals
  - modems

- Software security:
  - databases
  - applications
  - operating system
  - user interfaces

- Data integrity security:
  - integrity rules
  - replications
  - communication with other programs

- Network security:
  - network hardware
  - communication software

- User security:
  - passwords/user names
  - application authorizations
  - database authorizations
  - operating system authorizations

- Computer area security:
    - access security
    - fire prevention
    - escape routes.

Security at file level

Working out all of these issues is not easy in a large organization. Good security has a preventive function, but it also provides structure: it prevents problems, but it also describes standard procedures to be taken in the case of, for example, calamities.

Security can be implemented not only in the operating system, but also in the database or applications. In many organizations, passwords and user names are currently a topic of discussion. In principle, every level can be protected by security measures: the operating system, applications and databases.

Security at directory or file level must be implemented to prevent unauthorized access. If the organization uses products such as NFS and communications software, security at the operating system level is a necessity.

Security and authorization via menus

Usually, applications are protected via menus which can be modified to fit the individual user. Many software product suppliers are able to deliver dynamic menus. These menus allow the user to be authorized for certain applications, to which he obtains access via a screen which displays only the applications for which the user is authorized.

As there is a database in which all applications with all users are stored, the dynamic menu can be set up in such a way that it is automatically controlled. Menus also exist which allow the user to view all of the applications, but to activate only those applications for which he is authorized.

Security server

A security server can define a database containing all applications or files for which a person, department or a group of persons is authorized. A security server can be an absolute necessity for optimal security execution. Modern security services use DCE as a tool for security management and single logon (Figure 8.11).

A security server can act as a buffer which intercepts unauthorized users before they can log on to other servers. These security servers are frequently used as a sort of firewall against undesired users: the organization effectively erects a dam against them. Maintenance is simple and works as a separate module in

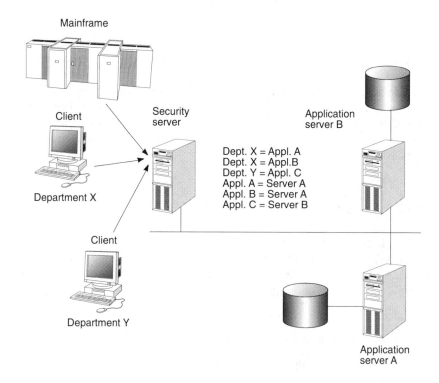

Figure 8.11 Log on through security server.

the client/server concept, since it is not linked to the rest of the programs. Communication with other computer systems outside of the organization runs less of a risk of unauthorized use if it occurs via the security server. A security server can control other security servers in order to execute local authorizations.

Database security

Security at database level is an independent security component. Every good relational database can secure tables and authorize certain persons to read, change and complete tables. Security at the database level is an especially important requirement in environments which make use of query tools to request data from databases and spreadsheets.

Personal computer security

The security of PCs requires closer attention. Partially due to deficiencies in the DOS operating system, the PC is a very weak link in the area of security. Often, simple password and user name security does not exist. Any user can log on to the system, with nothing to prevent him from modifying local files.

The influence of the user on the client/server concept implementation makes PC security an issue worthy of special consideration. Use of certain client/server concepts entails the use of software on the PC which allows access to certain servers, for example application software and network software, including TCP/IP, but also products such as NFS, the diverse SQL Net products and possible local databases. All of this software can be located on the PC's disk. In a client/server environment, the user name and server passwords are usually stated in the various communication software on the PC, which is a risky situation if security precautions are inadequate.

Backup and recovery

Making backups is important in every form of automation. The word 'backup' can be defined in a variety of ways: it can involve merely the copying of data, but it can also involve the double implementation of hardware and software products. There are many types of backups:

- placing data on a medium;

- double implementation of hardware components;

- double implementation of the network;

- working with more than one system so that if one system goes down the other takes over activity execution.

It is quite obvious that backup and recovery have a very close relationship with the rules defined in the security procedures. We first examine making a backup in the most generally used sense of the term – recording current data on a medium.

If the organization works in a large client/server environment, the data located on servers will usually be recorded regularly using backups. Large backup carousels, which quickly copy large database files to tape or optical disk, can be used for this purpose. These carousels can be centrally located and can access the servers via the network for backup purposes. A good administrative system includes the system from which the backup data was taken, the version number, and the date and time of the backup. A backup on floppy disks is sufficient for certain software.

In some cases, data will be immediately saved to a backup. This occurs in systems in which breakdowns must immediately be taken care of. In such situations, database files can be continuously copied from the original to another hard disk. If one of the hard disks goes down, another immediately takes its activities over, without the user noticing, and the system continues running without interruption. You can also use a third mirror on disk and make a backup on tape from this third mirror. After the backup on tape the second mirror copies the new information on the third mirror.

Careful consideration must be given to the relationships between applications and databases before backups are made. If two or more files are directly dependent on each other, they must be backed up at a single static moment. The simplest way to achieve this is to make the backup off-line at a time when the system is inactive. All data is frozen at that moment. It is, however, not always possible to bring an application down for a backup. In such cases, on-line backups are made. This is true of bank applications and reservation systems, for example, which are continuously accessed and updated. Software is available to create a log file during backups: first, all of the data is placed on tape; once that has been completed, all data that was changed during the backup is stored in the log file; the log file is then placed on tape.

This method can also be used during backups in a distributed environment. If databases are related to each other via tables, backups must be made with the utmost care. If a table with a foreign key from other databases is placed on tape while changes to another database on another server occur simultaneously, the backup will lack data integrity. This is easily solved via an off-line backup, but it is more complex in an on-line situation. The organization must carefully consider how strict its data security and integrity requirements must be before choosing the products to be used to carry out backup activities.

Another form of backup is the double implementation of hardware components. A double network, for example, can be implemented for backup purposes, as can double network cards and many other components. The PC should also receive special attention. Many organizations make no backups of the data stored on PCs, but this is actually a rather questionable policy. The following issues are of importance in this respect:

- Can software be quickly loaded on a PC via software distribution?

- How much time is invested in software installation on a PC?

- How much critical information is contained on a PC?

- Which files must be shared?

Critical software stored on PCs must be regularly backed up. This may be done fairly simply because most servers are able to copy the files via file transfer to other servers. In addition, tapes can be used or backup software can be activated via network management which can also copy PC data to the tape carousel. The time necessary to correctly install a PC within a client/server environment is often underestimated. The installation of network software on a PC, rules with regard to security, and so on, require many hours of work, making the backup of PCs quite desirable.

Mainframe communication in client/server systems also affects backup activities. If UNIX servers and the mainframe maintain copies of each others' information, this imposes extra requirements on the backup procedures.

Choosing the right software

We have used several examples in an attempt to describe the way in which the underlying relationships of management tasks can influence each other. In a large client/server environment, these tasks are supported by network, system and application management software. Optimal operation of these products requires effective tuning of the product relationships. The tuning of the tools of the organization is a completely separate function within the client/server concept, and definitely requires its fair share of attention. The creation of standards within each component of the client/server environment is an absolute necessity.

Besides the tasks already mentioned, other tasks can also be supported with management tools: for example, job scheduling, which allows us to monitor various daily operational tasks. Batches and printer control can also be supported with the help of such tools.

Management tools allow the client/server concept to be optimally implemented in its broadest form within an organization. The tools enable remote control of the complete environment via network management. They are extremely powerful aids which usually make use of information technology. Tools help support management task execution: they can send advice to the management departments or they can independently execute various functions. Such tools are of great importance during the implementation of larger client/server environments, and can greatly limit client/server management costs.

But how can we make the right decision for the tool? There are several steps in making the right decision. The first step is to set up an architecture in the organization, which gives a description of where all the hardware and software is located and how it works together. The second step is to set up the standards. The third step is the service levels that have to be supported. Out of these components you can come up with the requirements for the network, system and application management tools. During this phase you can compile a list of requirements and check if the tools on the market are able to support this (Figure 8.12).

Making a decision

We have now handled some of the issues that have a direct effect on the implementation of network and system management programs in a client/server environment. During implementation, the organization must take the existence of various separate modules for the various functions into account. Security, for example, can be taken care of by a security server, printer control by a printer server. The naming conventions for the various tables and data must be defined according to fixed standards. The standard naming conventions for tables, templates and libraries must be known by both the developer and the manager of the environment. The relationships between the various components must be

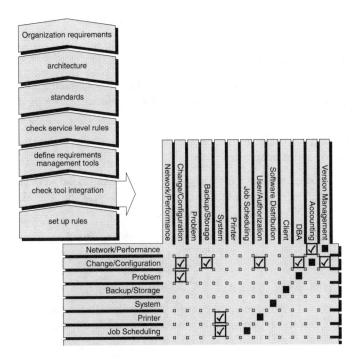

Figure 8.12 Seven steps, tool integration exposed.

recorded and maintenance in larger client/server environments must be carried out by management tools in as far as possible. Fine tuning of these components leads to a harmonious system with low maintenance costs and the necessary flexibility. This requires far-reaching standardization and modular construction.

In a large client/server environment you do need system and database management. Without them your maintenance costs will increase considerably.

GOLDEN RULES

- In each large client/server environment you have to invest in network and system management products.

- Firstly, set up an architecture for your environment.

- Secondly, make a decision on software products and see how they are related to each other.

- Thirdly, you have to set up standards for the network, the operating system, the database and the applications.

- Your network infrastructure must be able to support all of your applications.

- Network management tools can visualize your hardware infrastructure, and intelligent products will save you a lot of labor costs.

- See if your network management products can control intelligent hubs and virtual LANs. They should also have a connection with system management products.

- Your system management tools are dependent on your architecture, your standards and your service levels.

- Make a list of requirements for your system management products. See if each requirement is processed in each product. See if there is a relationship between the system management products.

- Choose products where you can specify the constraints of the organization.

- Modern network and system management tools are based on object orientation.

- See if your management tools use international standards like CORBA.

- Network and system management products will increase your investments initially, but the return on investment will soon start, and the return on investment of these tools is very big.

Chapter 9

International
standardization

Introduction

To ensure that costs remain under control, organizations are increasingly demanding international standards in the area of operating systems, network protocols, programming environments and databases. In addition to the organization's own standards, which are developed and implemented to ensure data integrity, and so on, international standards exist which ensure enduring investments in new techniques for the future.

Databases

An important standard in the area of databases is ANSI SQL, which is supported by most database suppliers. At present, 4GL products are able to communicate with several different databases. It is not true that all of the underlying differences between the various relational databases have been eliminated. The differences in, for example, the construction of triggers and stored procedures remain considerable. Extra precautions must be taken if the organization wants to use various databases in a heterogeneous environment. Gateways and middleware products are important solutions for this kind of situation. IBM's DRDA middleware concept, for example, allows different types of database to communicate with each other, and it allows organizations to work in a heterogeneous database environment.

Open Software Foundation (OSF)

Market demand for open systems is increasing, and the role of proprietary operating systems (systems that are not open), which are completely dependent on hardware products from a given supplier, is gradually decreasing. Open systems play a part in ensuring standard user interfaces, portability and interoperability:

- A *user interface* is of importance in communication with the user. It determines the manner in which communication is presented to the user, and largely determines the manner in which the user communicates with the system.

- *Portability* allows software to be transferred easily from one platform to another. Portability is made possible by standardization of the operating system.

- *Interoperability* allows simplification and standardization of the underlying communication between the various heterogeneous systems. This ensures that data can be exchanged easily.

DCE

Interoperability entails a standard international distributed processing framework. The Open Software Foundation (OSF) and Distributed Computer Environment (DCE) have taken the first steps in this direction. Large organizations such as IBM, HP, DEC and Bull have contributed to the standards contained in DCE. DCE enables the organization to work with computers from various suppliers within a single system, sharing the resources of that system. These resources can be computer power, data, printers and peripheral equipment.

DCE is not just for UNIX environments, but can also integrate other platforms such as mainframes and PCs. It enables users to communicate with several systems without logging on to various systems which perform specific tasks. A user working with DCE uses a system that manifests itself as a single homogeneous system. Optimal implementation of DCE allows users to work in a completely open environment within which tasks can be completely distributed (Figure 9.1).

DCE is a set of software tools and services which enables users to develop applications that work in a distributed environment. Although DCE offers utilities and services for direct use by the user, the administrator and programmer must remain conscious of the fact that certain conditions must be met for the

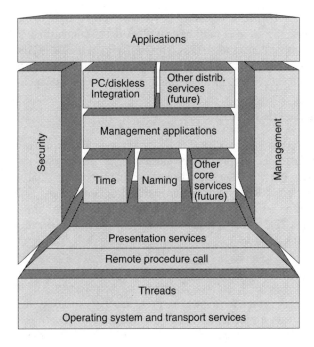

Figure 9.1 Elements of DCE.

successful introduction of DCE. Various security, registration and environmental items must be recorded and programmed according to fixed patterns.

DCE allows the organization to easily maintain distributed environments. Administrators can monitor all DCE components from a single management interface. The distributed computer environment makes use of cells. In complex environments with many users, systems, printers and other hardware, users must be able to call up all of the systems necessary to enable use of the facilities. To manage this, it is important that certain users, systems and other components are bundled in groups. A cell is usually a geographically determined group, for example a department of all users in a LAN. This enables simplified management and administration. The components covered by DCE are outlined below.

Threads

Most computer programs are single threaded: that is, processes are handled sequentially. Once a given process is completed, the following computer process is offered for handling. The subroutines within a given program are also processed sequentially. In an environment with several systems, however, realization of parallel processing must be possible. The programs usually have to be modified to realize this. Subprocesses can then be executed on various systems simultaneously. Of course, this process must be controlled and an administrative system must record and monitor the entire process. This is all part of the DCE Threads Service. Programmers can ensure that this thread system is implemented during programming. Use of threads allows the organization to increase performance considerably.

Remote procedure calls

An important component in client/server environments is the use of RPCs. RPCs allow the user to call up procedures located on the user's own system or on a remote system. The procedures can then be executed on the machine which is most fit for that purpose. RPCs must be separately programmed and activated by the application using a call statement. Use of RPCs allows multi-threaded working in DCE. DCE RPC allows greater flexibility in the implementation of diverse network architectures.

Time Services

Time Services is a function which ensures that the various system clocks are synchronized. Certain processes must be executed at a given time. DEC Time Services was developed to prevent systems from running out of synchronization with each other. This is especially important for management tasks. The tasks which are dependent on the network and must be precisely synchronized must be able to make use of DCE Time Services.

Naming/Directory Services

In DCE Directory Services, all the names of the sources with which the organization works are stored. Components such as printers, application servers, as well as persons or groups of persons, are allocated to cells. DCE allows the naming of just about everything, enabling simple identification of all systems. The request and answer processes in a client/server environment make use of these references.

Diskless support

If the organization uses diskless systems, DCE can enable communication by these systems in a client/server environment. This means that systems can be started from servers which support the operating system.

Security

If the organization operates in a heterogeneous environment within which users must be able to call up various systems and carry out various systems tasks, it is important that security in DCE is centrally arranged independent of the operating system. Databases working in a distributed environment must also be secured centrally. DCE enables the organization to set up security procedures in such a way that the user can work with various systems without having to log on to each of those systems. The DCE security rules are stored in a database, which the activated servers can access. These servers then know exactly which information and systems the user is authorized to access. All system components can be protected, including directories, printers, RPCs, databases, files, applications and operating systems, as well as cells. When the user logs on, his security authorizations are automatically processed by the DCE Security Service. The administrator can implement any changes to security levels or authorizations in his database, and all modifications can then be centrally processed for the entire distributed environment. The clients and servers for which a given user is authorized can also be centrally recorded and maintained.

Distributed File Services

A distributed environment has a complex internal structure, but must manifest itself to the user as a single entity. Files stored on the hard disk of another system can be accessed from another local system. To realize this function, the Network File System (NFS) or Sun is usually used. Files or other systems can be mounted with the help of NFS. 'Mounting' is a technical term which means making file systems accessible. This can play an extremely important role in management tasks such as software distribution, version management and the logon of various PCs to servers, for example in the case of local PCs which use NFS to realize mounts with application servers, security servers and database servers. Sun's NFS product is very important in this regard. NFS control becomes increasingly difficult, however, in mounting a large number of systems. DCE does not make use of NFS due to that system's security limitations and market demand for simultaneous LAN and WAN management. Instead, it uses DCE Distributed File Services (DFS). DFS offers various functions which unburden networks. In addition, DFS maintains a record of which cells have access to which systems. Files can simply be transferred over to systems which are less heavily burdened. A DFS server can easily replicate/copy files so that the files are always available to the user. DFS is also completely integrated in DCE, which strengthens DFS's relationship to the DCE Security Services. DFS also offers easier backup facilities, and it can be implemented in diskless systems. Another positive point for DFS is that it can cache, or temporarily store in internal memory, a great deal of the data, guaranteeing high performance. The ability to create links with file servers and to monitor whether the latest version is in cache is especially important in client/server environments. This is all handled by DCE. The tasks carried out by the Distributed File Service can become more complex as the environment increases in size and as relationships are created between the various systems. DFS allows the construction of such complex distributed environments.

At present, the first components of DCE are complete and the software is on the supplier's shelves. This does not mean, however, that the organization is finished with the construction of the environment after it has installed the software. Many of the components must still be programmed. DCE delivers software tools and services, which can also be used in non-UNIX environments. An application can make use of all or just some of DCE's functions. Programs such as On-Line Transaction Programs (OLTP), however, can integrate all DCE functions. One new OLTP product which makes full use of DCE functions is Encina. This product has been adopted by HP and IBM, among other companies, as the on-line transaction product for their UNIX/DCE environment. Encina makes use of DCE functions such as threads, security and RPCs. More OLTP products, which use DCE functions, will be developed.

DCE in action

In the client/server world there is a great need for international standards. At present most standards are still set by the products of the market leaders, but within a client/server world we need interoperability and policies on how we can work together not only at the client level, but also at the server level with databases, security and many other tasks. At present, large mainframe users turning towards the client/server concept are asking for an international standard like DCE. This will encourage the market leaders to work together. Within DCE we find some important client/server tasks handled properly. If you want to share systems and applications in your organization you need a good framework for the corporate IT infrastructure, and DCE will support you in this.

Let us give an example of DCE in action within the client/server environment.

In a large organization you have made a workflow document. You now know exactly what procedures and rules there are within your company. You have decided to develop a three-tiered architecture. On the clients we see several different software modules running, depending on the end user needs. The procedures are placed on special servers so that every application can use them. There are also distributed databases working on several database servers. When you start to work you first have to be authorized. From your client you ask for an authorization and you are connected to the security server. All your users are related to cells, and each cell is controlled by this security server. With the support of remote procedure calls you are connected to the server.

When the user is identified, DCE takes care that he is connected to all the other databases, printers or other systems he needs. The user does not have to log in on each server, and each server can work with a different operating system. With DCE you can create a single logon environment on all your platforms. The user can be a part of a group of servers who all belong to a cell. Within your application you work on a client, and with RPCs you make calls to your standard procedures stored on a server. If needed, they can make a connection to the database server.

If something changes in your workflow you need change only your procedure and nothing else.

By using the directory server, everyone in the software environment can find the server or the client they need. Within the directory server, your client will find all the locations of the devices required, like the address of the database servers or print server. Your developers can set up some standard RPCs or they can use existing libraries.

If you work on several database or other servers there is no need to be concerned about your time being inconsistent. The time is the same on each server as they are all controlled by the time server. Therefore, you can always make calculations based on time and dates. Regardless of which system you work on, each system connected to the DCE world works with all the other systems as if on one big distributed computer. This can be a mainframe or a UNIX server, any personal computer or other systems that support DCE. By using the distributed file system, the users are logged automatically onto files on hard disks from other computer systems. This is fully secure and replication can take place without any problem. The operator has full control over his site and system management tasks are made easier.

Can we have this type of client/server environment without DCE? It has in fact been done without DCE for many years, but by using DCE it is easier to set up a large distributed client/server site, and by using standards we can save a lot of time. For instance, the end user has to log on only once (single logon). In the past, a lot of code had to be written before all the systems could be connected together – now we can use standard libraries offered by DCE. While it is still necessary to write code oneself and use libraries, by using DCE every vendor can work together easily with products from other vendors, and this open world makes it possible to choose the right hardware and software products that you need for your organization. The systems can all work together, and it saves you a lot of time in setting up your own rules and in maintenance. DCE offers complete interoperability throughout the whole organization and over all platforms.

OMG

As already discussed, the management of a client/server environment becomes more complex as the organization increases in size and more use is made of heterogeneous hardware and software environments. The network and system management are of great importance in this respect. DCE does not regulate the network and system management, but delivers the tools necessary for a heterogeneous approach to security and time services.

Nowadays we are moving toward the world of objects. The client/server concept sets a standard for communication between many platforms, but a software program is split up into a user interface, application logic and the other parts described earlier. But that is only the first step in moving toward a completely distributed world. In future we will work with all kinds of multimedia applications or objects on screen. In every object you can store data like names and addresses, but also logic, such as the salary of a certain function having a certain maximum. All this information can be stored in one object. End users can copy these objects to other applications or make their own objects. Objects are reusable, and this is one of the most powerful parts of object technology which can be used in many types of application. Finally, you will want to use your objects not only in standard applications, but also in word processor files, spreadsheets, email and many other applications. This means that objects must become completely open to communicate with all kinds of operating systems, applications or computer languages. If you want to reuse objects you do need a dictionary, so that others can use them in any type of program you build. To be able to reuse objects and transfer them to applications you thus need an international standard for objects. The difficulty with object orientation is that it can work only if there is an international standard. This role is handled by the Object Management Group (OMG).

OMG and CORBA

The OMG group was founded to create distributed object standards and an architecture for objects in a heterogeneous computer environment. Most vendors understand that the object orientation world can be succesful only if all the objects used by several vendors can communicate with each other. Most existing computer companies, though not Microsoft, are members of this group because they understand the need for it. In 1990 the Object Management Group published the Object Management Architecture Guide.

Object Request Broker

There are several important components of the Object Management Architecture. One of them is known as the Object Request Broker (ORB). This middleware, in the world of object orientation, allows objects to communicate so that you can make requests to and receive responses from objects. The ORB receives a call, is responsible for finding the right objects, and then returns the results. This works like the client/server architecture, where clients make a request to a server. In the object world you need a communication medium between all the computer systems, and that is done by the ORB (Figure 9.2).

It is real middleware, and is independent of operating system and programming languages.

ORB guarantees portability and interoperability of objects in a heterogeneous environment. This architecture is known as CORBA, or the Common Object Request Broker Architecture. It includes a very important specification for the Interface Definition Language (IDL) which allows you to define the interfaces to objects using ORB. This IDL is the 'glue' in object land, and it allows you to communicate with all the other objects. Without this IDL we could never create a real object-oriented world.

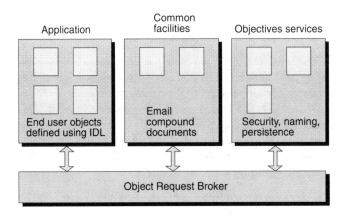

Figure 9.2 Object Request Broker.

Object Services
Other important functions created by the OMG are the Object Services. These provide functions like the object name, object notification and other functions for using and implementing objects.

Common Facilities
The Common Facilities in the OMA guide are a collection of end user services, such as email.

Application Objects
These objects are specific for end users, and they must be defined using the IDL.

With IDL and ORB we have the most important part of the object world. We can now make objects and plug them into any other program, and thus become truly independent. If we really turn to the object world we will also go to the world of the Object Database Management Systems (ODMS). Such systems will become the successors of the relational DBMS. ODMS stores objects instead of only data, as in relational DBMSs. We can already see some relational DBMS vendors turning to the world of ODMS, and in new releases of many relational DBMS we will find the first object functionality.

SOM and DSOM

We now have the foundations of the object world based upon OMG, but how do we build and package class libraries? In class libraries you have all your objects stored, including the logic, but the class libraries can be built in many programming languages, and we want to communicate between all types of libraries without making any changes.

This can be done with the System Object Model (SOM) developed by IBM. SOM is based on the Object Managment Group's description of CORBA.

Until now it has been hard to be completely open in the world of object orientation. Some C++ class libraries cannot be used by others, and a lot of libraries built in other languages cannot be used. SOM packages the objects and makes them portable to Windows, UNIX, OS/2 and other operating systems. This makes it possible for objects built in C or Smalltalk to be used by C++ objects. SOM will become a part of the operating system of the future, so that real interoperability can be achieved. An SOM IDL interface must be used to make the classes and define their interrelationships with other objects.

To work in a network with multiple machines, operating systems and applications means working in a distributed environment. To work with objects in this world you need a Distributed SOM (DSOM). This adds object locations to the objects. DSOM is a CORBA compliant Object Request Broker.

What are the advantages of object orientation and why do we need a new technique? The answer to this is simple. We are moving into a new era of interoperability where all computer systems must have the ability to work together and share information very easily. This can be done with objects. Within the object world we have inheritance, meaning that you can change one item and it will be changed in all the other objects as well. Compare it to the foreign key relationship in a relational database. The real benefit is that it saves time and relieves you from having to do it yourself. Objects are reusable, and that means that codes need not be rewritten. Objects are independent of computers and are easy to handle for end users. The end user can develop applications by himself, and a lot of things like connectivity, networking and relationships with other applications are solved automatically. What is needed now is to find a good operating system that can work with it, establish international standards for developing objects, and choose one language like IDL to work with and support in a distributed world. It now looks as if all these things can be handled with CORBA.

OLE and the Open Doc world

We have looked at the end user, at connectivity and at the effect of integration. What do end users want to gain from the client/server world? The end user wants to integrate all his information himself and develop his own applications. Information from a database and applications must be integrated with other products. Information in one application must be sent to other applications using point and click interfaces. This interaction between applications can now be done with objects from compound documents.

Foreign data can be embedded in a compound document. This can be data from a database, a spreadsheet, a word processor, email or pictures. End users are able to make their own applications by manipulating all kinds of data from different sources: it is the first step towards the object-oriented world.

Microsoft introduced OLE 2 (Object Linking and Embedding) for Windows in 1993 as their technology for integrating multiple applications and multimedia within a compound document. It can work only in the world of Microsoft Windows and the Macintosh, and not in any other world like UNIX. The great benefit of this product is that it is already on the market, and end users can become familiar with how to integrate all kinds of data. Many vendors like Oracle offer OLE interfaces for their products. OLE version 2.0 introduced the Component Object Model (COM), which allows you to drag, drop, edit and |transfer data. It provides you with encapsulation but no real object-oriented inheritance.

The real power of OLE is found in Windows 95, and it will be the start of end users integrating their data in documents which they will also develop themselves.

Open Doc

This product can be regarded as the competition's answer to Microsoft's OLE. It offers the same functionality as OLE 2.0, and is developed by a consortium that includes Apple, IBM, Novell, Oracle and Talligent. Its aim was to develop a product to allow users to work with compound document technology in a Windows, Mac, UNIX and OS/2 environment.

The technology is based on CORBA and the Object Request Broker. The product is able to work in a distributed and open world using DSOM. The strength of Open Doc is that it allows you to work in a distributed world, and not only on one single personal computer like OLE 2.0. The expectation is that Microsoft Cairo will solve this problem in the Microsoft world. Open Doc is open and not vendor dependent – all kinds of vendor can use the technology. Both OLE and Open Doc offer the user the possibility of working on compound documents, and it is likely that both worlds will converge in the future. In using these techniques, the end user will move towards the interoperability of all the applications which run on his local client.

Desktop operating systems and client/server

Over the last few years we have seen that the implementation of large client/server sites with desktop operating systems has made it possible to move toward a client/server environment. Client/server cannot work without powerful and stable desktop products. The client/server world would not exist without the current desktop products, but to turn to a more powerful environment with multimedia, graphical support, networking, object orientation and multiuser capabilities we need at least a 32-bit desktop operating system and object-oriented operating system. The world of the desktop operating systems must support international standards like DCE. One of the most important tasks of desktop systems in a client/server world is creating full and problem-free integration with the rest of the environment, and for that reason we can work only with powerful and stable operating systems that allow end users to run their applications and work flexibly.

The worlds of client/server and desktop systems are closely related. The personal computer brought computer power to the end user. Today we are able to build advanced products on personal computers and on mainframes. The computing power of personal computers has increased so much that they have taken over the role of the mini systems. With developments in the world of the graphical user interface and in networking possibilities on desktop operating systems, the world of client/server has started to really open up. We can now run CICS on OS/2; we run multimedia and all kinds of products on personal computers. There is no end to this local computer power: the future will give us parallel processors on personal computers, and the computer will become as normal a part of every household as the television. We will be connected to all kinds of network, and will do our shopping, study and holiday reservations with the support of the computer. We will get dedicated client computers that are able to make a connection to the Internet. We will work more from home, and will be connected to our office wherever it may be in the world. The only real problem remains the user interface. This is the key to success for the home computer. If we really want to make a user-friendly interface we shall have to move to object-oriented interfaces. Even the current interfaces of Windows 95 and OS/2 Warp are still not the most amenable products for the end user at home. The real future direction of the desktop will be based primarily on user-friendly multimedia capabilities, networking connections and object orientation that can support user-friendly tools for the consumer market at home. This will be based on client/server techniques.

Desktop future

With techniques like OLE and Open Doc, with groupware and office tools, we see that the world is turning toward the object world. End users are able to collect all kinds of different data themselves and point and click between applications. With applications using these techniques, advanced 32-bit operating systems, multi-processing machines and standard objects, the end user is becoming more capable at developing his own applications. These are all based on client/server techniques, and on architectures that allow all the different data to be integrated. In the client/server world we have to decide in which way we want to connect desktop systems to servers. Integration between the products, user-friendly systems, interoperability and connectivity are the keys to a successful implementation. Products like Netscape and Java will change the desktop future. With these tools we shall move faster to the Internet world. We shall use them inside and outside the company and they will become completely independent of operating systems.

GOLDEN RULES

- The client/server worlds needs international standards.

- DCE makes it possible to set up a heterogeneous environment.

- Make sure that at least your servers are able to work with DCE.

- Object orientation will become very important, and international standards, like CORBA, are needed.

- Products like OLE and Open Doc will become very important for the end user. They will ensure that the end user can develop his own applications.

- End users are being connected to international networks like the Internet, and communicate with their locally built applications all over the world.

Chapter 10

Hardware and multiprocessing

Multiprocessing

Current software demands will increase the need for more computer power. Software like multimedia voice and sound, the increased use of decision support systems, data warehousing, the need for end users to connect all this software together in windows with drag and drop functions into spreadsheets, word processors and many other applications – all these functions need computer power. The end user wants to work interactively with all kinds of multimedia software and object-oriented applications. There is a growing demand for computer power at the end user level, but also at the central computer level where all the servers or the mainframe are located.

At present we are very limited by the single processor function of the computer system. In most computers, one processor alone takes care of all the processing power. Even when we work with hundreds of users on a single computer, only one processor takes care of all the activities. The need for more computer power will increase dramatically with the use of this advanced software. In fact, over the last few years the computing power of the processor has increased by almost 100%, but even this is too limiting if we want to use all the advanced software just described.

Several years ago, the computer industry saw the sense of connecting several computers together and sharing their power. One of the companies that connected computers and tried to share computing resources was Digital with their VAX VMS cluster. Databases like Oracle and Rdb could speed up in a cluster. In a

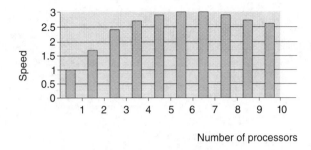

Figure 10.1 Speed of multiprocessing system with DB2/2.

cluster environment, the number of processors that could work together was limited; for example, if we connect three computers in a cluster the speed will not increase to 300% of the original processor, but is limited to perhaps 200%. In addition, the number of processors which can be used to increase the performance is limited to a certain maximum (Figure 10.1).

Over the last few years, research into forms of multiprocessing other than the cluster has increased. At this stage, the number of operating systems and the applications which are able to run with multiprocessing is increasing. Even products like OS/2 from IBM or Windows NT can work with multiprocessing. In the UNIX environment we can already work with multiprocessing for a longer period of time. In addition, the mainframe is able to work with multiple processors.

This means that, at the end user level and the server level, we will see an increasing use of multiprocessing. The desktop of the future will run with multiple processors, and then we really will be able to work with all kinds of advanced software. We then have to move to a 32-bit operating system on our desktop machines and connect it to parallel database servers.

At company level we can see an increasing demand for mission-critical applications, information warehousing and decision support systems. These types of applications need multiple processor computers. With the current price of hardware this is no longer a problem, which is why the computer industry is coming up with so many new types of multiple processing, hardware and software to support this growing demand at the end user and company level. Today, such an investment is cost effective and beneficial for organizations.

To work with multiple processors we need software that can work in this environment. First, we need an operating system that supports this, but in a client/server environment with a database server we need database software that supports multiple processing. By now most of the leading database vendors like IBM, Oracle, Sybase, CA Ingres and Informix can support one or more types of multiple processing. These databases distribute processing across multiple processors. This combination reduces the cost of decision support and OLTP through open systems. The software must be able to work with parallel data management to carry out parallel queries, parallel indexing, parallel backup and other functions like parallel recovery.

There are several types of multiprocessing:

* shared memory with shared storage

* shared storage

* shared nothing.

Symmetric multiprocessing

The first type of multiprocessing is symmetric multiprocessing. All the processors in such a computer are equal and communicate together with the shared storage. There is a rule which says that the more you share the more you must coordinate and the more performance this will cost. This type of multiprocessing must coordinate a lot of functions so it is limited to a maximum number of processors. The maximum number of processors is dependent on the software that runs on this computer, because the software must do most of the synchronization and coordination between the processors, but is also dependent on the computer's bus. In a commercial environment, a lot of information is updated and retrieved, all of which shares the same hard disk and internal memory (Figure 10.2).

The fact that all the memory and storage is shared slows down the performance at a certain number of processors. This can be improved if each processor uses caching, in which each processor gets a certain amount of memory for itself and the memory is not always shared completely.

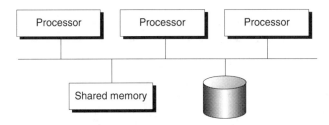

Figure 10.2 Shared everything.

Cluster

The second type of multiprocessing is best known as the cluster. Digital is one company that introduced this type of parallel technology successfully within its VAX VMS world. Today this cluster technology is also used by UNIX vendors like IBM in its most advanced form of High Availability.

In this type of multiprocessing each computer uses its own operating system and internal memory. The communication between systems is done via message passing. When we start a new process we first look at which processor is limited in its processor use, and then this process is sent to this system: this is a kind of load balancing. This type of multiprocessing is not dependent on the same processing structure: several computers work together and each machine can have a different processor (Figure 10.3).

The connection between systems takes place at the hard disk level. In this form we can also have a limited number of computers working together, and this is often used as a form of security.

With both of these types of multiprocessing there is a limit to the number of processors. The problem is the internal communication between the hardware and software. All kinds of checks and control functions are important, such as locking and queuing mechanisms, and remembering that the structure of the application will influence the performance. The improvement in performance is dependent on these factors. Database vendors that support these types of multiprocessing design parallel server software that supports these locking mechanisms.

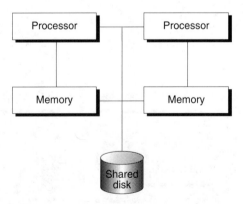

Figure 10.3 Cluster.

Massively parallel

The third type of multiprocessing is better known as being massively parallel. In this case we share nothing – each computer has its own operating system, its own memory and its own hard disk, and there is no shared bus structure (Figure 10.4). Each processor is independent and can do specific things. The communication takes place with message passing. In this environment we can work with from 100 to 1000 processors, which explains the name 'massively parallel'. The set up of a configuration is very important in this type of parallel system, and it will take some time to install the hardware, the operating system and databases before it can work together. These systems provide an enormous advantage, and a lot of companies are starting to work with them. In the field of large datawarehouses, with more than 300 gigabytes of information, and in the field of datamining we can benefit greatly from the use of this technology. Successful companies with this kind of parallel server are IBM with its SP2 system and Tandem.

The world of parallel systems has created a completely new field for database vendors. Especially in the field of data warehousing, there is a demand for query mechanisms that support parallel query options. In most cases, a part of the database is replicated from the OLTP to the decision support systems running on a multiple processor computer. The end user is now able to create his query.

A parallel query divides a single query into separate operations that are performed by multiple processors in parallel. All kinds of functions like joins, aggregations

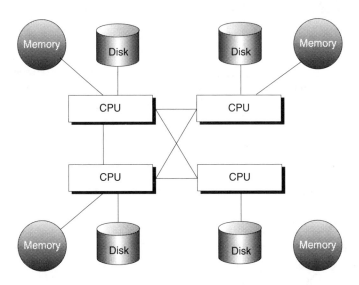

Figure 10.4 Massively parallel.

and so on are parallelized, making it possible to run them on parallel systems. The world of parallel systems, while just starting, is already one of the most successful. In the client/server field where we work with multimedia, many types of databases, queries on data warehouses, and so on, it is one of the most promising hardware techniques for the future.

Parallel systems are also used for security reasons. The cluster mechanism can be used for critical applications within an organization. They are now often used in large organizations like banks, government departments and insurance companies. An example of this type of parallel technique, known as High Availability, is given below.

High Availability

In large organizations which use a mainframe, it is often possible to switch over to another mainframe if the system goes down. This other system can be located in another computer center within the organization, but is usually at a different location from the original mainframe. This is often the case in organizations in which information systems are such an important link in the execution of business activities that the organization cannot afford system breakdowns.

This type of requirement was, until a short time ago, one of the reasons why many organizations did not work with UNIX systems. These systems were unable to guarantee meeting the high system operation continuity requirements of many organizations. This situation has changed greatly in the last few years. The UNIX platform presently offers more alternatives than many mainframes. High Availability (HA) is especially important in this regard. High Availability is a UNIX server feature based on the cluster technique, which ensures system availability at all times, even during system breakdowns. All components in a HA system are dual, so there is no single point of failure. Software continuously checks which components are active, monitoring the following components:

• CPU

• hard disks

• monitors

• memory

• network.

If a component goes down, HA records this and automatically executes the activities to keep the whole system operating. Since HA is very important at client/server sites, we shall examine it more closely. There are various forms of High Availability, of which a few are examined below.

Option 1

In this environment two systems are available, but only one is active. The inactive system does not take part in program processing. Both systems have their own hard disk, which are linked to each other. Data on the disks is continuously copied.

If one disk goes down the other is able to take over its tasks. The inactive system is activated only if the main system goes down. The tasks of the first machine are taken over by the previously inactive machine after the start-up phase, which takes several minutes. In the more advanced version of the concept, both systems are active but only one carries out the main tasks. The other machine remains on standby, but carries out no actions. The standby machine actually starts working only if the CPU of the main machine goes down and a script activates the standby system (Figure 10.5).

Option 2

In this form of High Availability, the extra server is not only suitable as a backup server, but also delivers extra processing power, allowing, for example, a relational database to run in parallel on several servers. We call this type of system a 'loosely coupled' system. The disks are continuously shared by both systems, and the systems can be connected in a cluster. If servers coupled in this way go down, the user does not notice anything. The other server takes all transactions over

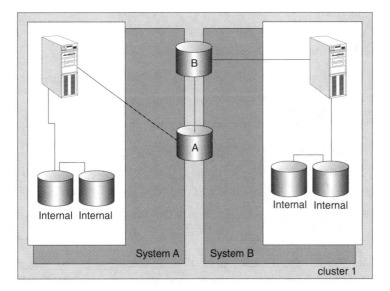

Figure 10.5 High Availability Option 1.

from the failed system. Of course, total system response slows down, but the system tasks carried out by the server which went down are immediately taken care of, since the other server was already an active participant in processing.

If, in addition, all hardware components are also placed in a no-break environment, the hardware can also continue operations if the power goes down, offering the highest level of operation continuity. Two components are active in this environment: cluster management and the lock manager. The cluster manager runs on every system and controls the cluster topology. If cluster management notices a problem it starts a special script. The cluster is modified by the script so that users can continue working optimally with the existing servers. The distributed lock manager ensures that users are able to run their software on several different servers, which is necessary to guarantee data integrity. This form of High Availability also offers extremely high performance. The parallel cache management provided by this form allows optimal use of memory. The locking mechanism is also optimally matched to this environment, allowing UNIX systems to be connected to each other in a cluster, which allows so much computer power to be bundled that the power and performance of a mainframe is easily equalled. To achieve this, software which can run in parallel on several systems must be used. The larger database suppliers currently offer this capability. This form of High Availability offers many more possibilities than fault-tolerant systems, it offers better performance and is much cheaper (Figure 10.6).

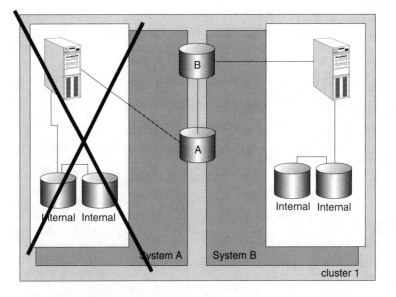

Figure 10.6 High Availability Option 2.

GOLDEN RULES

- Multiprocessing techniques will become very common, even on personal computers.

- Use SMP machines for heavy tasks within your organization.

- Make sure that your software is able to work with these hardware.

- High Availability can be used in organizations working with critical applications.

- Data warehousing environments are very suitable for multiprocessing techniques.

Chapter 11

Client/server and the Internet

The Internet is the biggest client/server network in the world. A worldwide network (WAN), its initial explosive growth rate continues unabated. It is used daily by millions of people in their homes, and by large companies such as banks and other commercial organizations. It is, in essence, a network of networks that makes possible communication between hundred of thousands of databases, and is fast becoming the international means of computer communication.

The Internet began as a project at the American Ministry of Defense, known as the Advanced Research Projects Agency (ARPA). Essential to this project was the certainty that, regardless of a failure in a network connection, every message sent would be received by the machine to which it was addressed. In the event of a network failure, the message would simply be rerouted until successfully transmitted. For example, a message prevented by network failure from going from New York to Tokyo would select an alternative route and travel via London. For the Internet today, this means extreme reliability: it will always work, and that is one of its big attractions.

The Internet uses the TCP/IP protocol, and is connected to other networks by a number of routers. Gateways make connections between the TCP/IP-based network of Internet and other types of network protocol. Each computer that is connected to the Internet has a host name and a unique IP address. Everybody at work or at home can connect up to the Internet by using any type of computer – even the simple PC. It is this that makes the Internet so important. Its basic accessibility makes it possible for all types of computer and user to work together. In addition to electronic mail, electronic newspapers and the wide variety of information that can be accessed, many types of computer files can be received by file transfer (FTP) and downloaded onto a local computer.

The Internet has literally millions of clients and numerous servers. In its initial stages, the information on the Internet was very often simple text; however, the graphical user interface encouraged an increasing demand for graphical communication. The Internet now also uses the World Wide Web (WWW) in support of the global move towards multimedia communication methods. The WEB is based on hypertext within which we can link all types of text with multimedia effects such as sound and movies.

In order to develop a WWW hypertext, we need to use a specific type of hypertext language known as Hyper Text Mark-up Language (HTML), developed by the CERN laboratory in Geneva, Switzerland. The hypertext mark-up language is designed to specify the organization of a text document. It requires that you construct documents with sections of text marked as logical units. These logical units are lists, titles, and paragraphs, and a browser displays these elements on your screen.

To present a program written in HTML codes, we need a Web browser on the client. One of the first browsers, Mosaic, was developed by the National Center of Supercomputer Applications in Champaign, Illinois.

If a Web browser wants to transfer its resources it needs a protocol. HTML uses the Hyper Text Transfer Protocol (HTTP). A resource can be an ASCII text or HTML documents, graphics files like GIF, sound or movies. Each connection can use only one resource at a time, which means that for each resource that a HTML document needs from the same host, it must make a separate connection.

If you have connection to the Internet you want to go to the right server. All the information that is on the Web is identified by a Universal Resource Locator (URL). This is a unique code for a hypertext document, and uses the following format:

<Protocol>://Internet adres>:IP port/resource pathname.

Protocol can be FTP file transfer or Telnet or HTTP. The *Internet adres* is the address of the host computer where we find our information, and the *port* is the number of a service on the host. The *resource pathname* is the directory, and the *file name* is where we find our information.

One of the problems with HTML is that there is no international standard for this language, and the current version has limited functionality for a worldwide market. This problem is one of the reasons why commercial organizations are taking over this HTML language and trying to improve it and make it a more powerful environment for international Internet connections. This world has been waiting for a better product, and this has now been developed by Netscape. The Netscape browser environment is a new presentation of HTML, and is fast becoming a world standard for Internet browsers. Netscape is found on the client and is used to connect to the host computers. It is much faster that the first versions of Mosaic, and gives us many more functions. Any client using a browser like

Netscape can make a connection to the WWW. On the host computers we can find any type of information – anything from a simple file to a complete relational database.

What makes Netscape HTML different from the fourth generation languages like PowerBuilder and SQL Forms from Oracle? These fourth generation languages are in many ways proprietary environments. They have their own database server, and all the clients must have the same front-end. This is no problem if you know each client and if you can work in a closed environment. However, if you want to make contact with a worldwide market using the Internet with unknown clients, you are faced with a dilemma, because each user will have a different front-end application. Web browsers like Netscape can solve this problem by using HTML and the hypertext transmission protocol. At the moment, many organizations are Wetting up Web servers, and this works well for most of the applications. In most cases, we have a client connection to a server, and we use the HTTP as a simple protocol for static information; we can look up a Web page and ask for information. For more dynamic interaction, such as working with databases, we have to use the Common Gateway Interface (CGI).

How can you connect a user to this client/server world and get information from a relational database running in the Internet environment? This can be done by setting up a three-tier client/server environment. On the client we build an application in Netscape by using HTML. This application is connected to a host computer using the CGI. From the client we send some information on a customer to the WWW server. There we can run a program that can build in C or in any other language. The WWW server can react by retrieving the appropriate files or by executing a so-called gateway program. This gateway program can do any type of processing, like manipulations of a database. The gateway program also returns an HTML page to the WWW server, which send it back to the client. The mechanisms by which the WWW server communicates with gateway programs are defined by the CGI. All the processing is done on servers, and the answer is sent back to the client. In this way we are able to set up a client/server environment application running on the Internet.

But there is more. We need a fully integrated world of multimedia with expanding capabilities.

The HTML is a world for text and documents but not for interactive multimedia. Products like Netscape have a number of functions that can support this, but one product with different capabilities is Java from Sun Microsystems Computer Corporation. Java is a programming language that is very similar to C++ and Objective C. It is an object-oriented environment that is optimized for distributed environments, and which can run on many platforms. Java creates platform-independent applications. It has many capabilities for multimedia, and can be linked to HTML environments like Netscape. Compiled Java applications run on a host, and can be sent as a resource to an HTML document running on a client. The client must run a browser that is able to connect to Java code. You do not have to install any Java software on a client. The complete software, middleware and compiled application is sent over the Internet to the client. You can also develop a browser in Java: this is the so-called Hot Java environment. Hot Java is very flexible and dynamic. End users don't need specific software; this product is open, and has many multimedia capabilities.

Hot Java is galvanising the Internet. Other browsers are limited in their functionality; with Hot Java you can create interactive applications, and the client does not need any software because the compiled software is sent from the host to the client on request.

As it continues to develop and grow, we shall see many types of new products coming on to the Internet market. Most of these products are operating system independent, and with them we shall find a completely new type of industry. For instance, one of these new products is the Virtual Reality Modeling Language (VRML) – an environment of three-dimensional pictures. This software was developed by Silicon Graphics, and makes it possible to develop 3D applications.

Setting up a complete Internet environment with a WWW server means that you have to install a Web server and a client. The client needs a browser like Netscape. On each machine you need TCP/IP as network protocol. You need a modem and a line connection to the Net. In most cases we see fast UNIX servers storing the HTTP software on the host. The first servers used UNIX because this operating system is able to respond to simultaneous HTTP service requests. But today we also see OS/2 and Windows NT working as Web servers. The protection needs special attention. We can solve this by using a firewall between the client and the servers. This can be a router, a gateway or a specific firewall hardware and software product.

How will this affect our offices? We shall work on our local groupware products like Lotus Notes, and connect them to Netscape and other products. Information from the Web can be transferred from and to clients and hosts. We shall move to a world with incredible possibilities, whereby the network becomes a central nerve centre. We shall move towards a world that IBM calls Network Centric Computing. Client/server technology is one of the first and most important steps toward making this possible. The next steps are open systems, high-speed networks and groupware products that are able to combine and connect all this information. Information in any form will come to us. Text, documents, movies all kind of information from organizations can be entered by using the Net. Banks and many other organizations will offer their services by using the Net. Education will be offered by using multimedia, and all the information that we collect will be up to date.

We shall find software on several types of platform all over the world, and with new software products like groupware, Netscape, Java and object languages it will become possible for all these modules to work together. This means that we are moving toward a world with object-oriented modules that can integrate on many platforms and which can be connected to all kinds of local applications. The network is opening up a huge new spectrum of communication possibilities.

Chapter 12

Glimpse into the future

In this book, we have tried to indicate the importance of careful consideration on the part of management tasks during implementation of the client/server concept. Client/server is not so much a technique as a way of working with multiple techniques that are dependent on each other. Client/server and distributed databases are also extremely closely linked to fundamental change processes presently occurring in our society. The organization of the future will require intensive coordination of activities, which will require optimal use of informatics tools. Only the use of the most modern techniques such as client/server and object-oriented programming will enable systems to meet these new requirements.

Client/server means division of labor between computers. The tasks are optimally distributed over various systems. This leads to the existence of dedicated hardware: database servers, graphics workstations, file servers, routers etc. Software will be much more modular in structure. Programs in client/server environments are split into a number of loosely related functions which are run on various different systems. Programs consist, as it were, of separate multifunctional components. Print routines, for example, will no longer be hard coded in individual programs, but central printer servers will offer print control services to the programs. The software consists of libraries which can be maintained with exchangeable components.

This all corresponds closely with the central concepts of object orientation. In client/server environments, clients and servers communicate via request and answer structures. In the object-oriented approach, objects communicate with each other via messages. The operating systems of the future will offer this kind of functionality as standard. Programming of new applications will resemble the connection of a number of multifunctional standard objects.

Object orientation will also have an effect on the development of databases. The database of the future will not only contain information structured in records, but also texts, video images, photos, and scientific models.

Construction of computer systems according to the client/server concept leads to an environment which can easily be modified in response to new developments. In the past, an entirely new system usually had to be purchased in order to be able to take advantage of new techniques. Client/server allows the organization to grow organically. The new systems need only be dropped into the network in order to be integrated in existing systems. This flexibility also allows the traditional mainframe to be easily integrated into the client/server environment. Mainframes are not yet threatened with extinction. They can still be well used as central database servers and OLTP systems for thousands of users.

On the other hand, PC and mini users can learn a lot from the way in which the management of mainframe sites is set up. The management of client/server environments is a crucial issue and in itself a separate area of expertise. Setting up and implementing good standards within the organization is of great importance. The mainframe world is a treasure trove of experience in the area of maintenance of vital business systems. The situation in the LAN and mini worlds is somewhat different. Client/server offers an alternative which is the best of both worlds. Island automation and isolated systems which require too much attention from the organization can be avoided. The PC user retains his flexibility, but also makes optimal use of infrastructural information systems, on line, without difficult batch jobs or retyping data. Users in client/server environments are no longer dependent on a central automation department. If users conform to the standards, they are themselves able to build local applications or to contribute local standard applications to the infrastructure.

What will the future bring for the average office employee? He will very probably spend a great many of his working hours at home. His home will be connected to a variety of communication facilities, partially via glass fiber, partially via traditional methods or wireless. Geographic movement will become less necessary due to home–office communication. The traditional office building will gradually disappear. The office of the future will no longer be a building in the traditional sense of the word. The organization's facilities will be geographically spread throughout the world: accounting in India, programming in the USA. Meetings will be supported by multimedia. Computer interfaces will change. Speech technology, handwritten texts and virtual reality will be used to communicate with computers. Amusement will take on other forms. Interactive, multidimensional films will be available on call. The viewer will be able to influence the film, requesting another star in the leading role, e.g. Casablanca with John Wayne. The new technology will also have an influence on education. The student of the future can determine his own individual course of study, in his own tempo.

Doctors will consult their international colleagues using optimal forms of communication. Designers will use graphical, or 3D programs to develop their own objects and make their own products.

The question of which organizations will benefit from these developments is quite interesting. In any case, we can expect a major shift in power structures and commercial importance. We now live in a transport economy and are moving toward an information economy, which will have an effect on, for example, the role of oil companies, transport companies and banks. The political effects will be substantial, and the service industry will be especially strongly influenced. This may sound like quite a vague future vision to many, but certain industries, the airline, banking, telecommunication and automation industries, are already adjusting their infrastructure to these new developments. What exactly the future will bring is known to no one, but that interesting developments await us is certain. The client/server market is developing rapidly and the concepts we have discussed here are subject to change. Although our intention in this book is merely to provide an impression of developments in the framework of present changes, we hope that we have provided the reader with enough information to participate in these developments with confidence.

Bibliography

Baker, R. (1990) *Case * Method, Tasks and Deliverables*, Addison-Wesley, Wokingham.

Berson, A. (1992) *Client/Server Architecture*, McGraw-Hill, New York.

Boar, B.H. (1993) *Implementing Client/Server Computing: A Strategic Perspective*, McGraw-Hill, New York.

Critchley, T.A. and Batty, K.C. (1993) *Open Systems: The Reality*, Prentice-Hall, Hemel Hempstead.

Date, C.J. (1986) *An Introduction to Database Systems*, Volume 1, fourth edition, Addison-Wesley, Reading, MA.

Donovan, J.J. (1992) *Business and Technology: A Paradigm Shift, Strategic Weapons and Tactics for Executives*, Cambridge Technology Group Inc., Eaglewood Cliffs, New York, USA.

Geraghty, J. (1994) *CICS Concepts and Uses: A Management Guide*, McGraw-Hill, London.

Glines, S.C. (1992) *Downsizing to Unix*, New Riders, Carmel, IN.

Graham, I.S. (1995) *The HTML Sourcebook: A Complete Guide to HTML*, Wiley, New York.

Gray, J. and Reuter, A. (1993) *Transaction Processing: Concepts and Techniques*, Morgan Kaufmann, San Mateo, CA.

Hugo, I (1993) *Practical Open Systems: A Guide for Managers,* second edition, National Computing Centre/Blackwell, Oxford.

Inmon, W.H. (1993) *Developing Client/Server Applications*, Wiley, Chichester.

Inmon, W.H. and Hackathorn, R.D. (1994) *Using the Data Warehouse*, John Wiley & Sons, Inc., New York, USA.

Inmon, W.H., and Kelley, C. (1993) *Rdb/VMS: Developing the Data Warehouse*, QED Publishing Group, Wellesley.

Kern, H. and Johnson, R. (1994) *Rightsizing the New Enterprise*, Prentice Hall, Mountain View CA.

Khoshafian, S., Chan, A., Wong, A., and Wong, H.K.T. (1993) *A Guide to Developing Client/Server SQL applications*, Morgan Kaugmann, San Mateo, CA.

Koch, G. (1993) *Oracle 7: The Complete Reference*, McGraw-Hill Osborne, New York.

Open Software Foundation (1991) *Distributed Management Environment: Rationale*, Bull Nederland NV.

Orfali, R., and Harkey, D. (1993) *Client/Server Programming with OS/2 2/1*, John Wiley & Sons, Inc., New York.

Orfali, R., Harkey, D., and Edwards J. (1994) *Essential Client/Server Survival Guide*.

Palmer-Stevens, D. (1992) *Guide to Local Area Networking*, Cabletron Systems, John Wiley & Sons, Inc., New York.

Rosenberry, W., Kenny, D. and Fisher, G. (1992) *OSF Distributed Computing Environment: Understanding DCE*, O'Reilly & Associates Inc., Sebastopol, California.

Salemi, J. (1993) *Guide to Client/Server Databases*, Ziff-Davis Press, Emeryville, California.

Smith, P. (1994) *Client/server Computing: All-in-one Reference for Total Systems Development*, Sams Publishing, Indianapolis, IN.

Tanenbaum, A.S. (1992) *Computernetwerken*, Academic Service, Schoonhoven.

Ullman, J.D. (1982) *Principles of Database Systems, second edition*, Computer Science Press, Maryland.

Vlist van der, P. (1987) *Telematica Netwerke, een organisatorisch perspectief*, Uitgeverij Tutein Nolthenius, Amsterdam.

Wheeler, T. (1992) *Open Systems Handbook*, Bantam Professional Books, New York.

Zantinge, D. and Adriaans, P.W. (1994) *Client/Server en gedistribueerde data-bases*, Lansa Publishing BV, Leidschendam.

Zdonik, S.B. and Maier, D. (1990) *Readings in Object-Oriented Database Systems*, Morgan Kaufmann San Mateo, CA.

Glossary

4GL
Fourth Generation Language. Class of programming languages, with accompanying development environment, specifically aimed at building form-based applications for mostly administrative tasks.

ACID
The basic transaction properties of atomicy, consistency, isolation and durability.

AIX
Advanced Interactive eXecutive. IBM's UNIX implementation.

Algorithm
A process or set of rules necessary for a computer to perform a task.

Alias
An alternative name for a data element or a device.

API
Application Programming Interface.

Application
A software program designed for a domain-specific task.

Architecture
The specific hardware and software components and the way they interact with one another. It describes how the hardware or software is constructed and can work together.

AS/400
Application System/400 is a midrange computer system from IBM. The AS/400 is designed for character-based administrative environments with large numbers of users.

Asynchronous
A way of transmitting data or processing a job one by one in a certain unit of time.

Asynchronous Transfer Mode (ATM)
One of the new protocols being utilized to support different network packet structures and higher network bandwidth requirements.

Atomic
The smallest addressable unit within a system.

Atomicity
For a transaction it means 'all or nothing'. All actions happen or none happen.

Attribute
A property that can assume values for entities or relationships. Entities can be assigned several attributes (e.g. a tuple in a relation consists of values). Some systems also allow relationships to have attributes.

Authorize
To allow system or user to perform a requested operation on an object.

Backbone
Generic term for LAN or WAN connectivity between subnetworks across the enterprise. The subnetworks are connected to the backbone via bridges and/or routers, and the backbone acts as a communications trunk.

Backup
A copy of software or data on a diskette, tape, or disk of some or all of the files from a hard disk.

Bandwidth
Defines how much data can be transferred per unit of time. This is the range of signal frequencies that can be carried on a communications channel.

Batch
Asynchronously processing of many jobs as a single group. A batch transaction is one that accesses many records or runs for a long time. Environment in which programs (usually long-running, sequentially oriented) exclusively access data, and user activity is not interactive.

Bridge
A device that connects two or more physical networks, and forwards packets between them. Bridges are used to connect networks. They do not carry out any interpretation of the information they are carrying.

Bus network
A LAN where all the workstations are connected to a single cable.

Business Rules
The standard rules in the organisation and described in a software program. This rule can be used by many computer programs.

Cache
A subset containing parts of a larger memory.

CASE
Computer Aided Software Engineering. Software environment to build business, form-based, applications. Upper CASE starts with providing a means to record data and process flow in diagrams. Lower case is focused more on solution design, especially designing a data structure (entity–relationship diagram).

CA Unicentre
The systems management product of Computer Associates.

CDE
Common Desktop Environment. The window manager brought forward by COSE to succeed OSF Motif.

CICS
Customer Information Control System is the transaction monitor product from IBM. It runs on most IBM platforms and on some (not IBM) UNIX systems.

Client
A computer system that can work locally or in a client server environment, and which is able to send requests to a server.

Client/server
A process in which software is split over clients and servers, and clients makes a request to the server.

Coax cable
A transmission medium in which a copper conductor is surrounded by insulation and a shield.

Collision
Two devices sending data on the same transmission medium at the same time.

Column
A part of a table in which values are selected from the same domain. The column is named in the head.

Commit
A condition or transaction when the changes to a database or other software system are concluded satisfactorily and can no longer be cancelled or rolled back.

Configuration (management)
A database with a description of all software and hardware modules.

Connectivity
The way different network devices and computers are connected to each other.

Consistency
Any action of the program does not violate any of the integrity constraints. All transactions can only be made if any program is a correct one.

CORBA
Common Object Request Broker Architecture. Software agent acting as a post office for messages between objects in an object-oriented program. One of the advantages of using an object request broker (ORB) is location independence; the message-sending object need not know that its object actually lives on another machine under a colleague ORB. The OMG produced a standard for the interfaces and behaviour of an ORB.

COSE
Common Operating System Environment. Industry cooperation body formed primarily by IBM, HP, DEC and Sun to revitalize cooperative work that lost progress while under the supervision of OSF.

Data Definition Language (DDL)
The language used to define internal tables, indexes, buffers and storage.

Data dictionary
The roadmap of how data objects relate to one another. It defines ownership and where the data can be found, and provides information on the data structure of the objects.

Data dictionary system
A software tool that allows the recording, storing, and processing of such metadata as data definitions, descriptions, and relationships between programs, data, and users.

Data highway
The concept of a worldwide network that connects organizations and end users all over the world. Via the network they have a connection with computer systems attached to the highway, so they are able to send the data all over the globe supported by the network highway.

Data Manipulation Language (DML)
A programming language that is supported by a DBMS and used to access a database; language contracts for addition to higher-order language for the purpose of database manipulation.

Datamart
An extract of the company-based data-warehouse. A datamart is a complete installed but smaller part of the company warehouse and mostly used in a department or by a specific number of users.

Data Mining
Analyzing the data of a warehouse (or any large data collection) in order to recognize patterns and trends, using neural networking or machine learning techniques.

Data model
The logical data structures and the relations within a database, including operations and constraints.

Data warehouse
A concept of bundling (replicated) data from all parts of an organization in one data system for flexible exploitation of this data.

DB2
An SQL-based relational database from IBM.

DBA
Database administrator.

DCE
Distributed Computing Environment. Standard by OSF to provide secure distributed services.

DECnet
The communication protocol from Digital Equipment Corporation.

Device name
The name that the system uses to identify a device.

Disk
A memory device that rotates a platter of memory medium past an electronic readwrite head.

DME
Desktop Management Environment. OSF initiative to standardize an IT management framework, commonly regarded as 'failed' by 1994.

DOS
Disk Operating System. The most common form for PCs is Microsoft's MS-DOS, which is derived from the Microsoft version.

Down-sizing
Migration of application from a mainframe to midrange servers.

DRDA
Distributed Relational Database Architecture. IBM middleware product for vendor independent remote (relational) database access, supported by IBM (DB2), Oracle, CA(Ingres), Informix, and others.

Dumb terminal
A terminal without any local intelligence.

Durability
Once a transaction completes successfully, its changes to the state survive failures.

Emulation
To imitate another hardware and software system on a local system.

Foreign key
A relationship between two tables or files. An attribute that is not a primary key to a relation in a table, but whose values are values of the primary key of another table.

Environment
The conditions under which a user works. It refers to the computer systems, but it can also refer to the physical environment, such as office, power and products.

Ethernet
One of the oldest LAN technologies. It was originally developed by Xerox, Intel and DEC. It was developed to run over coaxial cable, although it can now run over twisted pair.

FDDI
Fibre Distributed Data Interface. An emerging high-speed networking standard. An ANSI standard for use of fiber optics to provide networks up to 100 Mbits/s.

Firewall
Security processes installed on a router or a gateway that allow each network packet to be monitored, and which detect any unauthorized access or virus.

FTP
File Transfer Protocol. Remote file copying protocol; part of the TCP/IP suite of protocols.

Gateway
(1) A combination of hardware and software that interconnects otherwise incompatible networks or networking devices.

(2) Any program that translates between one protocol, or between software like databases, and another.

Graphical User Interface (GUI)
An interface that enables the user to work with graphics on his computer.

HA
High Availability. Dual hardware components, which can take over each other's functions in case of a failure so as to achieve only short service interruption upon failure of a component.

Hardware
The complete set of mechanical and other components of a computer system.

Host

A central computer system that runs all the applications and database. Communication is mostly based by terminal connection.

HP Openview

The network and systems management product of Hewlett Packard.

HP-UX

A version of UNIX from Hewlett Packard.

HTML

HyperText Markup Language. Hidden codes with which the layout for documents for WWW is created.

HTTP

HyperText Transfer Protocol. Rules for transferring WWW documents via the Internet.

Hub

The centre of a star topology network or cabling. A multinode network topology that has a central multiplexer with many nodes feeding into and through the multiplexer or hub.

Hypertext

A system in which documents or parts of documents are mutually connected.

IBM

International Business Machines.

ICS

IBM Cabling System. Proprietary naming by IBM for STP cabling with a particular type of connector.

IMS

Information Management System. Database from IBM.

Informix

A relational database and 4GL products from Informix, available on many platforms.

Ingres

A relational database and 4GL products from Computer Associates, available on many platforms.

Intelligent hub

A network hub that has the intelligence to allow software execution that monitors the desktop.

Internet

A network of networks, that enables the user to consult a huge number of datasets all over the world, using the TCP/IP protocol.

Interoperability
The ability of systems of different architectures to pass data and commands to one another to a useful extent and to interpret the information passed correctly.

Isolation
When transactions execute concurrently, more transactions cannot be executed at the same time. Each transaction is isolated and is handled one by one.

Join
An operation on a relational database that makes a connection between two or more tables and produces a new relation by matching the corresponding columns.

kbit/s
Kilobits per second.

Key
A data item or combination of data items used to identify or locate a record in a table.

Key, primary
A key is used to identify a record instance uniquely.

LAN
Local Area Network. A data communications network that can cover a limited area.

LAN Manager
A network operating system developed by Microsoft for PCs running IBM's OS/2. It is a second generation operating system developed jointly by Microsoft and IBM for PCs based on microprocessors.

LAN Network Manager
IBM's proprietary network management software for Token Ring networks.

Lock manager
A body of code that provides operations to acquire and release locks.

Logical Unit (LU)
An IBM term for a session endpoint, which is an important part of SNA.

Logical Unit 6.2 (LU6.2)
IBM's communications protocol used for program-to-program communication.

Login (single login)
The process to gain access to a system or to software products. A user must mostly enter a user name and a password. In single login, a user is connected to more than one system, but only types in the username and password once.

Mail
A computer system facility that enables the sending and holding of mail messages via the computer.

Message

A data object sent from one process to another.

MIB

Management Information Base. A network management database that can be accessed by using SNMP.

Middleware

Products that make the connection between the front end and the backend system in a client/server environment. Middleware is the glue between all the computer systems, and is able to make the connection between them. It can transport the data between the computer systems, and is a extra layer on the network protocol.

Motif

Window manager on top of X-Windows, brought forward by OSF.

MVS

Multiple Virtual Storage. Most frequently used IBM mainframe operating system. It is the flagship IBM operating system for 370-architecture (large) machines.

Name server

A process that maintains a database of names and addresses. Servers can register their names and addresses with the name server, and clients can ask for a server's address by name.

NetView

The IBM network management product.

Network

A collection of nodes that communicate with each other.

Network administration

Tasks of the person who maintains a network.

Network management

The management of network devices.

NFS

Network File System. Set of UNIX protocols for file sharing.

Normalize

To decompose complex data structures into normal form structures.

Object orientation

The property of a system that deals primarily with objects rather than images, text, etc, explicitly.

ODBC

Open DataBase Connection. Standard API to access data storage and retrieval facilities from a program. ODBC can also be looked upon as a database-independent driver library. The standard is most popular in PC environments.

OLTP
On-Line Transaction Processing, a generic term for applications that involve entail a number (usually large) of terminals.

OMG
Object Management Group. Industry standards cooperation founded to create distributed object standards.

OO
Object Oriented.

Open system
A term to describe any computer or peripheral design that has published specifications. This enables third parties to develop hardware or software for an open architecture so that all the systems made by several vendors can work together.

Operating system
Software that enables a computer to supervise its own operations, automatically calling in programs, routines, language, and data as needed for continuous throughput of different types of jobs.

Operational data
Data used to support the day-to-day operations of an organization – usually at a detailed level.

Oracle
The relational database and 4GL products from Oracle.

OS/2
The multitasking operating system designed by IBM for personal computers.

OSF
Open Software Foundation. Industry collaboration body initially founded by IBM, HP and DEC to balance the power in UNIX-land when AT&T (when they were still the owners of the UNIX source code) and Sun joined forces.

Packet switching
A method of switching data in a network in which individual packets of a set size and format are accepted by the network and delivered to their destinations.

Portable
Describes program or design that may be easily moved from one computer to another, or from one computer architecture to another.

Query language
A language that enables a user to interact with a DBMS to retrieve and possibly modify its data; mostly done with SQL in a relational database.

Queue
A data structure for managing the time-staged delivery of requests.

RDBMS
Relational Database Management System. A database management system that is based on relational algebra, and uses tables and columns. The relations between the tables are handled by foreign key relations.

Referential integrity
A principle of the relational database that specifies how a database must respond in one table and the table that has a dependent foreign key on a delete, update or insert action of a user. The integrity of a database must always be consistent and well designed.

Reliability
A module will meet its specification.

Remote Procedure Call (RPC)
A procedure call that invokes a local procedure, or invokes the remote server via a message and returns the server reply message to the caller as though it were the result of a local call.

Repeater
In a LAN, this is a device that repeats a signal from one cable to the next.

Roll back
To undo the effects of a transaction by a complete abort.

Routers
Routers operate at level 3 (network layer) of the OSI seven layer model. Routers are protocol specific routing information carried by the communications protocol in the Network layer can choose the best route for a layer 3 packet to follow.

RPC
Remote Procedure Call. A mechanism used by most versions of distributed processing systems to allow a program running on one processor to cause a procedure to be carried out on another.

Security
The protection provided to prevent unauthorized access to systems or software.

Server
A computer system offering a service from a client request for example, a database server or a print server.

Screen painter
A programming tool that is able to design a front end screen for the end user almost completely automatically. Changes in the screen are made by only using a mouse by using klick and drop functions or by function keys.

Simple Network Management Protocol (SNMP)
The open protocol of choice for TCP/IP-based network management systems.

Single logon

The transaction in a client/server environment whereby the end user is connected to many computer systems but only has to log in once by using a password or username, and not again for every computer system. A security and authorization server then controls the access to all the other hardware and software products. See Login.

SLA

Service Level Agreement.

SMP

Symmetric MultiProcessor.

SNA

Systems Network Architecture. IBM's network protocols 'standard'.

SNA (System Network Architecture)

IBM's network architecture.

Snapshot

A database dump from a part of a master database to another database.

SNMP

Simple Network Management Protocol. A protocol that can be used in a TCP/IP environment.

Solaris

The UNIX implementation from Sun Microsystems Inc.

Solstice

The network management product from Sun Microsystems Inc.

SQL

Structured Query Language. An ISO standard relational database language defined in 1986. Database query language developed originally by IBM and now subjected to international standardization effort. A language used in relational databases. A language to interact with relational databases; query, insert, update data and configure the database itself.

SQL2

An extension to SQL.

Star

A network topology in which each node is connected to a central hub.

Stored Procedure

A business rule or a application rule stored as a separate procedure in a database. Only when the stored procedure is called by a program will it be executed.

STP

Shieled Twisted Pair network cabling. Two pairs of intertwined leads shielded from electromagnetic disturbances.

Sybase
The relational database and 4GL products from Sybase.

Synchronous
All transactions are processed in the same time and not one by one.

System
A generic term that generally means a complete entity.

Systems Management
All tasks involved in managing the systems in a computer environment. Examples of these tasks are backup, printing, configuration management, change management. These tasks can be automated by using systems management tools such as Netview from IBM, HP Openview, Tivoli. These tools can work well only if you have defined your architecture and your standards.

Systemview
The network and systems management product from IBM.

Table
The SQL and relational database word for a defined set of columns.

TCP/IP
Transmission Control Protocol/Internet Protocol (TCP/IP). It was originally developed by the US Department of Defence and is able to operate in most environments. TCP/IP operates at layers 3 and 4 of the OSI model.

Third generation language (3GL)
A general-purpose programming language used to create any type of computer program. Examples of third generation languages are COBOL, C, Fortran and BASIC.

Tivoli
The systems management product of Tivoli Systems Inc.

Token Ring network
A local area network formed in a ring, which uses token passing as a means of regulating traffic on the line. A network architecture by which the workstations on the ring are given leave to transmit data while they are in possession of the token, which passes from node to node continuously. It operates at 4 Mbit/s with incipient versions at 16 Mbit/s. A local area network structure based on token passing round a ring.

TP monitor
Transaction processing monitor.

Transmission Control Protocol (TCP)
A protocol of the transport layer, and thus lies above the IP. Its main task is the reliable transportation of data through the network.

Trigger
An application or business rule stored in a database.

Tuxedo
A transaction processing monitor from AT&T and now from UNIX System Laboratories (USL).

Twisted pair
Two insulated copper wires twisted together, with the twists or lays varied in length to reduce potential signal interference between the pairs.

Two phase commit
A protocol that allows a set of autonomous processes on agents or servers like database servers to commit a transaction on all the systems or to abort the transaction on all systems. Very often used in a distributed environment.

UNIX
An operating system from AT&T and now from Novell. The operating system adopted the open systems movement as the basic operating environment for machines from workstation/large PC size up to high-end mid-range/small mainframe systems.

UTP
Unshielded Twisted Pair. Network cabling consisting of two intertwined leads without a shielding mantle. AT&T level 5 standard quality level is the highest and currently most used variation.

VAXcluster
A collection of VAX/VMS computers that act as a single computer.

View
An external relation that consists of attributes retrieved or derived from one or more base relations joined and projected as given in the view definition.

Virtual LAN
LANs shield users groups based on physical connection into a single piece of equipment. VLANS can achieve this based on software; physically dispersed users can be tied together in a VLAN and enjoy the same level of protection.

WAN
Wide Area Network. A network that transfers information over a large physical area. It can be a worldwide network.

Windows
A way of displaying information on a screen so that users can do the equivalent of looking at several pieces of paper at once. Each window can be manipulated.

Workstation
A term used to mean a PC, node or terminal. It is a device that has data input and output and is operated by a user.

X-Windows

A graphical user interface developed at the Massachusetts Institute of Technology (MIT). It has received wide acceptance.

X/open

User organization aiming to provide standards for open systems environments.

Index